Helena Paderewska

Helena Paderewska, 1919

Helena Paderewska

MEMOIRS, 1910–1920

*Edited with an Introduction
and Annotations by*

Maciej Siekierski

Foreword by

Norman Davies

HOOVER INSTITUTION PRESS
Stanford University | *Stanford, California*

hoover.org

Hoover Institution Press Publication No. 660

Hoover Institution at Leland Stanford Junior University,
Stanford, California 94305-6003

First printing 2015
27 26 25 24 23 22 21   9 8 7 6 5 4 3 2

Cataloging-in-Publication Data is available from the Library of Congress.
ISBN 978-0-8179-1864-4 (cloth)
ISBN 978-0-8179-1865-1 (pbk)
ISBN 978-0-8179-1866-8 (epub)
ISBN 978-0-8179-1867-5 (mobi)
ISBN 978-0-8179-1868-2 (PDF)

Contents

[*Illustrations follow page 52 and page 172.*]

List of Maps and Illustrations

Maps

Illustrations

PHOTO SECTION 1 *(following page 52)*

Helena Paderewska, circa 1900.

Wedding photo of Helena and Ignacy Paderewski, Warsaw, 1899.

Announcement of Helena and Ignacy's wedding, 1899.

Helena Paderewska, Antonina Wilkońska, and Ignacy Paderewski at Riond-Bosson, the Paderewski's estate in Morges, Switzerland, c. 1900.

Helena with Alfred Paderewski. Riond-Bosson, 1900.

Ernest Schelling, c. 1900.

Photographs of the Riond-Bosson Paderewski mansion during 1890–1930.

Map of the Riond-Bosson estate, Morges, Switzerland.

Ignacy Paderewski speaks during the unveiling of the Grunwald Monument in Cracow, July 15, 1910.

Helena and Ignacy with accompanying persons standing on the rear platform of their Pullman car during tour in USA, c. 1900.

Photo of concert for two pianos, Vevey, May 1913.

Portrait of Helena Paderewska, drawing, 1911.

The Paderewskis on the HMS Adriatic on the way to USA, April 1915.

Helena Paderewska, Monte Carlo, c. 1914.

Paderewski speaks at a Polish rally in Chicago, May 30, 1915.

PHOTO SECTION 2 *(following page 172)*

Helena Paderewska, c. 1920.

Children waiting for a meal being sponsored by the American Relief Administration, 1919.

Helena and Ignacy Paderewski welcoming Herbert Hoover to Warsaw. Hoover was then the director of the American Relief Administration, August 1919.

Mass on the Saski Square. Sitting from the left: Józef Piłsudski, papal nuncio Achille Ratti, and Herbert Hoover. Ignacy Paderewski stands behind the nuncio, August 1919.

Reception in the Belvedere palace in honor of Herbert Hoover. In the middle: Paderewski, Hoover, Piłsudski, and Hugh Gibson, USA representative, August 1919 [with inset detail].

Hugh Gibson speaks to the American Poles, soldiers of the Blue Army, in Warsaw, 1919.

Handwritten invitation to dinner from Helena Paderewska to Hugh Gibson, Warsaw, 1919.

Blue Army soldiers playing baseball, Warsaw, 1919.

Ignacy and Helena Paderewski in Poznań, December 1919.

4th of July celebration in Warsaw. Statue of Liberty is on the balcony of the Grand Theatre, 1921.

Unveiling of the Monument of Gratitude of the United States on the Hoover Square. The sculptor of the monument, Xawery Dunikowski is in the first row (with a scarf). October 1922.

Major Ernest Schelling receives the Distinguished Service Medal for his intelligence work, in the presence of his teacher Ignacy Paderewski, May 1923.

The Paderewskis at Riond-Bosson, Morges, Switzerland, 1929.

Poster of General Jozef Haller, commander of the Polish "Blue Army," 1919.

"Follow the Impulse," poster for the Home for Polish Girls Fund, 1917; artist: W. T. Benda.

"Come to the Polish Booth" poster/sign, New York, 1917.

"Armia Polska we Francyi. Polish Army in France," Polish recruitment poster, 1917; artist: W. T. Benda.

"Polacy! Idźcie na bój na prawy. Under the Polish flag on to the fight." Polish poster, 1917; artist: Witold D. Gordon.

Foreword

The body of literature devoted to Paderewska's husband, Ignacy, is already substantial, but Helena Paderewska's memoirs, edited by Maciej Siekierski, is the jewel that has long been missing from the treasure-house. It contains one extraordinary person's reflections on another, written at a juncture when both were in their prime, and when both had spent a decade closely involved in their homeland's cause.

Despite the passage of the years, no Polish name resonates round the world more strongly than that of Ignacy Paderewski. One of the earliest of globe-trotting pianists, he created an indelible image: with flowing mane, golden quiff, piercing eyes, and the dancing fingers that commanded a marvelous sureness of touch, he was by general consent one of the supreme virtuosi of the age. At the same time, through long-standing commitment, he combined his celebrity as music maker with political activism. He was an advocate for Poland's rebirth long before the cause became either popular or practical. Born in Podolia, a province deep in the Russian empire (and now in Ukraine), the son of an ancient landed family, he began his advocacy in an era when both Germany and Russia were doing their utmost to erase all traces of Polishness from their empires. Yet he persisted, adopting the technique of prefacing his concerts with a short talk about his suffering country. "I am a Pole, a faithful son of the fatherland," he told an audience in 1915; "I think of a Poland, great and strong, free and independent. Poland is the essence of my being." Helena Rosen Paderewska—the maestro's second wife—came to be an inseparable part of the act. Headstrong and explosive, she nonetheless surmounted obstacles to establish an undisputed position in his life and to devote herself to the progress of his career. In due course, she contrived to develop her own parallel career in national and charitable work.

One hundred years before Paderewski's birth, the Commonwealth of Poland-Lithuania was still standing firm as one of Europe's most ancient and most extensive states. It stretched some seven hundred miles from Germany in the west to Smolensk on the confines of Muscovy in the east and a still larger distance from the Baltic coast to the borderlands of the Black Sea. It occupied the area that is largely taken up on the contemporary map of Europe by Poland, the Baltic states, Belarus, and Ukraine. It was a "noble democracy," and as such completely at odds with the absolutist practices of the neighboring empires. Yet thanks to the misrule of its Saxon kings, which came to an end in 1763, it was a greatly weakened and chaotic state, and the rulers of its rapacious neighbors, Prussia, Austria, and Russia, made little attempt to hide their designs to control it and eventually to carve it up among them. In his distress, the last king of Poland, Stanisław August Poniatowski, appealed to the French philosopher Jean-Jacques Rousseau for an opinion. Rousseau's judgment was prophetic. "You may not be able to prevent your neighbors from swallowing you," he opined, "so you should do everything possible to prevent them from digesting you." In other words, because the political and military game would probably be lost, the preservation of the Commonwealth's language, culture, and traditions should be given absolute priority. And so it proved. In 1773, Poland-Lithuania launched Europe's very first Ministry of State Education. Secular schools were opened up and down the land; the arts and sciences were encouraged; and the seeds were sown for a cultural harvest whose benefits would be reaped long after the Commonwealth was destroyed.

A century later, in the decades when Paderewski was growing up, the cultural contest between the descendants of the "noble democracy" and their hostile foreign rulers was in full swing. The old Polish-Lithuanian state had disappeared during the Partitions of 1773–95, and had not been restored by the Congress of Vienna of 1815, when the post-Napoleonic order was established. The partitioning powers had even signed a treaty stating that the very name of Poland should be suppressed forever. Oppressive Russian rule in particular provoked repeated insurrections. The Polish language, once the vehicle both for government and for a literature more extensive than its German or Russian counterparts, was sidelined. Polish literature, whose pedigree went back to the Renaissance, was forced into dissident messianic channels, yearning in vain for the national resurrection that was fading from view. Polish Catholics were discriminated against, and Polish Jews, who had sheltered for generations in the refuge of the defunct Commonwealth, were obliged to live under strict police control in the so-called Pale of Settlement. The mass of the population, illiterate peasants, still lived as serfs under conditions little better than slavery. Aspirations were curtailed and hope was scarce. In such circumstances, Polish music received a very special mission. A branch of the arts that could not be easily curtailed by the state censors, it became the platform for resistance and for the promotion of patriotic attitudes.

Nor was it unusual for the arts in general, and music in particular, to become embroiled in politics. Verdi's tussles with the censorship in Rome, Naples, and Austrian Milan became famous. He was a passionate supporter of the Italian Risorgimento, and his brilliant "Va, Pensiero" (The Chorus of the Hebrew Slaves) from *Nabucco* was widely taken as the anthem of all national liberation movements. The trouble was that some of those movements were successful, and others were not. The unification of Italy was achieved, partially in 1861 and fully in 1870. Germany was united under Prussian auspices with the creation of the German empire in 1871. But Poland was foremost among the losers. Indeed, in the decades after the suppression of the January rising in 1863–64, it was all but invisible. Thoughts of independence had been crushed for a generation. The ruling empires were riding high. Germanization and Russification were proceeding apace; it was only in the Austro-Hungarian sphere, in Galicia, that Polish culture was permitted to flourish freely. Cultural Wars broke out on many fronts. When the Poles wished to erect a statue to their national bard, Adam Mickiewicz, on the centenary of his birth, they could not erect it at his birthplace, for it was in the Russian Empire. So they erected it in the Market Square of Krakow, in Galicia. And when Paderewski joined a committee that sought to unveil a monument on the five hundredth anniversary of the Battle of Grunwald, celebrating a victory of the Poles and Lithuanians over the Teutonic Knights, they were barred from carrying out their plans at the site of the battle in East Prussia. Instead, they built yet another monument in Kraków.

In 1910, when the Grunwald monument was unveiled, though the European powers were lining up in opposing political camps and a rearmament race was in progress, few people were thinking about imminent war, and almost no one was thinking of the possibility of Poland regaining its independence. As Helena Paderewska wrote of the same period, "In the councils of the world, Poland was voiceless." In 1910, Ignacy Paderewski was approaching the height of his worldwide fame. In addition to his concert tours, he had entered the new world of the phonograph and sound recordings, which would put him into a star cast that included the baritone Enrico Caruso and the violinist Fritz Kreisler. In the intervals between tours, he and Helena spent their time either in their Swiss home at Riond-Bosson or on their California ranches near Paso Robles. Yet, as the war clouds gathered, Paderewski was inexorably drawn into political discussions on the war's impact on Poland. Helena Paderewska's memoir covers just one decade of the eight decades of her husband's life. Yet it refers to the most turbulent events of his lifetime—before, during, and immediately after the First World War—and it presents a vivid picture of Paderewski's transformation from a maestro pianist to a savvy politician and spokesman for his homeland, whose efforts were crucial in realizing Poland's right to international recognition and independence.

NORMAN DAVIES
Oxford, July 2015

Editor's Acknowledgments

I have the pleasant duty to express my appreciation to a few individuals who have assisted me in this project: Annette Strakacz-Appleton, the recently deceased last member of the extended Riond-Bosson family, who shared with me her reminiscences of Helena Paderewska; Professor Marian Drozdowski, Joseph Herter, and Eugenia Szymczuk from Warsaw; Justyna Szombara from Kraków; Professor Marek Żebrowski, director of the Polish Music Center at the University of Southern California; Christopher Onzol from Los Angeles; and my Hoover Institution colleagues Katherine Jolluck, Bertrand Patenaude, Dale Reed, Małgorzata Szudelska, Eric Wakin, and Ann Wood. I also thank my daughter Victoria, who transcribed the whole text; my sons, Nicholas and Maximilian, who assisted with occasional technical difficulties and problems; and, finally, my wife, Anna, without whose patient support the whole project would not have been completed. In addition, I gratefully acknowledge the Polish Music Center at the University of Southern California, the Archives of Contemporary Records in Warsaw, the Paderewski Center for the Documentation of Polish Music at the Jagiellonian University in Kraków, the Polish Museum of America in Chicago, and, of course, the Hoover Institution Library and Archives as the sources of the illustrations for this volume.

Editor's Introduction

Ignacy Jan Paderewski (1860–1941), probably the best-known and most celebrated pianist of the early twentieth century, was the rave of Paris, London, and New York audiences, with annual concert tours across the continents. During the Great War, Paderewski set music aside and turned to politics, becoming an eloquent spokesman for the country of his birth, Poland, then occupied by the empires of Russia, Germany, and Austria. Using his personal fame and charisma, Paderewski gained access to the top political leadership of France, Britain, and the United States. His devoted wife and collaborator, Helena, facilitated and accompanied virtually his every move. Helena Paderewska's memoirs, written in English for a US audience and as a tribute to the US contribution to the Allied victory and help in the restoration of Poland, are the story of this great international adventure, which ended with the signing of the Treaty of Versailles. Although written not by an American, the memoirs document an American story of grassroots efforts to influence the political process and the course of history. It is a story of an exceptionally talented self-made man who accomplished his boyhood dream of freedom and independence for his homeland. The memoirs are also one of the few examples of a woman's look at the world of international politics during the Great War and its immediate aftermath. Indeed, Helena Paderewska was one of only several women, among hundreds of men, in the Hall of Mirrors when the Versailles treaty was signed.

The cause of Poland's independence was shared by more than twenty million Poles living in a country hopelessly divided by a cabal of its neighbors and by the large emigrant population residing mostly in the United States. The outbreak of the war in August 1914 ended the solidarity of the three empires occupying the lands of Poland, with German and Austrian armies engaging and eventually pushing back the invading Russian armies. About three-and-a-half million Poles were drafted into the occupying armies and frequently forced to fight one another, with nearly seven hundred thousand killed or missing by the war's end. Civilian casualties were equally staggering. The battles of the eastern front, fought mostly in Poland, brought death, devastation, hunger, and disease to the country. The belligerents made cautious political overtures to the Poles with promises of limited autonomy but never of full independence. The western powers were equally cautious, as any official expression of sympathy for the Polish cause was impossible without angering ally Russia, which claimed most of the territories once belonging to Poland.

The political situation in the United States, where some two-and-a-half million Polish immigrants made their home, was more favorable for educating the public and fund-raising for Polish relief supplies, though here also some major difficulties existed. The vast majority of the Polish immigrants were first-generation arrivals, barely literate, and poor; they came from three different parts of occupied Poland, and their concerns and sentiments for the home country were local and regional rather than national in scope. Finally, any agitation on behalf of a free Poland was vigorously resisted and countered by the considerably larger and better-established German American organizations and press, assisted until the first months of 1917 by the Imperial German embassy in Washington. Against all these odds, relying mostly on his own charisma and eloquence, Paderewski succeeded in uniting the Polish American community around Polish independence on the side of the western Allies and gained the support of the Wilson administration and the Allied governments for his program. Paderewski's accomplishments, however, would not have been as effective without his greatest supporter and collaborator, his wife, Helena.

She was born Helena Rosen in 1856 in Warsaw, the daughter of a Polish father and a Greek mother. Baron Władysław von Rosen, member of a Polish branch of an old Baltic aristocratic family and an officer in the Russian army, met Helena's mother during the Crimean War; she died shortly after moving to Warsaw and giving birth to Helena. Władysław soon remarried and left his daughter in the care of his mother, Katarzyna Rucińska Rosen, and his sister, Emilia Rosen Jaszowska. Helena became an avid reader, but aside from an intensive study of foreign languages, especially French, she received little formal education. Not quite eighteen years of age, and lacking her father's permission, Helena married an older man, Władysław Górski, a violin soloist with the Warsaw Opera orchestra. In 1877, she gave birth to a son, Wacław. A year later, she met an eighteen-year-old pianist, Ignacy Jan Paderewski, who played concerts together with her husband. Thus began a relationship that after several years turned from friendship into romance. Ignacy was briefly married to Antonina Korsak, who died in 1881 after giving birth to a disabled child, Alfred. Some years after the death of Antonina, Helena began to care for Ignacy's son and was like a mother to him until his death at the age of twenty. Her marriage to Górski deteriorated, in part because of her involvement with Paderewski; nevertheless, she was eventually able to get a Church annulment of her vows. Helena and Ignacy married in Warsaw in 1899, and they moved to Morges, Switzerland, to a palatial villa, Riond-Bosson, overlooking Lake Geneva. Although they devoted most of their remaining years to traveling on concert tours and political missions and spent the summer months in the hot springs and wine country of California's Paso Robles, they called Riond-Bosson home, a place where they came to rest and to entertain neighbors and international visitors. It was there that Helena died in 1934, after several years' struggle with depression and neurological disorders.

In addition to being a loyal and devoted spouse, as well as constant companion and confidant of her famous husband, Helena was a woman with a broad range of practical interests and commitments, some of which were direct extensions of Ignacy's ideas and programs and some of which were more personal. Like Ignacy, she had a strong interest in agriculture and animal husbandry, from the walnuts, almonds, and prunes she planted at her Rancho Santa Helena near Paso Robles, to the purebred, prize-winning chickens she raised at Riond-Bosson. This hobby had a practical application when she founded an agricultural school in Poland to train country girls in poultry farming and gardening and donated three hundred of her Swiss chickens for breeding by the Warsaw Agricultural Society. Her humanitarian and social work projects ranged from a care home for elderly female veterans of the struggle for independence, to a club for Warsaw newspaper boys, to care homes and feeding stations for refugee children, to her flagship endeavor, the Polish White Cross, an organization with some twenty thousand members, over which she presided. She collected money for her programs with innumerable fund-raisers and sales, spending countless days writing letters and appeals, visiting potential donors, and initiating local undertakings. Ignacy and Helena worked as a team: he met with the high and mighty, wrote memoranda, and delivered eloquent speeches; she worked at the grassroots level, meeting parish priests, leaders of women's organizations, and anyone else willing to help the cause of Polish relief and independence.

That huge undertaking was successful. Paderewski's efforts, augmented by those of his wife and supported by dozens of loyal associates and thousands of less well-known Poles and friends of Poland in Europe and in the United

States, brought about the Allies' recognition of Poland's right to an independent existence within secure borders and helped organize and equip a national army, soon to expand into a force able to decide local territorial conflicts and resist the Bolshevik plans of international revolution and conquest. Regrettably, neither Ignacy nor Helena nor any of their staff kept a detailed diary of these active years. She began one in 1915 but gave up after several weeks. Not until her husband left government service and they moved back to Switzerland in the early months of 1920 did she find the time and peace of mind to begin writing. Wanting to reconstruct the basic chronology and to remember the main characters in the dramatic events of the past several years, she especially wanted to pay tribute to American friends of Poland, including President Woodrow Wilson, his foreign policy adviser Edward House, and the one she called the "miracle worker from California," Herbert Hoover. This is why she decided to write the memoirs in English, not in Polish or French, and most likely she had American publication in mind. Her ideal collaborator in this work was her husband's only American student, and a dear friend and neighbor in Switzerland, Ernest Schelling.[1]

Although Schelling was recognized as a pianist and composer, and later as a conductor with the New York Philharmonic, little has been known of his life outside music. His papers and memorabilia, recently received by the Hoover Institution, document his work during the world war, work that discreetly but significantly contributed to the success of Paderewski's mission. Moved by patriotic fervor, and no doubt influenced by Paderewski's involvement on behalf of Poland, Schelling joined the army in the spring of 1917. After several months of training at the Army War College, he was given a commission and appointed assistant military attaché at the American legation in Bern, in neutral Switzerland, a key US intelligence gathering post. Major Schelling was aided in his work by a network of Polish émigrés in Switzerland and France; he reciprocated by sharing with Paderewski his contacts in the command of the American Expeditionary Forces and the State Department. Immediately after the armistice, he began working with prisoners of war and the American Red Cross and went on a mission to Warsaw, where he consulted with Paderewski and the Polish military command. Schelling also facilitated much of the dip-

---

1. Ernest Schelling (1876–1939), American conductor and composer, student and friend of Paderewski; during the war, he served as a major in the Military Intelligence Service in the American legation in Bern; his Swiss summer home, Château de Garengo, was a few miles south of Riond-Bosson.

lomatic and military communications and travel between Warsaw and Paris, which was the American and Allied military and political command center during the Peace Conference. The Polish government recognized Schelling's contributions several years after the war with the order of Polonia Restituta; however, later his services were forgotten, and he is unknown to historians of Poland. Although Paderewska was well aware of the role played by their special US friend in support of the Polish side, she omitted it in her account to protect his confidentiality. In early 1920, when Helena was writing her memoirs, Schelling was still in Europe, moving between Bern, Paris, and his Swiss residence of Château de Garengo in Céligny, only twenty miles south along the shore of Lake Geneva from Riond-Bosson. There is no doubt that he or his wife, Lucie,[2] or both, participated in Helena's project; the dominant languages of the Paderewski household were Polish and French, and though Helena and her secretary, Helena Lübke,[3] knew English reasonably well, they would have needed help with the language. In any event, after the memoirs were completed in May 1920 in Riond-Bosson, they were apparently turned over to Schelling, who put them in his New York safe, where they were undisturbed until his death in late 1939. Schelling's second wife, Helen "Peggy" Marshall,[4] found the two typewritten copies of the memoirs some months later while going through Ernest's papers. Peggy sought the counsel of her husband's and the Paderewskis' old friends, Mildred Bliss[5] and Charlotte Kellogg[6] and then tried to send a package of papers, probably containing Helena's memoirs, via the Swiss diplomatic pouch to Paderewski. Apparently, nothing came of it; by that time Paderewski had left Switzerland and, via Spain, embarked on his final voyage to the United States. When they met in New York, Paderewski most likely told Peggy to keep the papers until he had a home to return to. He died several months later in New York. The memoirs went back into storage and

2. Lucie How Schelling (1872–1938), French-born wife of Ernest Schelling.

3. Helena Lübke (1893–1987), Helena's secretary from 1919 until 1934.

4. Helen "Peggy" Marshall (1918–2007) married Ernest Schelling several months before his death in December 1939. During the war and immediately after, she was active in the Paderewski Testimonial Fund, which financed the Polish hospital in Edinburgh, Scotland. Later, she married another musician, Janos Scholz. The Schelling papers were donated to Hoover by her son, Christopher Scholz.

5. Mildred Barnes Bliss (1879–1969), art collector and philanthropist, wife of Robert Woods Bliss (1875–1962), secretary and lawyer at the US embassy in Paris from 1912 until 1919.

6. Charlotte Kellogg, author and biographer of Paderewski, widow of Vernon Kellogg (1867–1937), Stanford biologist, member of the American Commission for Relief in Belgium, and, in the first months of 1919, the American Relief Administration's representative in Warsaw.

remained there until several years after Peggy's death in 2007, when, along with Ernest Schelling's papers and memorabilia, they were donated to the Hoover Institution.

Why wasn't the manuscript published in 1920 or soon after? The obvious answer is that the text was out of date soon after its completion date, May 29, 1920. That day, the Polish offensive in Ukraine was at its peak, but only a few days later, the Red Army retook Kiev, and the Poles were in retreat. Two months later, the Bolsheviks occupied half of Poland, and they were ready for the final assault on Warsaw and a planned campaign into western Europe. Paderewski's great accomplishment was on the verge of collapse. It took a great national effort, the second in two years, and Western supplies, to beat back the Red Army and save the country from destruction; the Paderewskis were no longer directly involved in that effort. The memoirs thus needed a new epilogue, but Helena was not in a position to write it. Disappointment with politics and staggering debts incurred during several years of campaigning for Polish relief and independence made a return to music and the concert circuit a financial necessity and a welcome diversion. The declaration that Ignacy "will never play in public again" had to be withdrawn. Paderewski also had plans of his own to write his political memoirs; as always, Helena deferred to his wishes. The memoirs, which Paderewski dictated to Mary Lawton in 1932, detailed his artistic career, with the contract specifically noting his unwillingness to discuss his political activities. When Lawton interviewed Ignacy, Helena was ill and unable to participate in the project, her much earlier writing effort long forgotten. Lawton published the interviews in 1938 in a book that recalled Paderewski's career through 1914, though the interviews covered the period through 1932. She concluded the book with a note that said, "Later memoirs in preparation," in hopes of nudging Paderewski into providing additional material for a full second volume, one that would deal substantially with politics. Despite the book's great success, Paderewski refused to cooperate, and a second volume never came out.[7] Nevertheless, Mary Lawton's notes survived, and in 2011, the Paderewski Music Society of Los Angeles published the remaining Lawton interviews, covering the years 1914–1932, in a book of some 130 pages, about half of which deal with the same topics as Helena's own much longer and

7. Some of the correspondence regarding the controversy over the continuation of the Paderewski *Memoirs*—the letters of Hugh Gibson, Ernest Schelling, and Sylwin Strakacz—can be found in the Ernest Schelling papers in the Hoover Institution Archives.

more detailed memoirs.[8] The two texts occasionally overlap and comple-
ment each other, but Helena's story has the advantage of not only length and
detail but also a shorter time distance between the recorded narrative and
the events described.

Helena Paderewska was not an impartial observer of events she witnessed
and in which she participated. She freely admitted her preferences and biases.
She was a patriotic Polish woman and a devoted and loyal wife, who, like
her husband, held generally traditional social and economic views yet was
sensitive to the plight and the suffering of the poor and a strong believer in
Western-style parliamentary democracy, disdaining authoritarian demagogu-
ery and socialism in all its varieties. On occasion, she is prone to exaggerate
and dramatize somewhat, but her account of events is on the whole factually
correct and balanced and does not warrant constant editorial intervention and
evaluation. She is one of the key sources on the historical events in which she
participated or her husband told her about. Her near-adulation of her husband was readily reciprocated by Ignacy and shared by tens of millions in Poland and in the West. The level of worldwide admiration and popularity of this
great man can only be compared to that of another twentieth-century Pole,
Karol Wojtyła, John Paul II. Indeed, Ignacy was worthy of high respect not
only as a great pianist but also as a statesman and a man of strong principles
and selfless dedication to his cause, yet one endowed with sound judgment
and natural moderation, as well as personal simplicity and warmth to match.
Paderewska's view of her husband was certainly colored by spousal affection,
but in the main it was shared by most people who came into contact with him.
One American secretary of state, Robert Lansing, overcame initial reserva-
tions against an artist in politics and provided one of the best testimonies by
a professional diplomat:

> My . . . impression . . . was that Ignace Paderewski was a greater states-
> man than he was a musician, that he was an able and tactful leader of his
> countrymen and a sagacious diplomat. . . . What others, certainly more
> experienced than he in public affairs and credited with greater political
> shrewdness, failed to accomplish, Mr. Paderewski accomplished. . . . He
> made few mistakes and he never seemed to be in doubt as to the course
> which he should take. He was wonderfully resourceful and apparently

8. Ignacy Jan Paderewski, *The Paderewski Memoirs: Part II, 1914–1932*, recorded by Mary
Lawton (Los Angeles: Paderewski Music Society, 2011).

had an instinctive sense of the possible and the practicable. He held his imagination in leash as he did his emotions. He was not carried away with extravagant hopes or unrealizable dreams. His views were essentially sane and logical.[9]

Helena Paderewska's return to Poland after many years spent in western Europe and America came as something of a rude awakening. The homeland of her dreams, now independent in large measure thanks to the selfless efforts of her husband, was a devastated and hungry country, rocked by political instability, a veritable cauldron for competing, largely leftist, ideologies. Strikes, demonstrations, and shootouts by rival militias occurred daily. For the Polish people, Paderewski was a larger-than-life figure, worshipped by most and treated with at least a modicum of respect by the political elites and the press; however, his wife became fair game. The woman who had dined with presidents and royalty, spoke at least four languages, and spent a quarter of a century traveling the world was presented as being an unsophisticated, rude, and controlling wife who did not know "her place." Some of this antagonism stemmed from the fact that in the early months of 1919, much of the business of government was being conducted in the Paderewskis' suite in the Hotel Bristol, occasionally even in Helena's bedroom, which stretched her tolerance to its limits; some of it was pure nastiness, a way to attack Paderewski without mentioning him by name. When a coherent political argument could not be presented convincingly, critics resorted to the misogynist method of ridiculing Helena's physical appearance, style of clothes, and details of housekeeping—similar to what successive generations of American first ladies have experienced all too well. Helena, however, took the high road in her memoirs. She mentioned Poland's chief of state, Józef Piłsudski,[10] from whose direction most of the criticism came, always with respect and took in stride the doubtlessly irritating personal attacks by his youthful worshippers and older sycophants.

Historians have not given Helena Paderewska the attention she deserves. Two decades ago, the late Malgorzata Perkowska-Waszek, the foremost

9. Robert Lansing, *The Big Four and Others at the Peace Conference* (Cambridge, MA: Riverside Press, 1921), 204–7.

10. Józef Piłsudski (1867–1935), Polish statesman; one of the leaders of the Polish Socialist Party in Russia, later co-organizer of the Polish Legions fighting on the side of the Central powers; from July 1917 to November 1918 imprisoned in Germany; chief of state during 1918–1922; leader of the Second Polish Republic after the coup of May 1926.

specialist on Paderewski's life and works, lamented, "No one today remembers the extraordinary work of Helena Paderewska."[11] Nothing much has changed; there is still no full biography of Helena. She does have a substantial biographical outline, compiled by Andrzej Piber, in the *Polish Biographical Dictionary*.[12] Józef Orłowski's publication commemorating Paderewska's fifteen years of public service is mostly hagiographic in nature and lacks even basic biographical information, which should have been easy for him to establish because of his frequent visits to Riond-Bosson during the 1920s.[13] Mary Lee McMillan, Paderewska's American aide during 1915–1918, published a book of reminiscences about her work with Helena. Written more than fifty years after the events and with limited understanding of the historical background and attention to detail, the book provides only selected glimpses of Helena's and Ignacy's life and work in America during the war.[14]

Of the numerous biographies of Ignacy Paderewski where Helena receives some recognition, two authors deserve special note: Marian Drozdowski[15] and Adam Zamoyski.[16] For a general background and analysis of US relations with Poland, Piotr Wandycz's summary is unsurpassed, especially the chapter titled "Wilson and the Rebirth of Poland."[17] A recent monograph on the Polish question and the United States during World War I by Mieczysław Biskupski covers many of the same events described by Helena Paderewska but from a perspective much less sympathetic to Ignacy Paderewski.[18] The changing situation in the lands of historic Poland between 1914 and the end of 1918 is

11. Małgorzata Perkowska-Waszek, *Za kulisami wielkiej kariery: Paderewski w dziennikach i listach Sylwina i Anieli Strakaczów* [Behind the scenes of a great career: Paderewski in the diaries of Sylwin and Aniela Strakacz] (Kraków: Musica Iagellonica, 1994), 36.

12. Andrzej Piber, "Helena Paderewska," *Polski Słownik Biograficzny* [Polish biographical dictionary], vol. 24 (Kraków: PWM, 1979), 792–95.

13. Józef Orłowski, *Helena Paderewska: na piętnastolecie Jej pracy narodowej i społecznej* [Helena Paderewska: For the fifteenth anniversary of her national and social work], *1914–1929* (Chicago: n.p., 1929).

14. Mary Lee McMillan and Ruth Dorval Jones, *My Helenka* (Durham, NC: Moore Publishing, 1972).

15. Marian Drozdowski, *Ignacy Jan Paderewski: zarys biografii politycznej* [Ignacy Jan Paderewski: A sketch of a political biography], 3rd ed. (Warsaw: Interpress, 1986). An earlier edition is available in English.

16. Adam Zamoyski, *Paderewski* (London: Collins, 1982).

17. Piotr S. Wandycz, *The United States and Poland* (Cambridge, MA: Harvard University Press, 1980).

18. M. B. B. Biskupski, *The United States and the Rebirth of Poland, 1914–1918* (Dordrecht, The Netherlands: Republic of Letters Publishing, 2012).

chronicled exhaustively in Wiktor Sukiennicki's two-volume study on East Central Europe.[19]

Helena Paderewska's memoirs have been accessioned as an individual collection in the Hoover Institution Archives. The memoirs are in two carbon copies, untitled, and divided into fourteen sections. The original, which must have remained with Paderewska, probably did not survive. The present edition is a corrected version of the typescript, in which the form of most place names has been changed from German or phonetic English to modern Polish. Such names as Danzig and Posen, the forms commonly used in early twentieth-century English publications, have been changed to Gdańsk and Poznań, as these were the preferred forms for the author and have been in common usage for most of the past century. Some obvious typographical mistakes and errors in punctuation were also corrected. Finally, a few other errors were easily identified because of the context of the narrative, such as a reference to eastern Silesia instead of eastern Galicia, year 1917 instead of the obviously correct 1919, the transposition of names Gibson and Gilchrist, as well as other errors in the spelling of personal names. The mistakes have been corrected in the text without special annotation. The memoirs contain nearly three hundred personal names, of which it was possible to identify and verify all but a few. The information is provided in footnotes only the first time the name is mentioned. For the convenience of the readers, an annotated index of names follows the text. Dates of birth and death are provided unless they could not be located. I also added a brief biographical epilogue, summarizing Helena's and Ignacy's latter years, as well as a timeline of the 1910–1920 years in Helena's and Ignacy's lives. The fourteen chapters were provided with general chronological divisions. Finally, the typescript needed a title. Because it could be argued that Helena Paderewska's book is one in which her husband, inevitably, is the leading actor, and she has the key "supporting role," it could have been called "Memoirs of My Husband." Nevertheless, in recognition of the scale of that supporting role and the outstanding "coproduction" of the effort, I decided on *Memoirs, 1910–1920*. Indeed, there is no doubt that Ignacy had Helena playfully in mind when he would repeat one of his favorite aphorisms: "The road to success is full of women pushing their husbands along."

---

19. Wiktor Sukiennicki, *East Central Europe during World War I: From Foreign Domination to National Independence*, 2 vols., ed. Maciej Siekierski, preface by Czesław Miłosz (Boulder, CO.: East European Monographs, 1984). Distributed by Columbia University Press.

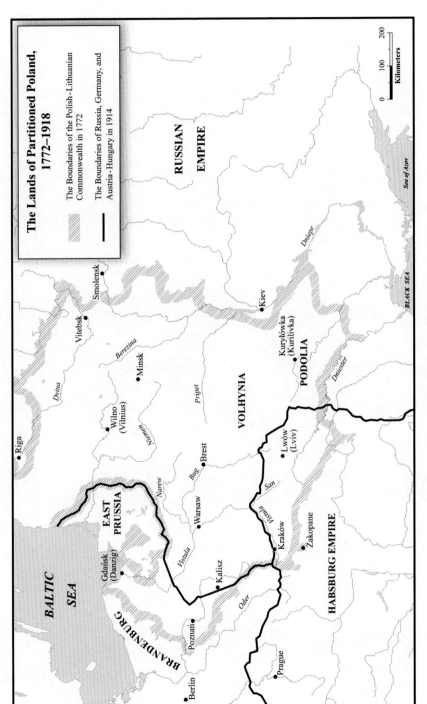

RUSSIAN EMPIRE

BALTIC SEA

BRANDENBURG

EAST PRUSSIA

HABSBURG EMPIRE

VOLHYNIA

PODOLIA

BLACK SEA

Sea of Azov

Riga

Smolensk

Vitebsk

Minsk

Wilno (Vilnius)

Kiev

Kuryłówka (Kurilivka)

Brest

Lwów (Lviv)

Warsaw

Kalisz

Kraków

Zakopane

Poznań

Berlin

Prague

Gdańsk (Danzig)

Dvina

Berezina

Niemen

Pripet

Narew

Bug

Vistula

San

Vistula

Oder

Dniepr

Dniester

Kilometers

0   100   200

Map 1. The Lands of Partioned Poland, 1772–1918

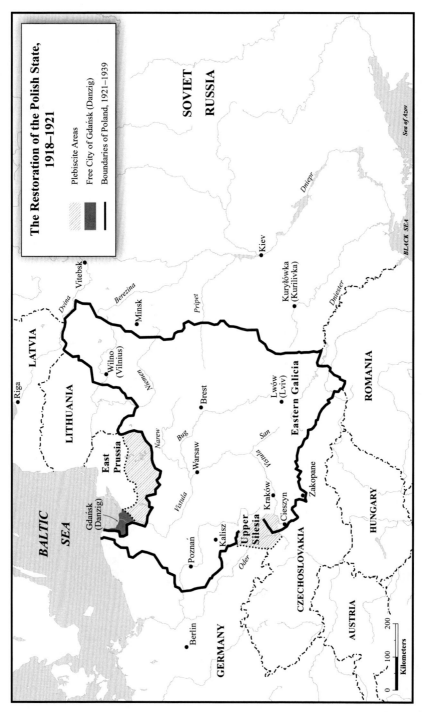

Map 2. The Restoration of Polish State, 1918–1921

The Restoration of the Polish State, 1918–1921

Plebiscite Areas
Free City of Gdańsk (Danzig)
Boundaries of Poland, 1921–1939

SOVIET RUSSIA

Sea of Azov

BLACK SEA

Kiev

Kuryłówka (Kurilivka)

Dniepr

Dniester

Berezina

Pripet

Minsk

Vitebsk

Dvina

LATVIA

Riga

LITHUANIA

Wilno (Vilnius)

Niemen

Brest

Narew

Bug

Warsaw

Lwów (Lviv)

Eastern Galicia

ROMANIA

San

Vistula

Kraków

Cieszyn

Zakopane

HUNGARY

East Prussia

BALTIC SEA

Gdańsk (Danzig)

Vistula

Poznań

Kalisz

Upper Silesia

Oder

CZECHOSLOVAKIA

AUSTRIA

GERMANY

Berlin

0   100   200

Kilometers

CHAPTER ONE

Husband, Artist, Patriot

On New Year's Day, 1920, in Warsaw, in the Sala Malinowa[1] of the Hotel Bristol, Mr. Paderewski has been listening to the addresses made by the leaders of the various clubs and societies that that morning had paraded in his honor. In his brief answer, it seems to me that he struck the keynote of his entire life. He said that he considered himself on that day the happiest of men because God had allowed him to realize his most ardent wishes, because his constant prayers since boyhood had been fulfilled. He had prayed that he might be allowed to serve Poland and to be useful to her. Even when as a boy he had prayed that it be granted him to build a monument to Grunwald,[2] so had he asked that he might live to see Poland free and independent, that he might help in its rebirth as a nation. He had asked that, when this moment came, he might stand before his countrymen with clean hands and pure heart. That day had come. His prayers had been answered.

It was a wonderful day, that New Year's in Warsaw, even as the Saturday before had been wonderful in Poznań.[3] The weather was abominable, but under a driving rain thousands had stood for hours in the streets before the Bristol where our apartments were. There had been a great procession in which were men and woman of all walks of life, from the aristocracy to the humblest laborers and peasants. They had come from all parts of Poland, artists, uni-

---

1. Sala Malinowa (Raspberry Hall), named after its art nouveau raspberry-motif decorations, is perhaps the largest room in Hotel Bristol. The hotel was constructed during 1899–1901 by a company of which Ignacy Paderewski was a shareholder. For more than a century it has been the most elegant and prestigious hotel in Warsaw.

2. Grunwald is the site of the 1410 victory of the combined forces of Poland and the Grand Duchy of Lithuania, led by King Władysław Jagiello, over the Teutonic Knights. The victory over this German military assured Poland's status as a major European power for the next three centuries. During the time that Poland lost its independence, the memory of Grunwald was an inspiration for Polish patriots.

3. The Paderewskis' visit to Poznań is described in chapter 10.

versity professors, teachers, students and schoolchildren, trades unionists, and businessmen, and a group of ancient veterans of the Revolution of '63.[4] For nearly two hours Mr. Paderewski had stood on the balcony reviewing the procession and for a half hour he stood bareheaded in the rain addressing the dense masses of people below him. The enthusiasm was tremendous, as it had been in Poznań the week before. It has been given to few men to have the experience that my husband had on these days. Not only did he know that the demonstrations were genuine in their spontaneity and affection, but he was conscious in the depths of his heart that he, who was their object, had done what they said he had done and had done it in absolute unselfishness, without thought of reward, without personal ambition.

New Year's Day had been chosen for the Warsaw celebration because on that day, the year before, my husband had arrived from America. Then he had been greeted as the savior of his fatherland, the man who more than any other man had made possible a free and independent Poland, who had brought back to her Galicia, Poznania, and the other provinces that had been torn from her by the iniquitous partitions, who had again stretched the boundaries of his country to the sea. Even more, he had been greeted as the one man who could bring order out of the chaos into which Poland had fallen since the armistice.

The demonstration in Poznań on the previous Saturday had likewise fallen on the anniversary of his arrival there the year before. They had been memorable days, those we had spent in Poznań at the end of December 1918. The German troops were not yet entirely out of the city, and there was fighting in the streets in front of the Hotel Bazar where we were staying. Some bullets even came in our room, one of them smashing a mirror. When Mr. Paderewski sailed from New York toward the end of November, nothing had been further from his mind than that he would go to Poland, and it was not really until the days we spent in Poznań that he realized that his work of the immediate future lay in his own country.

Until he went to Poland at the end of 1918, the great world knew him only as an artist. It was slow to believe that he could, as it were with the stroke of a pen, cast his career behind him and plunge with success into the greatest political battle history has known. It seems to be the general idea that if a man is an artist, especially a musician, that one fact precludes all possibility of his venturing into other activities with hope of success.

---

4. The January 1863 uprising, harshly suppressed by Russia.

I cannot speak of other artists, but of my husband I can, for I have been his wife twenty years and knew him well long before I was married to him. That he has been more than a musician I have always known. His friends, men who have known him well and intimately, have realized this. That he was able to almost at a day's notice to give up his art, to battle successfully for his country, in America and in Europe, in Warsaw, Paris, and London, to endure without complaint and without loss of courage the bitterest disappointments, to withstand for years without quailing a continuous nervous strain, to meet on equal terms and more than hold his own with the ablest statesmen of our time in questions involving the welfare of millions of people, all this was no surprise to me nor to those who knew him best.

For thirty years he had enjoyed success such as, perhaps, had been given to no other man in the history of his art. He had played throughout Europe and America. He had visited South America, South Africa, and Australia. He had won wealth and honors. He had written much music and as a composer had rivaled his fame as a pianist. His personality had provoked endless comment and had given rise to numberless legends concerning him and his life, more of them fanciful, many of them absurd.

Perhaps I am prejudiced, but it has always struck me as odd that the world was so slow, even unwilling, to grant that a man such as he could do more than one thing well. For so many years it had not only admitted his unusual personality but had insisted upon it, emphasized it, exaggerated it, and yet it could not read the significance of that very personality. I used to be amused, perhaps a little vexed, in America in the winter of 1915–16 when even our closest friends were astonished that he knew how to talk to an audience. During that time, in some of the larger cities, he prefaced his recitals by an address in which he pleaded the cause of Poland. As he put it, "I have to speak of a country which is not yours in a language which is not mine." It seemed to be most obvious that if he had the gift of oratory at all, the charm and personal magnetism that were such salient characteristics of his art would be just as potent when he spoke as when he played his piano.

It is not my plan to dwell long on his career as an artist. The world knows what he had been and what he is. The world must know by this time that never had music had a more ardent, devout, and humble servant. If there is one characteristic in him that overtops all others, it is his honesty, and to this must be added his absolute sincerity of purpose. Music, the most jealous of the arts, has never had cause to criticize his attitude toward her. Like all who have achieved greatness in the big things of life, he has always been a most serious man. I do not mean that his face is always long and that he never smiles, for when he throws off his work to play, no one can be more lighthearted and gay, more ready for a frolic; but he has never allowed play to interfere with his work. Few men, I believe, have worked harder than he; from the time as a boy he determined on music as a career and began his studies.

The world knows in a general way the story of his life. God gave him genius, but he developed that genius only by long years of privations and unending work, his capacity for continuous effort having been without limit. He has never spared himself, and only a man with an iron constitution and great physical strength like his could have endured the strain he has put on his mind and body. The greater part of his life he gave to music. There were the early years of hardships, privations, and trials during which he never lost his courage, his will to succeed. He was nearly thirty when success came to him, and with this success the days of privation were past. He had no longer to think of the means of existence; but with that success came more work, greater responsibilities, new tasks. He would not be content to accept himself at the world's estimation. He must go on and on, never satisfied with the goal he had reached. To the very end he prepared for his tours as painstakingly and as conscientiously as he did when he was fighting to secure recognition, always giving his best to his audiences, not only out of fairness to them but out of fairness to his art.

When he was not giving concerts, he was composing, putting into that work the same energy, the same honesty, the same sincerity he had given to his piano. The neuritis in his right arm that so troubled him in recent years and troubles him even today was the direct result of the manual labor involved in scoring his symphony, a great book of four hundred pages, which he did in three months.

During all the years the world knew him simply as a musician, and for many years before, there was another great impulse working within him. I have said quite truthfully that no man has lived more completely devoted to his art and to the best in his art, and yet from the earliest days music had been for him really a secondary consideration, I might almost say a means to an end. The real, final impulse that has ruled him from childhood, which has consciously and unconsciously governed his entire career, which has guided his almost every act, was his desire to serve his country.

The music that he served was in turn the servant of his one great ambition to serve his fatherland. While he gave his best to his art, he made his art prepare him for the day when Poland should call to him, never faltering in his belief that such a day would come. Sometimes I think he must have had an inspired vision. When he was fourteen years old, he had a boyish dream of giving Poland a monument to commemorate Grunwald. That dream he realized in 1910 when the monument was unveiled in Kraków amid festivities and ceremonies such as Poland had not seen even when she was at the height of her power. At that dedication I think it can be said that his real political career began, that for the first time he was accepted as a leader of the Polish people in their ambition once more to be free.

Again as a boy, he constantly dreamed of the return to Poland of Danzig, or Gdańsk, as we call it in Polish. Not only has he lived to see this dream at least partly realized, but he himself was the first Pole since the partitions who as a free man, a citizen of free and independent Poland, came to Gdańsk by sea, the British cruiser *Concord* taking him there from London in December 1918, six weeks after the armistice was signed.

And still another instance of his clear-sighted vision. Directly when the war began, he said that Poland's opportunity had come, but if she was to gain from it, there must be a Polish army fighting on the side of the Allies. He insisted always that it must be a Polish army, not an army of Poles, for only thus could Poland secure recognition as a nation, perhaps having in mind the historic saying of Bismarck[5] that Germany would be doomed the day that the Polish eagle spread its wings over the field of battle. Even at the very beginning of the war, there would have been no difficulty in recruiting Poles to fight under the French flag—in fact thousands did—but for Poles fighting under a foreign flag, the wars of the previous hundred years had shown what little benefit this was to Poland. They had given everything and received nothing. He felt that the time was then not ripe for such an army and he continually combated the idea of Polish legions under foreign colors. When he went to America, the Poles there were keen to send men abroad to help France, and he opposed the idea with all his force, in the end having his way. Although men of Polish blood volunteered to serve in the American army by the thousands—the first American soldier wounded in France was of Polish blood—when America went into the war he knew that the time had come for the realization of his dream, and in a short time the machinery was ready. Before the end of the summer of 1917, a training camp for officers was in full operation in Canada. Twenty-five thousand Poles from the United States and Canada were sent to France, this Allied and Associated Army, as it was called, giving to Poland a

5. Otto von Bismarck (1815–1898), first chancellor of Germany, 1871–1890.

place at the council table when the peace was negotiated. Without it, I question very much whether there would have been a free and independent Poland.

His country and its freedom were from his earliest days a veritable obsession. Waking and sleeping, the thought of Poland was always with him. Everything he did had really for its ultimate object the benefit of his country and his countrymen. All the time he was not giving to his music, he was studying Poland, its literature, its geography, its history, its politics, biography, and art, and there are very few men in Poland today who can be regarded as such final authorities on everything Polish.

When he composed, his music was dedicated to the glory of Poland, and, as the world knows, he filled it, saturated it with the spirit of his country as he felt it. A very large part of his fortune he invested in Poland, not because there he could get the greatest returns for it but because he felt it his duty to put as much money as possible into his own country. When the Hotel Bristol was built in Warsaw, he became the principal shareholder so that much needed work could be provided for the unemployed and that Warsaw should have a hotel worthy of a great European capital. And, really, built from plans following his suggestions, it was one of the first hotels in Europe in which were embodied the conveniences and luxuries of the great hotels of the United States. He did not expect to make money out of it and had not been disappointed.

With the same ideas in mind, he built a beautiful sanatorium for Polish people in Zakopane, that lovely resort in the heart of the Tatra Mountains near Kraków. He and I collected a sum of money, chiefly from the sale of his autographs, for the erection in Warsaw of a monument to Chopin.[6] That, by the way, makes an interesting little story. The money had been raised and the commission for the monument given to Szymanowski,[7] a well-known sculptor. A committee was formed in Warsaw to take charge of it. Of course, permission had to be secured from the Russian government to place the monument, and this was thought to be comparatively easy, for Emperor Nicholas himself had a few years before granted permission to the Poles to erect the great monument to their poet Mickiewicz,[8] this in fact being one of the first acts of the tsar after his accession, and every Pole will remember the joy it brought to the nation.

6. Frédéric (Fryderyk) Chopin (1810–1849), Poland's greatest composer and pianist of the Romantic era.

7. Wacław Szymanowski (1859–1930), Polish sculptor and painter; his Chopin monument, designed in 1909, was not unveiled until 1929.

8. Adam Mickiewicz (1798–1855), Poland's national poet. His Warsaw monument was unveiled on December 24, 1898.

Nor was the joy diminished because the governor of Warsaw refused to allow any speeches, any ceremonies whatever at the unveiling.

With this in mind and knowing that Chopin, unlike Mickiewicz, had never been active politically, the committee had little doubt that permission for the Chopin monument would be granted—but it was refused, and, of course, no reasons were given. It had been intended to push the matter further when the war came and drove it out of our minds. I will confess that I had forgotten about it until last spring in Warsaw I discovered that the statue was stored in the city, ready for erection and that the committee was still in existence. It will not be long, I hope, before it will be possible to set up the statue to which so many Americans and English have contributed.

As I have said, from the very beginning he made his music a handmaid to his desire to serve his country. He carried this to a degree that few could understand and many regarded as a pose. But how wisely he built, and how time has vindicated his judgment! He regarded his music not merely as a means whereby he could accumulate wealth, which would enable him to help his country in a material way, but, even more important, he considered the position his art gave him. For over a hundred years Poland had not existed. It was no longer even a name in the family of nations. The thirty million Poles were a subject race, and the world rushing on in its own affairs was rapidly forgetting that once it had been the greatest and most powerful nation of Central Europe, that it had ruled from the Baltic to the Black Sea, that for centuries it had been the barrier between the civilization of the west and the barbarism of the east. Two hundred and fifty years ago its army under Sobieski[9] had saved Vienna and western Europe from the Turks. For over a hundred years its youth, driven from home, had shed their blood for the sake of liberty wherever liberty was being fought for. The world was rapidly forgetting this, and for it Poland had come to be an almost legendary place, which had given it a Chopin, a Sienkiewicz,[10] a Modjeska,[11] a de Reszke,[12] a Sembrich,[13] and a Paderewski.

---

9. King John III Sobieski's troops, especially Polish heavy cavalry, were the deciding force in the defeat of the Turkish army besieging Vienna in 1683.

10. Henryk Sienkiewicz (1846–1916), journalist and Nobel laureate novelist.

11. Helena Modjeska-Modrzejewska (1840–1909), renowned actress specializing in Shakespearean roles.

12. Jean de Reszke (Jan Reszke) (1855–1925), internationally renowned Polish operatic tenor.

13. Marcella Sembrich (1858–1935), stage name of Prakseda Marcelina Kochańska, coloraturo soprano, with an international singing career chiefly with the New York Metropolitan and the Royal Opera House in London.

In the councils of the world, Poland was voiceless. After the last disastrous revolution of '63, Europe forgot her, and there was no one to plead her cause. Her emigrants were scattered to the four quarters of the earth. Over four millions of them were in America,[14] and while they maintained their language, their traditions, and ever nourished the fire of their patriotism, they were lost amid the myriads of people that surrounded them.

With success there developed in the mind of my husband the idea that he could be what he has been fond of calling an "ambulant ambassador" for his people. His art had given him the position that enabled him to mingle with the greatest and the best of all countries. His art likewise had brought him into contact with the masses of the people. He believed that by always insisting upon his nationality, he could with his art, with his social qualities, with his gift to persuade, keep alive the smoldering embers in the world's memory until the day came when they brightened into glowing flame, with Poland rising from its grave and demanding her seat in the council of nations.

And so it happened that during the more than a score of years that he traveled up and down the world giving concerts, he made it his business to meet people, to know men of intelligence, position, power, and influence, to know them intimately, and to gain their trust and confidence against the day when these acquaintances and friendships would be necessary to his country. To all of them he carried the story of Poland, its sufferings, its miseries, its heroic endurance, and his own absolute belief that such unrighteousness as a nation enslaved against its will could not forever exist in this world of ours and that the time of its deliverance was surely drawing near.

With his deep insight into European politics, he realized years ago what a menace to the world Prussianized Germany had become. But then he was as a prophet crying in the wilderness. He knew from the sufferings of Prussian Poland what Prussian domination in all its brutality meant. It was not because he was insulted as an artist at his first appearance in Berlin years ago that he

---

14. Paderewska's numbers, which she repeats later in the text, are inaccurate. American immigration records generally indicate country of origin, not ethnicity. Because Poland did not regain independence until 1918, most Poles arriving from Europe before that time were Russian, German, or Austrian citizens and listed as such. There may have been more than four million immigrants to America from the lands of historic Poland, but a very substantial portion of them were not ethnic Poles, but Jews or Ukrainians. An estimate of two and a half million ethnic Poles in the United States in 1914 is probably more correct. For more extensive treatment of Polish immigration statistics, see James S. Pula's summary in *The Polish American Encyclopedia* (Jefferson, NC: McFarland, 2011), 178–84.

refused ever to play in that city again.[15] It was because he was spoken of lightly as a Pole. Added to this was his fierce resentment against the cruel repression exercised by the Prussians over their Polish subjects. Time and again since then, he has been asked to play in Berlin. Extraordinary sums have been offered to him. Twice the emperor invited him to appear there, once formally through one of his ambassadors, but he would never consider it. After he had become famous, naturally he was persona non grata in Russia, and only twice did he visit Petrograd, the second time only for one concert. Since our marriage, only once have we broken bread with a Russian, and that was a gentleman who had been very kind to my husband long ago when he was a struggling boy of sixteen.

With the war came Poland's and his opportunity. The fruit of his years of labor was ripe for the gathering. He had reached the pinnacle of his career. His art had been such, his appeal so universal that he counted among his followers not only the musical but a large part of the non-musical public. His name was familiar to all, even in countries that he had never visited, and he counted among his intimate friends many of the greatest and most influential men of the day.

Moreover, and this must never be forgotten, for they were an enormous factor in bringing about the deliverance of Poland, he had early recognized the power, the vigor, and the force of the Polish Immigration[16] in America. Although it was not until he went to America in 1915 that he came to know its leaders intimately, he quickly won the confidence and trust of the men active in business, the clergy, and the rank and file, and so it was that when the hour struck, he had behind him for his work in Poland four and a half million Polish Americans, ready to follow him to the end, to give through him their lives and their wealth to the beloved fatherland.

As I look back on all that has happened in the past six years, more and more I wonder if my husband was not an instrument divinely chosen for this work. I do not believe that any but an artist such as he could have accomplished what he did. Only an artist's imagination could have endowed a man with that

---

15. Paderewski played with the Berlin Philharmonic Orchestra under Hans von Bülow on December 8, 1890. According to Paderewski, the director behaved rudely toward him, and the critics conspired to write hostile reviews (see Ignace Jan Paderewski and Mary Lawton, *The Paderewski Memoirs* [New York: Charles Scribner's Sons, 1939], 167–72).

16. Paderewska translates the Polish term *Polonia*, or Polish diaspora in the United States, as Polish Immigration, always capitalizing it out of respect for its decisive contribution to Poland's restoration after World War I.

wonderful intuition, that unfailing vision of what was to be. None but an artist such as he could have had the opportunities to make the friendships in all countries where he determined such friendships were necessary to his cause. None but an artist such as he, I truly believe, would ever have so won the confidence of President Wilson and of our beloved friend, Colonel House.[17] Without that confidence, without that trust, without all those years of devotion and sacrifice, I wonder if ever would have come that unforgettable interview on the afternoon of November 6, 1916, when President Wilson told him that if nothing else came of the war, Poland must be free, united, and independent.

Two and a half years he was in Paris and as prime minister of Poland was a member of the Peace Conference. Many of the men who were working there he had known for years, especially the English and Americans, enjoying their confidence and through them easily winning the confidence of the others. Moreover, his knowledge of all that concerned Poland, directly and indirectly, was so embracing, so complete, and so accurate that he was accepted not only as an advocate but as an expert whose word was not to be controverted.

I have dwelt somewhat at length on this aspect of his character because unless one realizes how patriotism and love of country filled his soul, how from the very beginning they had been his chief motives, the ruling passions of his life, it will be difficult to understand all that he has been able to accomplish. Even I, his wife, his constant companion in all his journeys, in his work and play, never realized until the war came how entirely he was mastered, how practically every act of his life was directed by his love for Poland.

17. Edward Mandell House (1858–1938), American diplomat, politician, and foreign policy advisor to President Woodrow Wilson.

CHAPTER TWO

July 1910–July 1914

On the banks of the turbid, swiftly flowing Vistula, almost in the shadow of the Tatra Mountains, Kraków, the ancient capital of Poland, is a gem among the cities of the world. There for a thousand years has beaten the heart of the Polish people. There are enshrined their most precious relics of a glorious past. There in the noble Wawel Cathedral their kings are buried, from the early Piasts[1] to John Sobieski. There they have lavished their wealth on the adornment of beautiful churches. There from all parts of Poland they brought earth to build great mounds to their three most heroic characters, to the legendary Krakus,[2] who slew the dragon that ravaged the country of its fairest youth, to the Princess Wanda,[3] who rather than marry a German prince and deliver her country to the enemy leaped into the waters of the Vistula, and to Thaddeus Kościuszko.[4] It was from Kraków that Kościuszko led his bands of peasants who with their scythes cut to pieces and destroyed the Russian army in the first of our revolutions.

Kraków being off the beaten track of travel, the average tourist, to his great loss, does not know it. There are few cities in Europe that retain to so great an extent their medieval charm, and not even in the old towns of Italy is it easier to reconstruct in one's imagination the glamour and brilliance of the Renaissance. In the fifteenth, sixteenth, and seventeenth centuries when Poland was at the height of its power, it was the nerve center of Central Europe. Its university attracted students from all parts of the world. Its life as we look at it now was one continuous pageant. Its power extended from the Baltic to the

1. The Piasts, the first historical house of Poland, ruled the country from the mid-tenth century until 1370.
2. Krakus, or Krak, was the legendary prince who founded Kraków.
3. Princess Wanda was the legendary daughter and successor of Krakus.
4. Tadeusz Kościuszko (1746–1817), Polish general, veteran of the American Revolutionary War, and leader of the abortive 1794 national uprising against Russia.

Black Sea and eastward almost to Moscow. It was the last outpost of Western civilization and culture.

Time has dealt gently with the old city, and the Austrians who were its masters for seventy years treated it with respect. Unlike so many cities of its kind, it has not dwindled and died away in modern times, for as a principal city of Galicia it has been, even since the partition,[5] an important seat of government and trade. The Congress of Vienna made it an independent republic, in which condition it remained until 1848 when the Habsburgs finally secured it for their own.

When Mr. Paderewski determined to erect a monument in memory of the victory of Grunwald, Kraków was the inevitable city in which it should stand. The project of such a monument had lain in his mind since he was a little boy. I have told how passionately he had studied Polish history, and of all the episodes of the past, none had appealed to him so strongly as this victory of the Poles over the Teutonic Knights on July 10, 1410. When he was fourteen years old, he began to lay aside money for this monument, even then certain in his own mind that he would some day build it. The project was with him always, and as he matured, developed, and studied, the significance of this victory continually grew in his mind. It had meant to Poland not only the possession of West Prussia and a secure hold on the sea, but the Teutonic Knights of the thirteenth, fourteenth, and fifteenth centuries had represented as truly the Prussian ideals of brutal aggression as did William of Hohenzollern in the twentieth. Liberty was as much at stake at the Battle of Grunwald as it was in the Battles of the Marne.

To many, that he should devote a large fortune to the erection of a monument celebrating a victory a half thousand years old, seemed quixotic to the last degree. None but an artist, and a hopeless idealist at that, would have done such a thing. Yet, while sentiment was undoubtedly the ruling impulse in his ambition to build it, he foresaw, perhaps dimly, perhaps he only hoped what has come to pass, that the dedication of such a monument would fan the fires of patriotism in the hearts of his countrymen into the whitest and hottest flame. Before the war the Poles, having no country of their own and

---

5. Russia, Prussia, and the Habsburg Austria colluded in destroying the Polish state in three partitions in 1772, 1793, and 1795. The south of the country, Galicia without Kraków, was occupied by Austria in 1772. Kraków was occupied and looted by Prussia in 1795. In 1809 it became a part of a rump Polish state established by Napoleon, the Duchy of Warsaw. It was made a "free city" by the 1815 Congress of Vienna, which restored the old order in Europe upset by Napoleon. Austria annexed the "free city" in 1846.

no prospect of one, had necessarily to live much in the past, and I sometimes wonder whether the Austrian government would have given permission to build the monument in Kraków had it realized what its effect on the popular imagination was to be. From the day it was dedicated, it has been the starting point in Kraków of all great popular movements that have had to do with the well-being of the Polish race, and its dedication itself was notable for a revival of national feeling such as Poland had not seen in half a century.

But when he determined to build the monument, Mr. Paderewski foresaw the difficulties that Austria might put in the way of its erection in Kraków. It stood to reason that the Austrian government would not consent to the celebration of a victory by what was now a subject race over the ancestors of their great and good friend, the German Empire, nor would they care particularly to offend their neighbor Russia by giving the Poles an excuse for an outburst of national sentiment. Therefore, until it was in place and unveiled, it was never spoken of officially as the Grunwald Monument, but as the monument to the memory of the great King Władysław, the first of the Jagiellons. Now it happened that one of the daughters of Władysław married a Hohenzollern, and one of his granddaughters became the wife of a Habsburg; wherefore he was a revered ancestor of both families, and the Austrian authorities could not with very good grace refuse to allow the erection of a monument to his memory, since the glory he won at Grunwald reflected on their reigning house. But we Poles have never limited the significance of the monument to the good Władysław. It was intended to be to the glory of Poland, and it is.

It was in 1906 or 1907 that Mr. Paderewski, having fully determined to build the monument and having the general plan of it clearly in his mind, discovered in Paris a young Polish sculptor named Antoni Wiwulski.[6] He was a native of Lithuania, and his lot had been even harder than that of most of the poor, unknown, half-starving young sculptors of Paris. When my husband found him, Wiwulski was ill, his system already having been undermined by years of privations. He was living in a garret under a leaky roof, and for months he had not known what it was not to be hungry or had proper clothes to keep him warm. Yet a brighter, braver, more indomitable spirit I have never known.

Mr. Paderewski saw in him a remarkable talent and gave him the commission to design the monument. We had him with us in Morges for several months, and later he was provided with a fully equipped atelier in Paris. He and my husband worked together over the designs, and in three years from

6. Antoni Wiwulski (1877–1919), architect and sculptor.

the time Wiwulski began, the work was finished. The pedestal was built of pink Swedish granite, and the figures and groups that are in bronze were cast in Paris.

The monument was unveiled July 10, 1910, on the fifth hundredth anniversary of the battle. The name of the donor does not appear on it, the only words its pedestal carries being the simple inscription of the two lines:

Praojcom na chwałę
Braciom na otuchę.

It is difficult to render into English the concise beauty of the Polish thought, but a rough translation would be "To the Glory of our Forefathers! To the Heartening of our Brothers!"

The ceremonies and festivities lasted three days. In all the history of Kraków, in all the history of Poland itself, there has been nothing equal to them. The long pent-up fires of patriotism burst forth in unexampled ardor. The population of Kraków swelled from two hundred thousand to four hundred thousand. Poles came from Russia, from Germany, from all the countries of Europe, and from America. The city threw its doors wide open. Rich and poor alike gave their houses to visitors, and by common consent there was no increase in prices either in the hotels or in the shops. The police and gendarmerie were withdrawn from the city, and in all the three days of the celebration there was not a single arrest, even for drunkenness. It seemed almost as if the golden age had returned.

Roman Dmowski,[7] who nine years later was to be associated with Mr. Paderewski in the Peace Conference, went with us to Kraków. He had

7. Roman Dmowski (1864–1939), Polish politician and statesman, with a conservative and anti-German nationalist orientation; cofounder of the National Democracy (ND) political movement. He sought Polish independence through nonviolent means and supported policies favorable to the Polish middle class. He was twice elected to the Russian imperial parliament, where he presided over the Polish caucus. Paderewski donated about $1,000 to his campaign. Dmowski lost the election of 1912 to a little-known Socialist candidate because of a united front of the Polish Socialists and Jewish parties. He treated this as a personal insult and responded with a well-organized boycott of Jewish businesses. He continued his anti-Semitic agitation with the help of a Warsaw daily, *Dwa Grosze* [Two Pennies], which he founded the same year. During 1917–1919, Dmowski was one of the leaders of the Polish National Committee in Paris. Along with Paderewski, Dmowski signed the treaties of Versailles and Saint-Germain-en-Laye.

been the president of the Polish Club of Petrograd,[8] the leader of the Polish members of the Duma.[9] As the founder of the National Democratic Party in Poland, he had been a figure of great prominence in the political life of his country.

Our reception in Kraków took us completely by surprise, far surpassing anything we had expected. In depths of sentiment, in genuineness it was equaled eight and a half years later when he [Paderewski] returned to Poland after the armistice to bring order out of the confusion left by the Germans, but in 1918 there was none of the festal gaiety that characterized his entry into Kraków in 1910.

During the celebrations we were the guests of the Towarzystwo Strzeleckie,[10] an ancient hunting society that has been in continuous existence since the thirteenth century. During all those centuries it had held shooting competitions every so often, first in archery and later with firearms. Years ago the king, Sigismund Augustus,[11] had given it an emblem in gold, half cock and half eagle, and among my most treasured possessions are a bull's eye with a bullet hole through its very center and a miniature reproduction of the emblem of the club. At the great competition that was a part of the celebrations, a rifle was given to me, out of courtesy, to shoot at a target, and by some absurd chance I hit the bull's eye, the best mark that was made, and thus won the prize. How it happened I don't know, but I preserve the bull's eye and the prize as witnesses to my skill as a marksman.

The interest in this celebration was by no means confined to the Poles. The various governments that had to do with them were not at all easy in their minds over the effect the unveiling of this monument might have on the people, and they were in no small measure distrustful of Mr. Paderewski. Up to then he had never taken an active part in Polish politics, but the Germans and the Russians feared him and his influence and sent representatives to observe everything and particularly to give verbatim reports of his speeches.

8. In 1910 the name was still St. Petersburg; name changed in 1914.

9. The State Duma or Imperial Duma was the legislative assembly in the late Russian Empire. It convened four times between 1906 and the collapse of the empire in 1917.

10. Towarzystwo Strzeleckie ("Marksman Society" in English), also known as Bractwo Kurkowe, was a paramilitary and defensive, not hunting, fraternity of Kraków burghers founded in the fourteenth century. Under Austrian occupation, the organization played an important social and patriotic role in Kraków.

11. Zygmunt II August (1520–1572), king of Poland and grand duke of Lithuania.

Before the end of the first day, when the monument had been unveiled, I felt instinctively that the die had been cast. I felt that in the future, whether he wished it or not, he must be an active leader of the Poles, and I realized as I had not before that he was ready for it, that all these years he had been preparing for it. It was not the speech he made at the unveiling that gave me this feeling. That contained nothing political in nature, nothing to which even the Russians could have taken exception. The spirit of the address was that the monument was a gift of love, not one of hatred, and his text was really the inscription cut into the stone of the pedestal.

It was the attitude of the people toward him that brought to me the revelation that henceforth he must take an active part in the politics of his people. They hailed him as a leader, and it would have been in the power of no man to refuse the leadership so offered. Two other incidents showed me how well prepared he was for the task.

The first of these was unofficial. Among those who attended the unveiling were the Polish members of the Duma who had come from Petrograd, members of the Polish Club of which Mr. Dmowski was president. A luncheon was given for them at the hotel, during which many speeches were made. Mr. Paderewski was there, and in the course of the discussion considerable heat was shown. The Polish members of the Duma were not by any means unanimous in their opinions and theories regarding the future of the country, and finally Mr. Paderewski took the floor, so to say, and developed at length his belief that the great menace to the future of Poland in particular and to the world in general was not Russia but the German Empire. The authority with which he spoke, the impression he obviously made on his hearers, revealed to me for the first time the qualities of leadership that lay in him and the thoroughness of his preparation for that leadership.

The following evening came the great banquet given in his honor by the Towarzystwo Strzeleckie, at which he was the principal speaker. It is impossible to convey in words the picturesqueness of that dinner. Entering the great dining hall of the club, we were immediately transported into the past. All the members wore the gorgeous ceremonial dress that had made Polish functions so impressive in days gone by: superb silks, satins, velvets and furs, rich brocades, and priceless jewels. It was all the more spectacular because the Poles, generally speaking, are big men and wear these national costumes with ease and grace.

At this dinner Mr. Paderewski made a vehemently patriotic speech and roused his hearers to great enthusiasm. Nor did he spare them or his people. I remember he said, among other things: "We are not a people capable of hatred. We spend so much energy and anger fighting each other that when the real fight comes, we no longer have the driving power of hatred left. I consider it a morbid symptom, our inability to hate an enemy as he deserves to be hated."

Wonderful as was the first day of the celebrations when the monument was unveiled, even more so were the second and third. The feature of the second day was the exhibition given by the Falcons, a Polish gymnastic and military society. It was an extraordinary sight, those thousands of men in their picturesque costumes, going through their drills and exercises with the perfection of a machine. In Russia and Germany the Falcons had long since been under a ban, but nonetheless they had maintained their organization in secret. Thousands of them came from Russia for the festivities. Hundreds of them came secretly over the frontier without passports or permits, and many of them, when they returned, were arrested and imprisoned for weeks and months.

The climax of the celebration came on the third day, when there was a procession, a cortege in which marched over eighty thousand men. I doubt that there will ever again be anything like it. All of them were in their traditional national costumes, each organization, it seemed, a little more gorgeous and picturesque than the other. Imagine ten thousand stalwart Galician peasants, each in the white woolen costume of his native country, a long peacock feather in his hat, all of them mounted on beautiful white horses. As they passed the reviewing stand hat in hand, they bowed low in their saddles, sweeping the ground with their feathers. It all seemed as if romance in its most fantastic trappings had returned to the world for the day.

Many Poles regard as a turning point in our history the dedication of this monument. The abortive revolution of 1904–5,[12] which had amounted to less than nothing, had had a most depressing effect on the spirits of the people, and they were rapidly falling into a mood of resignation with their lot, which was very dangerous to the idea of national liberty. The celebrations at Kraków showed them again that they were still a truly great people. They awoke in them again the slumbering spirit and prepared the way for the great events

12. The events of 1904–1906 in Russian Poland, sometimes called the Revolution of 1905, were part of the widespread social and economic unrest sweeping the empire, caused largely by recession and the unsuccessful war with Japan. In Poland the situation was aggravated by national oppression. Strikes and armed resistance were suppressed by overwhelming police and military force, and though the Russian government made some concessions in the area of education and social organizations, Russian Poland remained a conquered and occupied country.

that were to come in less than ten years. The monument became at once a point of national pilgrimage. It seemed to personify and make real not only the great past of the race but the certainty of a great future.

I must pause for a moment to tell about the tragic end of the sculptor, Wiwulski. The commission to design the monument brought him prosperity. He returned to Paris to work, always hampered, however, by ill health, for already tuberculosis had begun to develop. During the latter years of the war, he received a commission to design a church for his native city of Wilno. Against the advice of his friends, he went there to superintend its construction. When in the early months of 1919, following the departure of the German troops after the armistice, Wilno and Lithuania fell into the hands of the Bolsheviks, Wiwulski immediately volunteered as a private soldier. One night when on guard duty he gave his overcoat to a fellow soldier who was shivering with the cold. He caught cold, pneumonia set in, and he died within a few days. He was an artist of very real talent, a most lovable character, and a truly brave soul.

From Kraków we went to Zakopane, for Mr. Paderewski was thoroughly exhausted and in great need of a rest. Then we returned to Morges, only for a few weeks as we were due in Lwów in October for the first Festival of Polish Musicians. Mr. Paderewski was to have played but found himself unable to do so, and Ernest Schelling—now Major Schelling—played in his stead. Major Schelling is not only one of our dearest friends, but he is one of the three pianists who can call themselves pupils of my husband, and needless to say we were more than delighted with the very great success he had there. It was at this festival that my husband made his now celebrated address on Chopin, one that has been translated into several languages and has brought him many tributes for its scholarliness and literary beauty. Needless to say that in it, he constantly emphasized the thought that was uppermost in his mind, the fostering of Polish art, Polish literature, Polish nationality.

That winter we stayed in Europe, Mr. Paderewski giving a number of concerts, and in the following summer we were able to make a tour that both of us had long planned in our minds. We went to South America, to Brazil and Argentina, Mr. Paderewski giving concerts with his wonted success; in fact, in Buenos Aires he had the greatest concerts of his whole career. The tour was interesting to him from more than one point of view. Always an ardent traveler, he was seeing new countries and meeting new people, and it was really as much a holiday for him as it was work, the concerts being in a sense only incidental to his eager study of these countries and to the multitude of new impressions he received from them. We met many interesting people and made at least one very real friend in ex-president Roca[13] of Argentina, whose death a few years later gave my husband great sorrow. It was he who took us to his great estate on the Pampas, where Mr. Paderewski saw stockbreeding on a truly gigantic scale for the first time. The sheep we now have in Switzerland are direct descendants of some he gave to us.

While we were in Rio de Janeiro, we occupied two small cottages attached to a hotel situated on a height in the suburbs of the city; we chose to go there chiefly because from these cottages we had a most ravishing view of the wonderful harbor of Rio and of the city itself. One night I was in one of the cottages while Mr. Paderewski was playing piquet[14] with his manager, Mr. Chimène,[15] in the other. It must have been nearly one o'clock when there came a knock at the door, and, opening it, I found a man standing there, who introduced himself as Jean Jaurès.[16] He had come to Brazil to give lectures under the management of Mr. Chimène, and his ship had not been expected to arrive until the next morning; hence there had been no one to meet him, and at the harbor he had been directed to come to us.

I sent him over to the other cottage, and this informal introduction led to a very pleasant acquaintance that brought us much pleasure while we were in Rio. Mr. Paderewski had never met him before, although he was quite familiar with his work. While he had respected the great Socialist's ability and sincerity, naturally the two men were at opposite poles in their beliefs, but were big enough to be able to discuss questions of the day with each other, and they met several times. Mr. Jaurès attended one of my husband's concerts, and as a result I have in my memory book a most beautiful inscription from him. We went to his first lecture but were not greatly impressed, for he had neither the personality nor voice to give him success on the lecture platform. The news of his assassination three years later on the eve of the war brought back very vividly the days we had seen him in Brazil, for my husband never met him again.

Returning to Switzerland in November, we left in the following February for South Africa. That tour, frankly, was not an overwhelming success. The people there were hardly ready to listen to serious music, and we did not stay long, for we were back in Europe in May. I remember very well that while we

13. Julio Argentino Roca (1843–1914), president of Argentina, 1880–1886 and 1898–1904.

14. A card game for two players, very popular in France and less so in England until the early twentieth century.

15. Mr. Chimène, Paderewski's French manager and agent.

16. Jean Jaurès (1859–1914), French Socialist leader.

were in the charming town of Durban, one man had a grievance, and following the truly British custom he wrote a letter to the newspaper. A little while before, he had heard a man in the course of one concert play ten instruments, including a Jew's harp, with astonishing success, all this at a cost of two shillings. What right, then, had Paderewski to demand ten shillings when he was to play only one instrument, and a piano at that?

In the autumn, we took a house in London for three months, and my husband gave numerous concerts in London and in the British provinces. Mr. Dmowski was with us there for a month, and as he was one of the principal leaders in Polish politics, Mr. Paderewski was particularly active in introducing him to leading men of affairs. During these months, my husband kept constantly in touch with British statesmen Mr. Asquith,[17] Mr. Balfour,[18] Mr. Winston Churchill,[19] Lord Northcliffe,[20] Mr. Bonar Law,[21] to name only a few of them, and always regarding himself as, so he called it, the "ambulant ambassador" of Poland, he did not miss a chance to talk Poland to these men on every possible occasion. Nor did such talk come greatly amiss, for few statesmen of the countries that have since become our allies had any knowledge of Poland two years before the war, and he was unwittingly preparing their minds for the great events of 1919, when, as commissioner for Poland at the peace conference, he argued the cause of his liberated country before some of these very men.

Another of those incidents of vision, intuition, or call it what you will. We returned to Poland in the spring when Mr. Paderewski gave several concerts in Warsaw and Lwów. There was the usual success, heightened by a warmth of greeting that was unusual even for Poland. After the third and last concert in Lwów, he left the stage in a very serious, even depressed mood, which was not his wont, for usually at the end of a recital, his spirits are very high. I asked him what the matter was, and he replied: "This is the last time I shall ever play in Lwów."

Naturally I was astonished and asked him for his reasons.

---

17. Herbert Asquith (1852–1928), Liberal prime minister of the United Kingdom, 1908–1916.

18. Arthur Balfour (1848–1930), Conservative prime minister of the United Kingdom, 1902–1905; foreign secretary, 1916–1919.

19. Winston Churchill (1874–1965), home secretary, 1910; first lord of the admiralty, 1911–1915; minister of munitions, 1917–1919; secretary of state for war, 1919–1921.

20. Alfred Harmsworth, 1st Viscount Northcliffe (1865–1922), British newspaper and publishing magnate.

21. Andrew Bonar Law (1858–1923), British politician; leader of Conservative opposition, 1911–1915; chancellor of the exchequer, 1916–1919; Lord Privy Seal, 1919–1921.

He merely answered: "I shall never play in Lwów again. You wait and you will see whether I am right."

I have never referred to it again. I cannot explain it, and I doubt that he could. After this concert he played twice in Kraków and three times in Warsaw. These were his last concerts in Poland.

We spent the winter preceding the war in America in what was altogether the most successful tour Mr. Paderewski had ever made in the United States. Between October and May he gave some eighty concerts, going from the Atlantic to the Pacific and from Canada to the Gulf of Mexico. There were two important incidents during this winter, one of them decidedly unpleasant: the effort started by various Jewish interests to boycott his concerts.

The year before, a movement had started in Poland, with its center in Warsaw, to encourage the Poles to go into trade. In the interest of this movement, a paper had been established, called *Dwa Grosze*,[22] which was immediately successful. Its gospel was that Poles should trade with Poles and thus encourage the building up of Polish shopkeepers, and as the greater part of all the small trading was in the hands of the Jews, the latter deeply resented this so-called boycott. The movement started without Mr. Paderewski's knowledge, and the paper was an assured success before he knew anything about it. Nonetheless we had hardly arrived in New York when the entire Jewish press of that city began to make the most violent attacks on him. It accused him of having furnished the money needed to establish the *Dwa Grosze*, it charged him with aiding the persecution of the Polish Jews, in fact there was no end to what it did not make him guilty of, and it demanded that the Jews boycott his concerts.

All this was very annoying, and the annoyance was not decreased by the many anonymous letters that he received in which the writers called him all manner of vile names, accused him of all manner of crimes, and threatened him with bodily harm, the favorite threat being to blow up his private car. The agitation spread all over the country and while the proposed boycott did not affect the concerts in the least, the situation was so serious that Mr. Paderewski went to certain influential Jewish friends in New York, with the result that the New York campaign came to an end before we left for the west.

Although the *American Hebrew*, a most influential paper, in a leading editorial established the injustice of the campaign, outside of New York it contin-

22. *Gazeta Poranna 2 Grosze* [Morning Gazette 2 Pennies], Warsaw daily published during 1912–1929; organ of Roman Dmowski's National Democratic Party.

ued unabated. We found it particularly active, for example, in Cincinnati, and finally when we reached San Francisco, the whole city was filled with various handbills of which the following is a sample:[23]

WILL YOU CONTRIBUTE MONEY TO HELP MURDER

INNOCENT CHILDREN DELICATE WOMEN

AND HELPLESS OLD MEN?

Then stay away from the Paderewski concerts.

This is what Paderewski did with the money he earned in the United States.

Paderewski gave $20,000.00 to establish the newspaper *Dwa Grosza*, published for no other purpose than the agitation of killing the Jews of Russia.

Paderewski's generous contribution made that agitation successful, and today, everywhere in Russia, desolate women are weeping for their slaughtered babies, husbands and fathers. Will you help Paderewski again to contribute twenty thousand dollars for murder?

San Francisco, great music lover, but greater lover of humanity, will not help the slaughter of innocents.

Stay away from the Paderewski concerts.

Respectfully,

THE JEWISH PROGRESSIVE CLUB

THE JACOB GORDIN DRAMATIC CLUB

WORKMEN'S CIRCLE, NO. 114

WORKMEN'S CIRCLE, NO. 511

---

23. A photograph of the original handbill is reproduced in *The Paderewski Memoirs*, facing page 387. The text, probably composed by a Russian Jew who very likely never saw the newspaper, calls the periodical *"Dva Grosha."* Paderewski devotes a whole chapter of his memoirs, titled "Tragic Experience," to the *Dwa Grosze* affair. Though he does not mention Roman Dmowski by name, he admits sending about $1,000 (not $20,000 as in the leaflet, and certainly not a sum with which one could start a daily newspaper) to his failed election campaign to the Duma because he liked the program of promoting the rise of a Polish middle class. Dmowski's election committee used the donation and Paderewski's name, without Paderewski's permission, to establish and promote the newspaper, which was an immediate success. Paderewski was genuinely hurt by the charges of anti-Semitism and by Dmowski's apparent breach of trust, yet he never formally disavowed Dmowski and his National Democracy movement in Poland, fearing that such a direct condemnation would further fragment the Polish political scene. Nevertheless, though Paderewski remained on good terms with Dmowski, seeing him as an important conservative ally in the struggle for Poland, their relations were never particularly close.

This was quite too unbearable, and as a result, while we were in Paso Robles, Mr. Paderewski made a formal affidavit to the effect that he had had nothing to do with the anti-Jewish movement in Poland. It was generally published, and the agitation gradually died out, but we were to hear it again the next year when we were in San Francisco.

The other incident was what brought us to our beloved Paso Robles in California. During the entire tour my husband had been more or less troubled with neuritis in his right arm, a complaint he had had off and on for several years. While we were in San Francisco, it became unendurable, and he was ordered by physicians to take a complete rest of several weeks, else it might happen that he would never be able to play again.

There was nothing to do but to cancel the concerts scheduled for the immediate future. The question then came, where should he go, and Ernest Urchs of Steinway and Sons, who was with us, recommended Paso Robles as a place suitable for rest and quiet and with waters that were supposed to be excellent for all nervous troubles and the like. So to Paso Robles we went.

Were ever a man and a woman who were to fall in love with a place introduced to it under such ghastly conditions as those in which we first saw Paso Robles! And yet if it had not been for those very conditions, perhaps we would have left at the end of our three weeks with pleasant memories but rather bored—certainly not as extensive landowners.

When we arrived we were not particularly impressed. Paso Robles itself is not much to see, although the country nearby, where our ranches are, is enchanting. At first its chief recommendation with us was the immediate discovery that the hotel was excellent, but the first real impression we got was the storm on the day following our arrival. It began in the middle of the afternoon, and I had never dreamed that so much water could fall in a given time. For nearly three weeks we were there without light, water, except mineral water from the springs and rainwater gathered in cisterns, without mail or telegraph, absolutely marooned in the midst of a raging flood. All the bridges were down for miles around, all the roads were washed out, and we had as companions some three hundred and sixty forlorn refugees caught on weekend excursions. An old friend, Sir Henry Heyman[24] of San Francisco, came to see us for a day and was forced to stay a fortnight.

---

24. "Sir" Henry Heyman (1855–1924), Jewish American violinist and director, knighted by the king of Hawaii.

It is necessary to record here another driving passion of my husband, which follows his love of country and his art. It is land. Land hunger is very characteristic of the Poles, for they are above all else an agricultural people, and it has always been very strongly developed in him. He believes in land, and it is always difficult for him to resist the temptation to purchase it wherever it may be. He even owns land in Brazil. Besides, he has always had a shrewd sense of land values. As an illustration, once in an early tour in the United States, he gave a concert in Birmingham, Alabama, which was then at the very beginning of its great "boom." There everybody was "talking corner lots," and Mr. Paderewski, having some time on his hands, very naturally looked around. He was especially interested because it was one of the first of the American "boomtowns" he had seen. He met a number of the leading men, talked with them about the possibilities of the city, and finally discovered a lot that he decided to buy. It was not particularly attractive to look at as it was then, but the price was not alarming, and he told his secretary to finish the deal the next day.

A few days later while he was on his way north, he asked his secretary for the deeds to the property as he wanted to send them with some other papers to New York. To his anger and amazement, he discovered that his secretary had not taken him seriously and had done nothing about it. Mr. Paderewski's impulse was to send him back to Birmingham by the next train, for not only had he agreed to buy the lot but he was certain that it would be a good investment, but something prevented him, and the matter was dropped. At least ten years later, in January 1905, he was again in Birmingham. When my husband saw the changes that had come to the city, he immediately remembered the lot he had wanted to buy, and nothing would do but he must see it. It took some time to locate it, for it had come to be in the center of the city, one of its most valuable pieces of land. That he was chagrined was only human. At the same time, his judgment had been vindicated.

Besides Riond-Bosson, our home in Morges, which comprises about fifty acres, he had owned a large estate in Galicia, and when the war broke out he was preparing for development a great property on the shore of Lake Geneva at Prangina, near Nyon. The part of this that borders the shores of the lake originally belonged to Prince Jerome Bonaparte, and next to it, also a part of the original estate, is where the former emperor of Austria, Charles, found refuge after the revolution that sent him into exile. The nucleus of this property was a farm that he had had for many years. There he indulged in his love for scientific farming, particularly in the breeding of hogs—always with a view to the welfare of Poland. Farming always appealed strongly to him. His boyhood had been spent among the fertile fields of Podolia, where farming is the one and only interest, and he is a true son of his province. At Riond-Bosson he had given much attention to the raising of fruit, and his grapes were almost as celebrated as my poultry, which is a great deal for me to admit.

But to return to Paso Robles. Weather-bound with absolutely nothing to do, time dragged heavily on our hands, and my husband was frankly bored and very restless. So, chiefly because he had nothing else to do, he bought land. As a result, today we regard Paso Robles as our second home, and many has been the time since when, in hours of discouragement, I have wished it were our only home, that we could spend the rest of our lives there, quietly and in peace. There we fled for a few weeks in the summers of '15, '16, '17, and '18 to get away from the agonizing worries that beset my husband, and it was there that he decided once and for all to forsake his art.

Within a half-hour's drive of Paso Robles, we have two properties, the San Ignacio ranch, which now contains something over two thousand acres, and the Santa Helena ranch of three hundred and sixty acres, which my husband gave to me as my own. On the former he has planted three hundred acres in walnuts and almonds, while I have walnuts, almonds, and prunes planted on mine. Later he bought a property of some twenty-five hundred acres in Santa Barbara County, near the Santa Maria oil fields, and some day, I hope, we shall find oil there.

Our tour in America ended in May, and we sailed for Europe on the *Kaiser Wilhelm II.* She carried a full shipload of artists, a large part of those who had been singing and playing for the Americans through the winter, including a majority of the principals of the Metropolitan Opera Company. We left America planning to return the following autumn to Australia and New Zealand, where eight years before Mr. Paderewski had had a most successful tour and where we had made many warm friends whom we wished to see again. We planned to stay in Australia until the middle of the following winter, then return by way of San Francisco and spend a month or two on our new properties at Paso Robles. The last thought in my husband's mind was that in less than a year, in almost exactly eleven months, he would be back in America, direct from Europe, to plead for Poland devastated by the great war; that we should remain in the United States for three and a half years; and that when we left, it would be to go to a free and independent Poland of which Mr. Paderewski was to be the prime minister. How strange they all seem now, those weeks of calm and quiet that preceded the Boche rush into Belgium. Even in July we were still talking Australia.

CHAPTER THREE

July 1914 – January 1915

And then came the war. It broke on us in the midst of the festivities with which we were celebrating Mr. Paderewski's name day, July 31. With us Poles the great day of the year is not our birthday, although we celebrate that, but our name day, the day of the saint after whom we have been named, and St. Ignatius Loyola, being the patron saint of my husband, for many years July 31 had been a time of high festival. As it happens, my birthday falls on August 1; therefore, our celebrations usually lasted three or four days. Except during the war, when we spent four summers in America, we were rarely absent from our home in Morges at this time, and it was Mr. Paderewski's great joy to have about him as many of his nearest and dearest friends as could come to Switzerland.

Our house, Riond-Bosson, was always full to the roof, and the overflow of guests we "slept" some in the neighboring village of Tolochenaz, some in the hotel in Morges; but all of them met at our table for luncheon and dinner, and generally it was a problem how to seat so many even in our large dining room. There were rarely less than twenty, and the table furnished a confusion of tongues. At least three languages were heard there, and sometimes four and five were going at the same time, with Mr. Paderewski acting as interpreter and keeping the conversation general. Newcomers were always amazed at the ease with which he could keep in touch with one another people of three or four different nationalities, some of them ignorant of languages except their own, and how he was never at loss to translate even puns and plays on words. Many of us who live on the continent, especially in Slavic countries, can speak three or four languages because we are taught them as children, but Mr. Paderewski not only speaks several languages but mastered them. It is a common saying among our English and American friends that few of the native born have such a command of English as he, that few understand and appreciate more clearly the very spirit of the language. They tell me that it is very unusual indeed. And this is as true of his French and German as it is of his English.

It had always been the rule during this season to forget all our cares and worries and to do everything possible to make happy the hero of the hour. Gaiety and lightheartedness were the rule, and no prank was too foolish if it brought a laugh. From year to year, the program for the two days ran along much the same lines. After luncheon on the thirtieth, the kitchen was surrendered to the chef to make final preparations for the great day, "final" literally, for he had been at work for a fortnight or more preparing his sweets and his cakes, his awe-inspiring edifices of pastry. For dinner we used to take our houseguests to the little Hotel Mont Blanc in Morges. On the morning of the fête, such guests as would went with me to church, where a special mass was celebrated. At noon the master appeared, and we used to keep up the pretty old-time custom of Poland. He stood in the great hall of the house and there received the congratulations of his friends, presents from his family, servants, and employees, and addresses from different societies, while there was always waiting for him a great pile of congratulatory letters and telegrams from all parts of the world.

After that, luncheon. The table was spread in the orangery under the great stone balcony, which forms a terrace for the house. Never less than forty sat down; often there were sixty or more, all the house party and our dearest and most intimate friends. Here a majority of our guests were Polish, the cuisine was Polish, the decorations were always in amaranth and white, the colors of Poland, and Polish was the prevailing language. What with the many courses, the many speeches, and the many toasts, the afternoon was gone by the time we rose from the table, and in the evening came the more formal festivities. So far it had been an intimate, almost family affair, but for the evening, invitations had been sent by the hundreds to all our friends and acquaintances who were within reach.

For the evening there was always some particular feature planned to take Mr. Paderewski by surprise. One year we had a Polish fête. Another year it was a most absurd symphony orchestra, and still another year—and this happened to be the last one—it was a most gorgeously beautiful Chinese pageant. The organizers of the spectacle, whatever it was, were always our dear friends Major Schelling and his wife, whose home is a few miles from ours on the shore of Lake Geneva; the brothers Morax of Morges, René,[1] the poet, and Jean,[2] the artist; and Sigismund Stojowski[3] of New York. Each year these good friends

---

1. René Morax (1873–1963), Swiss poet and playwright.
2. Jean Morax (1869–1939), Swiss painter and theater and costume designer.
3. Zygmunt Stojowski (1870–1946), Polish American pianist and composer.

devised something different and sought to outdo their efforts of the past. After the spectacle came dancing, which lasted far into the next morning, and, weather permitting, the celebration ended with a picnic the next afternoon on our property at Prangins, this in honor of my birthday.

All who were in Europe in that last month before the war will remember how blind to reality most of us were. Not until the storm broke did we really believe that there would be war, and even then it took us days to realize fully that it had come. To the very end of the month we were talking of our projected trip to Australia in the fall, and had the war held off another week, it would have found us in Austria, at a watering place we had planned to try for the first time. Mr. Paderewski was thoroughly convinced that war was inevitable. He had made up his mind about this immediately after the assassination of the Grand Duke Franz Ferdinand, and the ultimatum of Austria to Serbia served only to convince him that war was near. He knew that Germany was prepared and that France and Russia were not; but he thought it was a matter of weeks or months instead of days, and Mr. Dmowski, who was one of our guests, scoffed at the idea of immediate war. Russia, he said, would not be ready for three years, and until then she would not fight, for she realized that it would be suicidal for her to enter into a war with Germany under such conditions. In fact, persuaded by Mr. Dmowski's certainty that there was no immediate danger of war, in the last week of July I deposited a considerable sum of money in my bank in Lausanne, so that when Saturday came and my guests, most of them penniless like almost everyone else at that time, were starting for Paris and England, I had hardly a franc in the house with which to help them and could get none from the bank.

Mr. Dmowski was so sure that there would and could be no war, at least then, that in response to an urgent telegram summoning him to Poland he started for Warsaw on the afternoon of the thirty-first by way of Germany. When he reached Basel he found the frontier closed, with a fully equipped division of German troops on the other side of the line. He succeeded in hiring an automobile and finally reached Berlin. From there he started for Poland and nearly made it. He was arrested in the town of Kostrzyń, in what was then Prussian Poland, and put into jail with a Russian high official as a companion. After two weeks he was released and ultimately reached Warsaw by way of Copenhagen, Stockholm, Finland, and Petrograd. All this is by way of showing again how even men who were directly in touch with international affairs refused to believe that war was so near.

Skeptical as we were that war was at hand, nonetheless the shadow of the world tragedy lay heavy on us. Mr. Paderewski decided that there should be no change in the program, and we determined to "carry on" as if everything were normal. And really, it was an extraordinarily successful day. Everybody who came seemed to have determined to forget for the moment what was in the future and to get as much pleasure as possible out of the day. Mr. Paderewski was in constant touch with Bern and Paris and knew the developments from hour to hour. Although his anxiety increased as the day went on, he did not allow his guests to see it. I remember well the morning of the fête he made it seem that his chief worry was the nonarrival of our friend Mr. Sharpe[4] from London, with the cigars he had promised to bring. Timothee Adamowski[5] of Boston, who was one of our guests, had complained that morning that he was unable to get a newspaper, so Mr. Paderewski had a kiosk put up before the entrance of the house, and Henryk Opieński,[6] most marvelously disguised as a Polish Jew, sold ancient papers and magazines to all who would buy. That kiosk remained standing for months, a mournful reminder of a past that had gone forever.

Toward the end of the afternoon, we knew that war was inevitable. At four o'clock the bells had rung in Morges warning the people that the mobilization of the Swiss army would begin that night. Telephone messages and telegrams began to flow in from all parts of Switzerland bringing regrets from friends who had decided against coming to the evening's fête. The exodus of foreigners had already begun. All the Swiss employed on the place received orders to leave that night, and within two or three days we had hardly a man on the place because even our Russian Poles had gone to France to join the French army. That night the Swiss government requisitioned our automobile and our horses, and my only consolation during the next few weeks was that our chef was physically incapacitated for military duty.

The fête that evening was particularly beautiful. We had sent out about five hundred invitations, and despite the threatening conditions we had over three hundred guests. Madame Sembrich, with her husband, William Stengel,[7] had

4. L. G. Sharpe, Paderewski's London manager after the retirement of William Adlington; went with him on several tours of the United States, South America, and South Africa.

5. Timothee (Tymoteusz) Adamowski (1857–1943), Polish-born American conductor, composer, and violinist; first conductor of the Boston Pops Orchestra.

6. Henryk Opieński (1870–1942), Polish composer, violinist, teacher, and musicologist.

7. Wilhelm Stengel, Sembrich-Kochanska's teacher at the Lwów Conservatory and later husband.

come from her home in Nice, which she has not seen since. She was a German subject, and not only was she not allowed to return to France but all her property in Nice was sequestrated, her money in the bank, her house and its furnishings, and the greater part of her wonderful collection of jewels—nor has she yet, I believe, succeeded in getting anything back. Among the guests that the Schellings brought were Enrique Granados,[8] the Spanish composer, and his daughter. Poor man! He was to be one of the victims of the *Sussex*[9] when he was returning to Spain from New York, where his opera had been produced at the Metropolitan Opera House. Edward de Coppet,[10] the founder of the Flonzaley Quartet, who has since died, was there with his wife and son. With them came the four inseparable members of the Flonzaley Quartet. Rudolph Ganz[11] was to have come, but he had been called to the colors that afternoon. Later, when it became evident that Switzerland would not be involved in the war, he was released and allowed to go to America.

With Madame Sembrich also came Alma Gluck,[12] the soprano, and her husband, Efrem Zimbalist,[13] the violinist. Felix Weingartner[14] and his wife came from the nearby town of St. Sulpice, and Mr. and Mrs. Josef Hofmann[15] came from Vevey. Among our houseguests were the Timothee Adamowskis of Boston, Miss Eleanor Comstock[16] of New York, and our dear old friend William Adlington[17] of London. In addition to all these were, of course, the mayor of Morges, several members of the Swiss government from Bern, and many others prominent in society and politics.

8. Enrique Granados (1867–1916), Spanish pianist and composer.

9. The *Sussex* was a cross–English Channel passenger ferry torpedoed and severely damaged by a German U-boat on March 24, 1916.

10. Edward J. de Coppet (1855–1916), American banker and music enthusiast; owned a villa on Lake Geneva called Flonzaley.

11. Rudolph Ganz (1877–1972), Swiss American pianist, conductor, and teacher.

12. Alma Gluck (1884–1938), born Reba Feinsohn in Bucharest, Romania; world-famous American soprano.

13. Efrem Zimbalist (1889–1985), Russian-born American concert violinist, composer, and conductor.

14. Felix Weingartner (1862–1943), Austrian composer, conductor, and pianist.

15. Josef (Józef Kazimierz) Hofmann (1876–1956), Polish American virtuoso pianist, composer, teacher, and inventor.

16. Elinor Comstock, former student of Theodor Leschetizky, founder of the Elinor Comstock School of Music in New York.

17. William Adlington, piano teacher and one of Paderewski's representatives in London; nicknamed "Governor," he accompanied the Paderewskis on several tours in America and Australia.

As usual the weather favored our fête. It had been a beautiful, bright, warm day, and in the evening, too, it was quite comfortable to be out of doors without wraps. I remember that never had the mountains on the opposite shore of Lake Geneva been more lovely than they were at dusk. From our house we have stretched before us the whole line of Savoy Alps, from the Dents du Midi to Mont Blanc, and never during the whole summer had the "Alpine Glow" been more exquisitely radiant. At nightfall the grounds about the house were illuminated with Chinese lanterns and hundreds of tiny electric lamps in various colors.

For weeks the brothers Morax had been at work preparing the Chinese cortege, which was to be the feature of the evening. We ourselves had some very fine Chinese costumes, the Schellings had some of very great beauty, and Mr. Jean Morax had secured others with which to costume the actors. The pièce de résistance was a wonderful dragon, several meters long, with a most horrific head of paper-mache. It had great green eyes and from its mouth and nose issued clouds of smoke and flame. Major Schelling had arranged the Chinese music, and Mr. Stojowski conducted the orchestra (composed of guests), which was placed on the upper balcony of the house. And there were some charming Chinese dances done by three young girls, of whom pretty little Miss Granados was one.

After the spectacle came the dancing. For the music we had two pianos in the drawing room with two pianists at each instrument. At one of these were Josef Hofmann and Efrem Zimbalist, at the other Major Schelling and Stojowski, and a part of the time Timothee Adamowski fiddled. A very distinguished orchestra this, although not more unusual than the one we had the year before, when at the two pianos at one time were Hofmann and Olga Samaroff,[18] Schelling and Rudolph Ganz. It had always been a question in my mind which was the more skilled exponent of ragtime, Josef Hofmann or Ernest Schelling. I have seen some exciting contests between them, and the honors have always been about even.

All this time, while the gaiety was at its height, in another room, always within reach of the telephone, was a group of serious men. Most of the Swiss had brought with them their rifles and valises containing their uniforms, for they were to join the colors at daybreak. Every Swiss of mobilization age has at his home all the time his complete equipment for war, which he must keep

18. Olga Samaroff (1880–1948), American pianist, music critic, and teacher; married to Leopold Stokowski, 1911–1923.

in order and for which he is held responsible, this being one of the things that enabled little Switzerland to have 350,000 fully equipped and trained troops on the frontier within two days, an impenetrable barrier to any desire or plan the Germans may have had to rush into France over the flatlands of the northern part of the country. Rifles stacked up in a corner of the reception hall brought grim-visaged war very close to us.

Among the men were some of the higher officials of the Swiss government from Bern, and in the group about the telephone was, I remember very well, Mr. David Jayne Hill,[19] once the American ambassador in Berlin. It was a very great contrast. In one room were people dancing madly to the raging music made by four strong men at two concert grand pianos. In the next room were these very serious men who were getting news every few minutes over the telephone from Bern, Geneva, and Lausanne, and messages came through even from Paris. Mr. Paderewski divided his time between the two groups, and as the evening wore on, he became more and more anxious and worried, but even then, although in constant touch with official sources of news in Switzerland, none of us really believed that war was but a few hours away.

Although some of our guests left shortly after midnight, it was after five when the last one had gone. At the end the partings had been full of sorrow, for none of us knew when we might see one another again. Some we have never seen since. With many, it was years before we met, not until we returned to Europe after the armistice was signed, and others we were to see next in the United States, where we were to go the following spring. After all had left, Mr. Paderewski stood on the steps of the house and talked for a little time about the situation. His one thought was Poland. It was the fate of the Poles that haunted him continually. If there was war, Poland would again be a battlefield. If there was war, the Poles would be fighting against each other, some in the Russian army, some in the German, and some in the Austrian. The prospect was very terrible and the outlook was very black for us that night. Germany, my husband knew, was prepared to the last minute, and Austria in good condition. Russia had not yet recovered from the effect of the war with Japan, and France was so thoroughly impregnated with pacifism and socialism that it was a question whether she still possessed her old fighting qualities. Of course, it was not known then that England would arm, and the idea of the United States entering was not even dreamed of, although there

---

19. David Jayne Hill (1850–1932), American diplomat and historian; ambassador to Switzerland, the Netherlands, and, during 1908–1911, Germany.

was a distinct feeling among the men, a feeling that Mr. Paderewski shared, that if war really came, it would involve the whole of Europe, if not the whole of the world before it ended.

The next morning was to have been my picnic, and I was pleased to see that the sun was shining brightly. That one of our American guests had taken the early morning train for Paris did not greatly impress me. He was expecting to sail in the middle of the following week on a German ship, and he wanted to be sure that he would make it. Ultimately I believe he went in the steerage of an American liner. We had heard the various rumors that France was to mobilize at once but had not taken them very seriously, and it was planned that such of our guests as were going to Paris and London should leave the first of the week. But at ten o'clock that morning I was called to the telephone for a message from Paris from a thoughtful friend who told me that the order would be posted at four o'clock that afternoon mobilizing the entire French army and that our guests must start at once as all passenger railway traffic would cease during the period of mobilization, which might be in the neighborhood of three weeks.

My birthday that year will always be memorable. I roused the people, gave them the news, and told them to pack because they all had to leave on the night train from Lausanne for Paris. Discovering that most of them were short of money, I took the train for Lausanne, our automobile having been requisitioned by the government, and went to the bank where they courteously but firmly refused to let me have even one franc of the several thousands I had deposited just a few days before. I returned to Morges almost in despair, but by putting all our resources together we finally scraped together enough money to send to Paris those who did not have their tickets. In the evening we managed to get all their luggage to the station and saw them on their way home, leaving us utterly worn out, completely unnerved, and absolutely penniless.

But our trials were only beginning. I went into Lausanne on Monday, August 2, to lay in a stock of provisions. I had no money, but fortunately our credit was excellent. When I returned I found our house full to overflowing. There were exactly fifty-three Poles there, friends and acquaintances who had been caught in Switzerland by the war where they were spending the summer holidays, who could not get home, and even if the way had been open, like everyone else they were penniless and could not get money, no matter how large their letters of credit might have been. Riond-Bosson became at once a great Polish refugee station, and for the next three months we never had less than fifty with us, and for two years the house was full.

The first break in our colony of exiles came in November, when we lost nine of them. It was quite a thrilling little incident for us. News had come that in Genoa there was a small Russian ship about to sail for Archangelsk and that she could take a very limited number of passengers who were brave enough to endure much hardship. It seemed madness to attempt such a journey, for although the submarines had not yet become very active, there were still German raiders at sea, and even without the prospect of being captured and taken to Germany, the mere idea of spending a month or more in November and December in the North Atlantic and the Arctic Ocean was formidable enough to discourage all but the most desperate. But there were nine of our friends quite desperate enough in their desire to get home to make the adventure. And adventure it was. The ship, as ships go, was tiny. Being Russian, she was dirty. She was very slow, and while it turned out that she was seaworthy, life on her during the storms that overtook her continuously from the time she left Gibraltar was hardly worth living, and in the Arctic the exiles were nearly frozen by the cold of midwinter. It was two months before they reached Archangelsk, battling always with storms and during the greater part of the last month with ice. Within a few days after their arrival, the harbor of Archangelsk was closed for the winter, but they finally reached Warsaw, most of them destined again to be refugees when the Germans came.

We took into the house as many as we could, and it was astonishing the number we put up in our comparatively limited space. We placed others in Morges and others in Tolochenaz. We were practically without servants, although by a piece of great luck, as I have already said, our cook was not taken from us. That Monday Mr. Paderewski, Mrs. Wilkońska,[20] Miss Alma-Tadema,[21] myself, and others of the household were the waiters at the table. It would have been great fun if it had not been so serious. I had been preparing for the summer and autumn shows my two thousand prize chickens, but during the first three months of the war thirteen hundred of them did their bit for liberty by helping to feed our refugee guests. I can attest that those chickens were probably the most expensive that ever appeared on a table, even now when the present cost of chickens is considered. Our bank in Lausanne allowed us two hundred francs a week, and on this we were expected to feed fifty or more people three times a day. What a blessing it was that our credit was good.

20. Antonina Wilkońska (1858–1941), Ignacy Paderewski's sister.

21. Laurence Alma-Tadema (1865–1940), Belgian-born English novelist and poet; friend of Paderewski and supporter of Polish causes.

Our guests who had left for England that Saturday night had much the same experience that all travelers had at that time. The Adamowskis were lucky enough to receive their trunks about three months after they left Morges. Miss Comstock was held up in Paris for three weeks before she could get enough money on her letter of credit to take her to London. Mr. Sharpe, who had his son with him, stood in a densely massed crowd on the pier at Dieppe for eleven hours waiting for a boat to take them to New Haven. Monday morning, the second, there arrived from Paris a director of the Banque des Pays Autrichiens who had barely been able to get out of the city with his daughter. He told us that he had put all of Mr. Paderewski's securities in the Credit Lyonnais and that he was sending his own valet to us with a trunk containing property of his own, and would we please keep it for him until he could call for it in a few days. He left the key of the trunk with us. The key we still have, but neither the valet, trunk, nor owner ever appeared, and we never heard from him or of him.

In the confusion, which came in the first weeks of the war, it took us some little time to get our bearings, but in the autumn organized work began for the Polish cause. Not only was Morges full of Poles but there were many of them in Lausanne, and, in a sense, Lausanne became the first capital, unofficial of course, of what was to be later the Polish Republic. Every Sunday afternoon Riond-Bosson was overflowing with Polish exiles. They came from Morges, from Lausanne, from Vevey and Montreux, from Geneva, from all parts of Switzerland, wherever they happened to be. The sole topic was how the war might bring about the deliverance of their country, but the most any of them imagined possible was the deliverance of Russian Poland, of the Congress Kingdom, that it might receive real autonomy. Mr. Paderewski, however, scorned all that. I really think that his fellow Poles considered him almost if not quite mad in those days because he was talking not merely of the freedom of Russian Poland but the rebirth of old Poland with Galicia, Poznania, Silesia, West Prussia, and, above all, Gdańsk. I admit that it must have seemed a rather large program in those first months of the war when, if the Germans had been stopped at the Marne, they had on the other hand destroyed the Russian army in the Masurian Lakes.

Those Sunday afternoons at Riond-Bosson were not only interesting but they were pathetic, in a sense tragic. Riond-Bosson became a tiny bit of Poland in a foreign country, and the meetings there became the great event of the week for the exiles. There they could talk in their own language with their own people, and, being quite human, they found consolation in the fact that others were having quite as difficult times as they themselves, for few of them had ready money, and the problem of existence for all was very difficult.

The excitement among our friends was great when the news reached us of the September manifesto[22] of the Grand Duke Nicholas[23] in which he promised Poland independence following the war. Because perhaps the wish was father to the thought, all of them accepted the news at its face value, all of them except my husband, who remained exceedingly skeptical. His judgment was vindicated later when it was learned that the manifesto had been issued without the knowledge of the grand duke, some say by Prince Lvov,[24] some say by a subordinate official. At any rate, its object was to avert the possibility of a revolution in Poland, and as it turned out it was not worth the paper it was written on so far as it meant anything for Poland in the event of a Russian victory. While, of course, my husband did not know at that time that the manifesto was really a trap, he did not believe for a moment that Russia would carry out its promises once the war was over.

I remember that the *Journal de Genève* sent one of its editors to interview him on the subject. When the journalist arrived, Mr. Paderewski was very busy; he was mowing the grass of the lawn, and the journalist greeted him as "Cincinnatus."[25] Mr. Paderewski refused to be quoted over his own name, this for very obvious reasons, for had his views been published then as coming from him, his usefulness to his country would have ended there. In his work for Poland, which was shortly to begin in earnest, he had sufficient difficulty with hostile Russian influences, and he realized then that if anything was to be accomplished, it must be through Russia's allies.

The gist of the interview was that Poland, in view of her own experience in the past with Russia, could expect little, and that little diminished to nothing when one remembered what Russia in recent years had done to Finland, how she had deprived her of her ancient rights in the face of the most solemn promises made a century ago by the Imperial Council and reiterated since by every tsar. He told the story of how when the Finnish question was up before

22. The manifesto was actually dated August 14, 1914, in St. Petersburg. It promised the Poles a united, autonomous country ruled by the Russian tsar.

23. Grand Duke Nicholas Nikolaevich of Russia (1856–1929), cousin of Tsar Nicholas II, commander in chief of Russian forces during 1914–1915.

24. Prince Georgy Lvov (1861–1925), Russian statesman; prime minister in 1917.

25. Lucius Quinctius Cincinnatus (519–430 BC), the "savior of Rome"; in 458 BC, he was plowing his land when he was asked to lead the forces of the republic against invading enemies; he became Rome's symbol of virtue and simplicity.

the Imperial Council, Baron Rosen,[26] who came from the Baltic provinces, protested most vehemently against this injustice, which he did not hesitate to characterize as a crime. The answer he received was that since he was only partly Russian he would never be able to understand that imperial Russia kept her promises or broke them as she pleased, that her only guide in such things was the welfare of Great Russia as interpreted by the true Russians.

Toward the end of October, Henry Sienkiewicz finally arrived from Austria, where he had been detained for weeks, the coming of the war having found him on his property near Warsaw, which had been given to him by the Polish people. The debt of Poland to Sienkiewicz is something very difficult to explain to other peoples. Abroad he is remembered chiefly as the author of *Quo Vadis*, which has been in such an enormous vogue throughout the world. There was a time when his Polish historical novels enjoyed a considerable popularity, especially in America and Germany, but never in the smallest degree comparable with their significance to the Poles. We were gradually coming completely under foreign, particularly French, influences in our literature and our art and thus had made a considerable advance forward to the first stages of denationalization. Our authors were following French models. The latest French book was as much an event in Warsaw as it was in Paris. French was becoming rapidly the usual language among the cultured classes, and we were on the highway to forget our own noble literature.

Then came Sienkiewicz, who awakened us with a shock. His *With Fire and Sword*, *The Deluge*, and *Pan Michael* appealed to foreigners as vividly picturesque historical novels that might or might not be true to fact, the latter being of comparatively small importance. What appealed to the Poles was the truth of the pictures of their glorious past. Sienkiewicz is to them not merely the greatest of their novelists but the man who through his books revived the dwindling fires of national life. No translation can carry into another language the beauty of his style, as no translation can bring to foreigners the truthfulness of the pictures of Polish life and characters he made with his pen.

Directly after war had been declared, he started for Switzerland, but when he arrived in Vienna he was arrested by the Austrian authorities as a Russian subject and held for several weeks. Then he came to Switzerland, and after staying a few weeks in Lausanne, he went to Vevey, where he lived until his death. He was a man of very unusual personal and intellectual charm. He had traveled widely and observed closely and was an admirable talker. If he

26. Helena Paderewska's maiden name was Rosen, so the story has a familial touch.

lacked the aggressive force to carry on a great campaign on behalf of Poland himself, his was a name around which all Poles would rally, for he was in a sense a national hero.

It was in November that Erasmus Piltz[27] suggested to my husband that he and Sienkiewicz organize a Committee for Polish Relief. A considerable part of our country had already been devastated by the war, suffering was already intense, and through lack of seeds the prospects for the next harvest were none too good. The immediate relief of the suffering of our people was to be the first and obvious purpose of this committee, but equally important was to secure publicity for Poland, to distribute propaganda.

Foreigners do not and cannot realize how completely without a voice in the world Poland was in those first months of the war. She had been almost forgotten, her very existence as a nation had become little more than a legend before the war began, and afterwards in the struggle of giants that was in progress she was utterly lost. This was especially true in the case of the Entente, for Poland—that is, the part of Poland that had been best known—was a part of the Russian Empire, and there was no desire on the part of England or France to do anything that might hurt the feelings of their powerful ally. This was brought home to us with great force a few months later in Paris and London.

The committee was formed with Sienkiewicz as president and my husband as vice president. The leading Poles who were then in Switzerland were in it, among them Erasmus Piltz, Marian Seyda,[28] Adolph Święcicki,[29] Vincent Lutosławski[30]—whose two brothers were to become victims of the Red Terror in Moscow—Professor Askenazy,[31] the eminent historian, and Kucharzewski,[32] who later was prime minister of Poland under the German regime.

Before this committee was able to function, it was necessary to secure the permission of the Swiss government. Mr. Paderewski went to Bern for this

27. Erazm Piltz (1851–1929), Polish journalist, politician, and member of the Russian Duma in 1914.

28. Marian Seyda (1879–1967), Polish politician, journalist, and member of the National Democratic movement.

29. Julian Adolf Święcicki (1850–1932), Polish writer and translator of Romance languages; member of the Frederic Chopin Monument Committee in Warsaw (1912).

30. Wincenty Lutosławski (1863–1954), Polish philosopher and author; member of the Polish National League.

31. Szymon Askenazy (1866–1935), Polish historian and professor at the University of Lwów.

32. Jan Kucharzewski (1876–1952), Polish historian; prime minister of German-occupied Kingdom of Poland during 1917–1918.

purpose with Sienkiewicz and Professor Kowalski,[33] now Polish ambassador to the Vatican, and was successful, having been able to show the Swiss authorities that there was no militant purpose behind the committee. The day that this permission was granted was memorable for Poland, as it was the first time in nearly a hundred and fifty years that any government had given formal recognition to a Polish organization as distinctly Polish.

In the beginning progress was slow. Poland above all else needed publicity, and, realizing that there was comparatively little literature available for those who knew only French or English, Mr. Seyda and Mr. Piltz undertook the preparation of the Polish encyclopedia in both of those languages, a book that was to be of great value in the work of propaganda that was soon to begin. Mr. Paderewski, in the meantime, was buried in his studies. His library was filled with maps and books relating to the war in general and Poland in particular. The more he studied and the more he observed, the more he was convinced that Poland's sole hope lay in the Entente. He was not certain how it would work out, but he was certain that if Germany won the war, the last hope of Poland would be gone. It was following this line of thinking that he decided that if Poland was to share in the victory over Germany, it was above all necessary that there should be not any army of Poles but a Polish army fighting with the armies of France and Great Britain.

It became evident very early that the central committee in Switzerland must necessarily be very limited in its work and if anything worthwhile was to be accomplished, centers must be established in France, England, and the United States. Therefore, Mr. Paderewski volunteered to go to Paris, London, and New York and establish committees in those cities. We left Morges at the end of January, expecting to be away three months at the most, planning to give three weeks to Paris, three weeks to London, and six weeks to going to and returning from the United States. We returned to Morges for one day at Easter, 1919, more than four years later.

---

33. Józef Wierusz-Kowalski (1866–1927), Polish physicist and diplomat; Polish envoy to the Holy See, 1919–1921.

CHAPTER FOUR

January–April 1915

It was only when he began his work in Paris that my husband realized how difficult the task he had undertaken was. That he finally succeeded in gaining nearly all he aimed at is true, but it was only after many disillusions, many disappointments, many hours of discouragement. He began to realize in Paris how little the world knew of Poland and how little it cared. In Paris and again in London, he was made to realize what the influence of Russia meant. In Paris, Russia was all powerful, for it was Russia during these first months of 1915 who was ready to win the war. In London, a few weeks later, they were still talking of the Russian "steamroller" that was to crush the eastern frontiers of Germany and Austria as if they were paper shells.

Hardly had we settled in Paris than he found himself, as it were, surrounded by a stone wall against which he beat himself in vain. Our friends greeted us with kind and cordial words, they expressed the deepest sympathy for our cause, but—we were subjects of Russia, we Poles, and they could do nothing, officially or semiofficially, without the consent, approval, and cooperation of Russia. The Russian ambassador was Count Izvolsky,[1] a man thoroughly anti-Polish in his sympathies and representing an aspect of Russia that we Poles hated the most. When my husband realized that no committee could be formed unless Izvolsky was, at least nominally, the head of it, the outlook was very discouraging.

In the meantime, some progress was being made in other directions. I must always recall with gratitude the kindness of Mrs. Bliss[2] of the American embassy, she who organized the first American ambulance service in France.

---

1. Alexander Izvolsky (1856–1919), Russian foreign minister during 1906–1910; ambassador to France during 1910–1917.

2. Mildred Barnes Bliss (1879–1969), art collector and philanthropist; wife of Robert Woods Bliss (1875–1962), secretary of the US embassy in Paris, 1912–1916, and counselor of the embassy, 1916–1919.

It was through her, at least at her house, that we met Mr. Denys Cochin,[3] who became one of my husband's most helpful friends and one of Poland's most ardent partisans. Her kindness also enabled me to get my first glimpse of what war really meant, for through her I was able to inspect the wonderful American hospital at Neuilly, and she obtained permission for me to visit the wounded Polish prisoners in the Val de Grace hospital. There were fourteen or fifteen of them, all of them from the province of Poznań, compelled to serve in the German army whether they liked it or not. I wanted to do something to make them more comfortable and happy, although they were a cheery lot of fellows despite the fact that most of them had lost one of both of their legs. What impressed me most was that while they were grateful for the chocolate, cigarettes, and soap I gave them, all of them wanted beyond anything else a looking glass, and when I had given each of them a little pocket mirror, they were quite happy and content.

We also secured permission from the government to look after the welfare of the Polish prisoners. This work was undertaken by Władysław Mickiewicz,[4] the son of our great poet and then a man of nearly eighty, and his daughter, Marie.[5] If the story of all the devoted service that was given during the war is written, there can be no brighter chapter than that which tells of the work of Władysław Mickiewicz and his daughter. For five years, until the last Polish prisoner was repatriated, they never ceased their efforts. They went from prison camp to prison camp, wherever there were Poles, and brought them comfort and words of cheer and alleviated their sufferings to a great degree. Both of them delicate, it is nothing short of wonderful that they were able for so long to endure the hardships and privations that this work brought with it. And beyond this, after the war they undertook to look after the well-being of the Polish laborers and artisans who came to France to help in the work of reconstruction.

It was during the early days of our stay in Paris that the idea came to me of selling in America dolls made by Polish artists in Paris. Miss Mickiewicz and I were walking along one of the boulevards when I saw in a window some most interesting French and Alsatian dolls that were being sold for the benefit

3. Denys Cochin (1851–1922), French writer and Catholic politician; during 1893–1919, he represented Paris in the French National Assembly.

4. Władysław Mickiewicz (1836–1926), Polish émigré activist and publisher in France.

5. Marie Mickiewicz (1868–1952), Polish émigré activist in Paris; granddaughter of Adam Mickiewicz.

of a war charity. That gave us the idea. In Paris at that time, there were many Polish students and artisans who were all but destitute, for they could receive no money from home, and there was little chance of making money in Paris. A Madame Łazarska[6] had already started a little atelier where small articles were being made, and taking this as a beginning, we started the manufacture of the Polish dolls that became so well known during the next two years all over America. With the motto "Buy a Doll and Save a Life," I carried trunks of them from one end of the United Sates to the other, selling them wherever my husband gave a concert. It was hard work, but it paid off. Not only did these dolls provide a means of existence to many Polish artists and refugees in Paris, who were well paid for making them, but with the profits I was able to buy milk for the babies in Poland and do many other things of value. In the two years that I carried the dolls around with me in America, selling them at concerts, at fairs, and at bazaars, I raised nearly $100,000.

In the meantime, Mr. Paderewski was working tirelessly on his committee. Everywhere he met with the same answer, that nothing could be done without Count Izvolsky. He even went directly to Mr. Poincaré,[7] the president of the French Republic, who gave him much the same answer. Poland was a part of Russia, and as Russia was the invaluable ally of France, it would be quite impossible for the French government, directly or indirectly, to sponsor any movement having to do with a part of Russia without the approval of the Russian ambassador. On this account it was impossible to arrange even a Polish Day in Paris, although all the other countries of the Entente were holding such days.

Having every reason to believe that Count Izvolsky would not of his own account have anything to do with such a committee, Mr. Paderewski resorted to a little ruse. He went to Emile Loubet,[8] former president of the republic, and presented the case to him. He found Mr. Loubet very cordial and in the end obtained his consent to be one of the heads of the committee if England and Russia were similarly represented. Then my husband went to Sir Francis Bertie,[9] the British ambassador, and asked him if he would allow his name to be used for this committee with Mr. Loubet's and Count Izvolsky's. Sir Francis readily agreed to this, and armed with these two powerful names he went to

6. Stefania (Krautler) Łazarska (1887–1977), Parisian doll maker and painter.

7. Raymond Poincaré (1860–1934), four-time French conservative prime minister; president during 1913–1920.

8. Emile Loubet (1838–1929), president of the French Republic during 1899–1906.

9. Francis Bertie, 1st Viscount Bertie of Thame (1844–1919), British ambassador to France (1905–1918).

Izvolsky himself. There was then nothing for the Russian ambassador to do but to accept the honor of serving on this Polish committee, which he did, but not with the urbanity one would look for in a distinguished diplomat. However, it was of no importance to my husband what Count Izvolsky really thought about the committee after he had agreed to allow his name to be used, for once Russia had approved of the undertaking, everything moved rapidly.

The Duchess d'Uzès[10] accepted the presidency, and the first meeting of the committee was held at the house of Princess de Brancovan,[11] an old friend of my husband, and the first five thousand francs were given by the Princess de Polignac.[12] Among the very first to join was Gabriel Hanotaux.[13] Others were Mrs. Denys Cochin, Briand,[14] Barthou,[15] Edmond de Rothschild,[16] Jean de Reszke, Count Michael Potocki,[17] Władysław Mickiewicz, Princess de Caraman-Chimay,[18] Princess de Brancovan, Princess Elizabeth Poniatowski,[19] Mrs. de Reszke,[20] and Countess Tyszkiewicz.[21]

Izvolsky was not at the first meeting of the committee and professed to be greatly aggrieved that he had not received notice of it in time. My husband called on him to explain that Mr. Hanotaux had been leaving Paris most unexpectedly and had particularly asked that the meeting be held before he left so that he could attend, for which reason it was possible to give only a few hours' notice, and Mr. Izvolsky had another engagement. That the Russian ambassador was unable to attend gave Mr. Paderewski no very great sorrow,

10. Marie Thérèse d'Albert de Luynes (1876–1941); d'Uzès is the premier title in the peerage of France.

11. Born Rachel Mussuros (1847–1923), pianist and socialite, she was the widow of Prince Gregoire Bibesco-Bessaraba de Brancovan (1827–1886), and the mother of Countess Anna de Noailles (1876–1933), writer.

12. Princess Edmond de Polignac (1865–1943), American-born Winnaretta Singer, heiress to the Singer sewing machine fortune; musical patron.

13. Gabriel Hanotaux (1853–1944), French statesman and historian.

14. Aristide Briand (1862–1932), served eleven times as prime minister of France.

15. Louis Barthou (1862–1934), French politician; prime minister in 1913.

16. Edmond de Rothschild (1845–1934), of the French banking family; philanthropist; supporter of Zionism.

17. Michael Potocki later in the war organized the League for the Care of Polish Soldiers.

18. Princess de Caraman-Chimay (1873–1916), born Clara Ward, American socialite married to a Belgian prince.

19. Not clear whom the author had in mind; Princess Elizabeth Poniatowski, born Elizabeth Sperry, and sister of Mrs. William Crocker, died in 1911.

20. Maria de Goulaine, earlier married to Count Mailly-Nesle.

21. Not clear whom the author had in mind.

and he had still less regret after the call he made on Mr. Izvolsky. To put it mildly, the ambassador was most unpleasant and said all the polite things his ingenious mind could devise to let my husband realize the contempt in which he held Poland and the Poles.

That Edmond de Rothschild became a member of the committee should practically be a sufficient answer to the charges that had been made in America the year before, that Mr. Paderewski had started a campaign against the Polish Jews. Not long after our arrival in Paris, Mr. Rothschild asked my husband to lunch with him, and at this luncheon the entire Jewish question was discussed with the utmost frankness on both sides. Later Mr. Rothschild asked my husband to put his views in writing, which he did.

Our stay in Paris turned out to be thoroughly successful from almost every point of view. Mr. Paderewski succeeded in forming a distinguished and influential committee through which a considerable sum of money was raised, and, more important still, he secured a large amount of publicity for Poland. The press was more than generous. The appeal that had been written by Sienkiewicz was printed in full, provoking much comment, and after the first meeting of the committee, most of the important papers carried leading articles on Poland. From that time on, there was rarely a week that Poland did not figure in the public press.

There was one incident during our stay in Paris that went far toward consoling my husband for the disappointments that beset him when we first arrived there. When we left Switzerland, of course, we had no money. Our bank allowed us two hundred francs a week, on which we were expected to maintain our full house of refugees. It was actually difficult to raise enough cash to take us to Paris, but once in Paris, we had been certain that there would be no more difficulty, for not only did Mr. Paderewski have a considerable sum on deposit there but the greater part of his securities was in the Credit Lyonnais. It is not difficult to picture his state of mind when he discovered that not only was he unable to draw on his funds but could not even negotiate a loan on his securities. We needed much money for our expenses in Paris, London, and New York, and for a time it looked as if we should not be able to get any.

Finally, one day, as a forlorn hope, we spoke of this to Mr. Chimène, who had arranged our tour in South America four years before. We thought possibly that he might have some influence with the Jewish bankers. When my husband explained his plight to him, he exclaimed: "Mon maître, Paderewski cannot borrow any money in Paris? What you need I shall give you, and I shall bring it at once."

As a result, this friend, on whom we had no claim whatsoever, put all his securities together, raised money on them, and was able to let us have sixty thousand francs. It was practically all he had in the world, and his wife came to us lamenting it was not more, this despite the fact that the loan left them nothing, and Mr. Chimène was soon to enter the service. To be sure, we thought we should be back in Paris in two months at the latest, but it was three years and a half before we returned, and only then were we able to repay him.

Reaching London, we found the city "Russia-mad," so to say. Russian art, Russian music, Russian literature, Russian dancing, everything Russian was the last word in London in that early spring of 1915. The Russian "steamroller" as it was called, was crashing through Galicia, smashing the Austrian army that opposed it. Przemyśl had fallen, Lwów was doomed, and everybody thought that Austria would be completely crushed within a few weeks. The disappointments on the western front were more than equaled by the unbroken series of victories the Grand Duke was winning in the east. Generally speaking, the time was not very propitious for the launching of a movement in favor of Poland, even when that movement had no militant significance, and we found the same condition in London that had met us in Paris, except for one very great difference.

When we arrived in London, we were met by our friend Miss Laurence Alma-Tadema, who had already started working for Polish Relief. She has been one of the most untiring friends of my country and did much for the Poles during the war. She organized the Polish concert in London when Sir Edward Elgar's[22] "Polonia" was played for the first time. She organized a school for Polish refugee children in Fribourg, Switzerland, and when the Swiss government forbade the bringing into the country of any more children, she took them to England, and there established three schools. The British government gave her the authority for final approval of all applications made for certificates of Polish citizenship and Polish passports, and her zeal for Poland was untiring throughout the war.

But when she met us she was thoroughly discouraged. The town, she said, had gone quite daft over everything Russian. It knew nothing of Poland and cared less. It would be a waste of time and effort to form a committee and raise any considerable sum of money; rather, she thought Mr. Paderewski might give two concerts, which were certain to raise at least two thousand pounds.

---

22. Sir Edward William Elgar, 1st Baronet (1857–1934), British composer. The concert during which Elgar's symphonic prelude "Polonia" was played took place in Queen's Hall on July 6, 1915, with all of the receipts going to the Polish Victims' Relief Fund.

But my husband had other ideas. True, he discovered almost immediately that he could do nothing in London without the approval of the Russian ambassador, but fortunately Count Benckendorff [23] was quite a different type of man than Izvolsky in Paris. Moreover, it was almost immediately evident that once the approval of the Russian embassy was secured, the rest would be easy. When Mr. Paderewski explained what he wanted, Count Benckendorff not only gave his approval but became active in forming the committee. Talking one day to my husband, he said: "I think you ought to direct most of your work on behalf of the Poles of Galicia. They are suffering the most. Their country in the east has been almost entirely destroyed, and although they are subjects of Austria, they are nonetheless Poles. Russia is big enough and rich enough to take care of the Russian Poles who are in distress."

I question whether any foreign cause ever brought together such a distinguished committee as that Mr. Paderewski succeeded in forming in London. At its head were Cardinal Bourne,[24] the French ambassador,[25] the Belgian minister,[26] and the prime minister, Mr. Asquith. Following the name of the prime minister came that of the Marquess of Crewe,[27] whose father before him had been at the head of a Polish Relief committee that had done much for our country before. On the list were the Dukes and Duchesses of Norfolk[28] and Somerset,[29] the Duchess of Bedford,[30] the Marquess and Marchioness of Ripon,[31] the Earl of Rosebery,[32] Lord Charles Beresford,[33] Lord Northcliffe,

23. Count Alexander Konstantinovich Benckendorff (1849–1917), Russian ambassador to United Kingdom during 1903–1917.

24. Francis Bourne (1861–1935), archbishop of Westminster, 1903–1935; made cardinal in 1911.

25. Paul Cambon (1843–1924), French ambassador in London, 1898–1920.

26. Count Charles de Lalaing (1856–1919), Belgian minister in London.

27. Robert Crewe-Milnes, 1st Marquess of Crewe (1858–1945), British Liberal politician and writer.

28. Norfolk is the premier duke in the peerage of England; Henry Fitzalan-Howard (1847–1917), 15th Duke of Norfolk, married to Gwendolen Constable-Maxwell.

29. Algernon St. Maur, later Seymour (1846–1923), 15th Duke of Somerset, married to Susan Margaret Richards Mackinnon (d. 1936), noted philanthropist.

30. Mary Russell, Duchess of Bedford (1865–1934), English aviatrix, ornithologist, and founder of hospitals.

31. Frederick Robinson, 2nd Marquess of Ripon (1852–1923), married to Gwladys Herbert, Marchioness of Ripon (1859–1917), patron of the arts.

32. Archibald Primrose, 5th Earl of Rosebery (1847–1929), Liberal statesman and prime minister in 1886; married to Hannah de Rothschild.

33. Lord Charles Beresford (1846–1919), British admiral and member of Parliament.

Sir Edward, now Viscount Grey,[34] Arthur J. Balfour, Austen Chamberlain,[35] Winston Churchill, Lloyd George,[36] Bonar Law, Reginald McKenna[37]—nearly every member of the government—the Lord Mayor of London,[38] Sir Edward Poynter,[39] Sir Ray Lankester,[40] Sir George H. Perley,[41] High Commissioner of Canada Thomas Mackenzie,[42] High Commissioner for New Zealand Peter McBride,[43] High Commissioner for Victoria John S. Sargent,[44] H. Gordon Selfridge,[45] Thomas Hardy,[46] Edmund Gosse,[47] Sir George Alexander,[48] Sir George Frampton,[49] Lady Randolph Churchill,[50] Lady Charles Beresford,[51] Mrs. Leopold de Rothschild,[52] Mrs. Asquith,[53] Mrs. Lloyd George,[54] and many others, representing the best in politics, art, and society.

Lord Northcliffe, who had been for more than a dozen years a friend of my husband, threw open the columns of the *Times* to him and brought him into

34. Edward Grey, 1st Viscount Grey of Fallodon (1862–1933), British Liberal statesman; foreign secretary, 1905–1916; ambassador to the United States, 1919–1920.

35. Austen Chamberlain (1863–1937), British statesman, half-brother of Neville; chancellor of the exchequer, 1903–1905 and 1919–1921.

36. David Lloyd George (1863–1945), British Liberal politician; prime minister during 1916–1922.

37. Reginald McKenna (1863–1943), British banker and Liberal politician; home secretary, 1911–1915; chancellor of the exchequer, 1915–1916.

38. Sir Charles Johnston, 1st Baronet (1848–1933), Lord Mayor of London, 1914–1915.

39. Sir Edward Poynter (1836–1919), English painter; president of the Royal Academy of Arts.

40. Sir Ray Lankester (1847–1929), British zoologist.

41. Sir George Halsey Perley (1857–1938), American-born Canadian politician and diplomat; Canadian high commissioner to the United Kingdom during 1914–1922.

42. Thomas Mackenzie (1854–1930), prime minister of New Zealand in 1912; later New Zealand high commissioner in London.

43. Sir Peter McBride (1867–1923), Australian politician and industrialist; appointed Victorian agent-general in London in 1913.

44. John Singer Sargent (1856–1925), American portrait painter.

45. Harry Gordon Selfridge (1856–1947), American-born British retail magnate.

46. Thomas Hardy (1840–1928), English novelist and poet.

47. Sir Edmund Gosse (1849–1928), English poet, author, and critic.

48. Sir George Alexander (1858–1918), English actor and theater producer.

49. Sir George Frampton (1860–1928), British sculptor.

50. Lady Randolph Churchill (1854–1921), born Jeanette Jerome, was the American wife of Lord Randolph and mother of Winston.

51. Lady Charles Beresford (d. 1922), born Mina Gardner.

52. Mrs. Leopold de Rothschild (1862–1937), born Marie Perugia; daughter of a Trieste merchant.

53. Mrs. Asquith, born Margot Tennant, Asquith's second wife.

54. Dame Margaret Lloyd George (1866–1941), born Margaret Owen.

contact with Mr. Steed,[55] the foreign editor of the *Times*. I very well remember a luncheon that Mr. Steed gave us during which he said:

> The future map of Europe is already settled [this being three and a half years before the end of the war—HP]. Poland will have autonomy under Russian rule. The Czechs will unite with the Moravians and Slovakians for a new country, free and independent. To the Serbs will go the greater part of Dalmatia, Herzegovina, and Bosnia, and a large part of Croatia. Russia will have Constantinople and the Straits, while to Italy will be given the Trentino.

The ignorance of most of these Englishmen and Englishwomen in all things regarding Poland was simply appalling to us, although I suppose we should not have been surprised. I remember that Lady Randolph Churchill, who was more than kind and worked very hard for the committee, said at a dinner one day that Poland would be free in two years and have a perfectly good king to rule over it. At a luncheon that Mr. Lloyd George gave for Mr. Paderewski, Poland was naturally the sole topic of conversation. Przemyśl had just been taken, and a considerable part of the time was consumed in attempting to teach our English friends how the word was pronounced. I was meeting Lloyd George, at whose side I sat, for the first time, and I remember how greatly impressed I was at the keenness and quickness of his mind. He frankly confessed that he knew little about Poland, and during the greater part of the luncheon, I underwent a cross-examination at his hands that left me quite exhausted.

In the meantime, Mr. Paderewski had embarked temporarily on a journalistic career. His first article in the *Times*, which was supplemented by a leader written by Mr. Steed, attracted much attention and won much praise. It even brought a note of warm approval from Count Benckendorff, who asked him, in his next article, to say something nice about the Grand Duke Nicholas, which he was very glad to do. He met all the leaders of the London press. One day, Mr. H. E. Morgan,[56] Lloyd George's private secretary, gave a luncheon for him at which the other guests were fourteen of the leading journalists of England. It was during this time, too, that he made an important discovery,

55. Henry Wikham Steed (1871–1956), British historian and journalist; editor of the *Times*, 1919–1922.

56. Herbert Edward Morgan, business executive; author of the 1914 book *The Dignity of Business*; later assistant to Lloyd George in Ministry of Munitions.

that it will never do to send an article to one paper one day and to another the next, thinking that both would print it. I remember he had an article of importance in the *Daily News* and was greatly concerned that the *Times* did not print it the following day. He called up Lord Northcliffe to ask him why. His mistake, I suppose, was a mistake that most apprentices make, but it was never repeated.

The work that began with such success in London did not stop there. It spread to Australia and New Zealand, where some of the best results for Polish Relief were achieved. An appeal was made to those countries, and thousands of dollars were sent to us in the next few months. Madame Melba,[57] who was in Australia at that time giving concerts for the benefit of the Red Cross, gave one for Poland that raised $60,000. She even put up her own dog for sale and received £2,000 for it.

In New South Wales the work of providing relief for Polish war sufferers was carried on with extraordinary activity, especially when one considers that Australia had to do so much for its own people during those years. It was only when the government was compelled to forbid the collection of funds for Poland that the schoolchildren of New South Wales ceased to contribute, and as soon as the armistice was signed, the work was resumed. Through the wonderful generosity of our Australian friends, Mr. Paderewski, on leaving Poland this February, was able to give the handsome sum of six million marks to various causes.

It was very interesting to observe the attitude of our English friends toward my husband during these weeks in London. His art and that he was an artist seemed to have been forgotten completely. He was accepted as a publicist, as if his whole life had been given to such work. Rarely was there any talk of music, the men and women we were seeing having little time and less inclination in March 1915 to talk of art. Mr. Paderewski was accepted at once and without question as an expert on the situation in the Near East[58] and, naturally, as a special representative of his country. Even then, when the war was so young, it was felt that one of the results must be a solution of the Polish question, and my husband's advice and opinions were constantly sought.

57. Dame Nellie Melba (1861–1931), born Helen "Nellie" Porter Mitchell, Australian operatic soprano.

58. During World War I the concept of the "Near East" included much of central and southeastern Europe as well as the Asian domains of the Ottoman Empire. After the war and the dissolution of the Ottoman state, the term "Near East" was no longer applied to parts of eastern Europe.

The concrete results of his work in Paris and London were of very great value. Not only had he succeeded in starting the work of relief but he had secured great publicity for Poland. He had made it possible that Poland was once more written about and discussed, and much information had been spread abroad.

But to my mind, much more important than any of the immediate results that came from his work in Paris and especially in London was the impression he made on the leading men of France and Great Britain. It is no exaggeration to say that he astonished even those who had known him well for years. His political knowledge, his grasp of the great problems, his farsighted vision, and above all his sincerity and obvious honesty of purpose won for him admirers and friends among the leading men of all parties. It was as if he had never been an artist. He seemed to be accepted at once as a trained statesman. At the time it was impossible to appreciate this in its fullness, but directly after the armistice was signed and we were again in Europe, it was the British government that asked him to go to Poland and rescue the country from the chaos.

We sailed on the *Adriatic*[59] on April 7. Although this was more than a month before the *Lusitania*[60] was sunk, everybody was taking precautions, and I remember at the last minute we had to have life jackets specially made for us, as there were none to be had in the London shops. The trip to New York was characteristic of such trips during the war, a dark ship, no wireless, boat drills, and all the other nerve-wracking accompaniments of those journeys. The ship's company was small. Of those on board I remember Charles Klein,[61] the dramatist who was a *Lusitania* victim six weeks later, and Miss Alice Kauser,[62] of New York, who in the next year or so was a most useful friend and did much to help me in my work. The ten days aboard ship were very restful, very welcome after the two tense months we had had in Paris and London, and they were really the last days of rest that my husband had until he left Warsaw to go to our home in Switzerland after he had retired from the government.

---

59. RMS *Adriatic*, ocean liner of the White Star Line.

60. RMS *Lusitania*, British ocean liner sunk by a German U-boat on May 7, 1915, near Ireland. Among the victims were many Americans.

61. Charles Klein (1867–1915), British American playwright and actor.

62. Alice Kauser (1872–1945), theatrical agent.

Helena Paderewska, circa 1900.
[Archiwum Akt Nowych, Warsaw]

Wedding photo of Helena and Ignacy, Warsaw, 1899.
[Polish Music Center, University of Southern California]

Monsieur I. J. Paderewski et Madame Hélène Baronne de Rosen ont l'honneur de vous faire part de leur mariage qui a été célébré le 31 Mai 1899 en l'Eglise St Esprit à Varsovie.

Announcement of Helena and Ignacy's wedding, 1899.
[Hoover Institution Library & Archives, Stanford, California]

Helena Paderewska, Antonina Wilkońska, and Ignacy Paderewski at Riond-Bosson, the Paderewski's estate in Morges, Switzerland, c. 1900. [Hoover Institution Library & Archives]

(Above) Helena with Alfred Paderewski. Riond-Bosson, 1900.
[Hoover Institution Library & Archives]

(Left) Ernest Schelling, c. 1900.
[Hoover Institution Library & Archives]

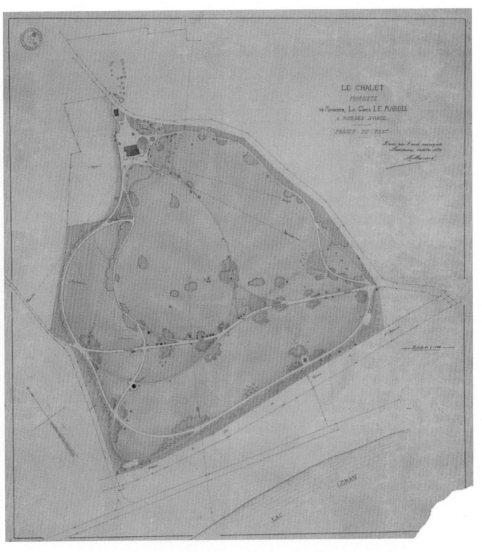

(Facing and above) Photographs and map of the Riond-Bosson Paderewski mansion during 1890–1930.
[Archiwum Akt Nowych, Warsaw]

Ignacy Paderewski speaks during the unveiling of the Grunwald Monument in Cracow, July 15, 1910. [Ośrodek Dokumentacji Muzyki Polskiej, Jagiellonian University, Cracow]

(Right) Helena and Ignacy with accompanying persons standing on the rear platform of their Pullman car during tour in USA, c. 1900. The Paderewski's cook, James Copper is sitting. [Ośrodek Dokumentacji Muzyki Polskiej, Jagiellonian University, Cracow]

(Below) Concert for two pianos. Vevey, May 1913. From the left side: Ignacy Paderewski, Rudolf Ganz, Count de Faria (Portuguese Consul to Lausanne), Lucie Schelling, Helena Paderewska, August Roussy, Jean-Baptiste-Paul Beau (French Ambassador to Switzerland), Eugene Couvreu (coucilman of Vevey), Ernest Schelling, and Camille Saint-Saens. [Hoover Institution Library & Archives]

Portrait of Helena Paderewska, drawing, 1911. [Archiwum Akt Nowych, Warsaw]

(Below, right) Helena Paderewska, Monte Carlo, c. 1914. [Hoover Institution Library & Archives]

(Below, left) The Paderewskis on the HMS Adriatic on the way to USA, April 1915. [US Library of Congress, Washington, DC]

(*Above, left*) *Paderewski speaks at a Polish rally in Chicago, May 30, 1915.* [Hoover Institution Library & Archives]

(*Above, right*) *Advertisement for photographs sold to benefit the Polish Relief Fund for War Victims.* Music Trade Review (*New York*), *November 20, 1915, p. 17.*

Ignacy Paderewski and Jan Smulski, at Riond-Bosson, Paderewski's estate in Morges, Switzerland. [Photo ©Polish Museum of America, Chicago; photographer: Zezbiorow L. T. Walkowicza]

The hotel where the Paderewskis stayed during their annual visits to Paso Robles. [Hoover Institution Library & Archives]

The Paderewskis visiting their ranchos in the Paso Robles area, California, 1921. [Polish Music Center, University of Southern California]

Handwritten note from Woodrow Wilson, 1917. "An independent Polish state should be erected. I take it for granted, for instance, if I may venture upon a single example, that statesmen everywhere are agreed that there should be a united, independent, and autonomous Poland. Woodrow Wilson." [Archiwum Akt Nowych, Warsaw. Gift of Przemysław Bloch]

Ignacy Paderewski and Woodrow Wilson at the White House (newspaper clipping), 1917. [Archiwum Akt Nowych, Warsaw]

(Left) Helena Paderewska with her collection of Polish dolls, c. 1918. [Photo ©Polish Museum of America, Chicago]

(Below) Helena Paderewska with Polish dolls, c. 1918. [Polish Music Center, University of Southern California]

(Left) Helena Paderewska, President of the Polish White Cross, in uniform, 1918.
[Hoover Institution Library & Archives]

Helena Paderewska distributes gifts to volunteers at Polish Army Camp at Niagara-on-the-Lake, Ontario, Canada, November 21, 1917. [Photo ©Polish Museum of America, Chicago]

(Below) Helena and Ignacy Paderewski at the reviewing stand at the Blue Army military camp at Niagara-on-the-Lake, Ontario, Canada, November 1917. [Archiwum Akt Nowych, Warsaw]

*Helena Paderewska with a group of nurses from the
Polish White Cross, New York, 1918.* [Hoover Institution Library & Archives]

*Wojciech Kossak,
Polish White Cross
poster, 1919.* [Source:
Maciej Siekierski]

Ignacy Paderewski and Wacław Gąsiorowski with the Polish Military Mission, New York, 1917. [Hoover Institution Library & Archives]

Standard-bearers of the Polish Army before the President of France, Henri Poincaré, Summer 1917. [Hoover Institution Library & Archives]

The Polish Army Orchestra conducted by Tadeusz Wronski, 1918.
[Hoover Institution Library & Archives]

General view of Warsaw under the German occupation, 1915.
[Hoover Institution Library & Archives]

*(Right) Hotel Bristol,
Warsaw, c. 1914.*
[Hoover Institution
Library & Archives]

*(Below) Royal Castle,
Warsaw, c. 1914.*
[Hoover Institution
Library & Archives]

(Left) Józef Piłsudski, 1919.
[Hoover Institution Library & Archives]

(Below) Major Zygmunt Iwanowski,
1919. [Hoover Institution Library & Archives]

Helena and Ignacy Paderewski,
Zygmunt Iwanowski; behind them
Józef Piłsudski. Warsaw, 1919.
[Hoover Institution Library & Archives]

Paderewski with his closet aides during the negotiations of the Paris Peace Conference in Paris; from Left: Sylwin Strakacz, Ignacy Paderewski, Jan Ciechanowski, Zygmunt Iwanowski, 1919. [Polish Music Center, University of Southern California]

Ignacy Paderewski and general Tadeusz Rozwadowski with the American volunteer pilots of the Kosciuszko Squadron, Paris, 1919.
[Hoover Institution Library & Archives]

CHAPTER FIVE

April—September 1915

Our arrival in New York, April 15, 1915, was the beginning of three and a half years of unending work for both of us, work from which we were never free at any hour of the twenty-four, for it seemed as if by the time my husband got to bed in the morning, I was up and started on the tasks of another day. Night has always been my husband's favorite working time. His day usually begins at about noon and ends some time the next morning, at two, three, and four o'clock, often five and six when there is work to be done. During the months in Warsaw when he was prime minister, it was usually at night, after our late dinner, that the most important conferences were held, and while the cabinet crisis was on in November and early December of last year, it was seldom that he went to bed before six in morning, and there were days when it was even later than that. They still speak of him in Warsaw as the man who never sleeps.

This does not seem as unusual to Poles or to those who have lived in Poland as it might seem to Americans and English. Late hours are the rule in Warsaw, rather than the exception, this being, I think, a heritage from the Russians. We rise late. Our luncheon—or dinner—is in the middle of the afternoon. Our dinner—or supper—is late in the evening after the theater or opera. When we dance all night, we dance literally all night, for no one thinks of leaving a ball before six or seven in the morning. Of course, this is not so true now as it was in the past. Shortage of coal and shortage of food necessitated early hours for everybody during the winter of '19–'20, and I shall be surprised if the old schedule is returned to. The servant problem alone may make this impossible, for Poland, with its independence, acquired among other things a servant problem, in common with the rest of the world. Our servants are no longer "servants" but are "domestic employees," and their work is to be arranged on a ten-hour basis if not on an eight. As one of the things they demand is no evening work, it looks as if there must be decided changes in the social life of the country, especially of Warsaw.

It will be remembered that even in April 1915, the submarines were causing much anxiety, and as there was no wireless, ships were not reported for New York until they had passed Fire Island. Nonetheless, although the notice was short, several of our friends were there to meet us at quarantine, including my son, W. O. Górski,[1] Herman Schaad[2] of the Aeolian Company, Ernest Urchs[3] of Steinway, Alexander Lambert,[4] and one or two others. At the pier there was a still more numerous company, among them a delegation from the Polish Central Relief Committee, which afterward became the Polish National Department of the United States. At the head of this delegation was its president, John F. Smulski,[5] whom my husband then met for the first time.

Mr. Smulski, who is the president of the Northwestern Trust and Savings Company of Chicago and was once the state treasurer of Illinois, has been a most vital and potent factor in all Polish work done in America not only during the war but since. At the head of the Polish National Department he has enjoyed the trust and confidence of all the Poles in America, and his untiring energy, his shrewdness, and keen business sense have been of invaluable service to the cause. A native of Poznań, he was taken to America when he was a child but not before he had experienced the heavy hand of Prussian displeasure. He was sent to jail when he was seven years old because he had worn a square-topped cap of traditional design.

His loyalty and unselfish devotion to my husband during those months we spent in America makes one of our most fragrant memories. There was never a time that he was not at Mr. Paderewski's call. More than once in the next two years when we were on tour, he would travel from one to three days for a talk that might last only as many hours. No man has had the welfare of Poland more at heart, and no man has worked more unselfishly for it.

At our very landing in New York, it seemed as if we were taking the first step that was to separate us from the past. The hotel that Mr. Paderewski went to when he first visited New York was the old Windsor, and he lived there as a matter of course on all his succeeding visits until it burned. When its

---

1. Wacław Otton Górski (1877–1936), journalist; Helena Paderewska's son from her first marriage to violinist Władysław Górski.

2. Herman Schaad of the Aeolian Company; Paderewski endorsed the company's organs and pianos.

3. Ernest Urchs (d. 1928), manager of Steinway and Sons; concert promoter.

4. Alexander Lambert (1862–1929), pianist, composer, and friend of Paderewski since student days in Berlin; later director of New York College of Music.

5. John F. Smulski (1867–1928), Chicago banker and Polish American leader.

proprietors, Hawk and Wetherbee,[6] took the Manhattan, he followed them there—which was most characteristic of him, for there are few men who more dislike change, who are more unwilling to break the custom of years. But in 1915 he went to the Gotham, which was really to be our American home for the next three years and a half, two things influencing us. At the time we could not get our old apartments in the Manhattan, and the other was that Madame Sembrich was living at the Gotham.

Mr. Paderewski was not able to maintain any illusions he might have had respecting the task he was about to undertake for long. During our first day in New York, friends told us that he would not be able to collect any great amount of money. America was not interested in Poland and in fact, was not very much interested in the war. They cited the case of that charming Belgian woman Madame Vandervelde,[7] who had been in America the greater part of the winter raising funds for the relief of the Belgians. With all the publicity that Belgium had had, with all the sympathy that had been aroused by the heroic stand of the Belgian army at the beginning of the war, with all the influence that had been used to help her, Madame Vandervelde had been able to raise only a paltry $300,000, which was nothing in comparison to the needs of her country and, with the wealth of America, nothing as compared with what Great Britain and her colonies, especially Canada, had given.

Frankly, in the spring of 1915, the Americans as a people were not greatly interested in the war. The vast majority of them regarded it as something entirely outside of themselves, as something that was none of their business. Moreover, German influence was never so strong as it was then. The persistent propaganda that had its headquarters in the German embassy in Washington had tainted the souls of many of those who naturally would have been in sympathy with the Entente. America was still largely under the spell of German "efficiency," and it would have been a brave man who at that time would have prophesied that in two years the United States was to become the deciding factor in the war. Even the *Lusitania* seemed to have only a momentary effect.

This is an oft-told tale now, but it is necessary to refer to it again so that some idea might be gained of the difficulties that confronted my husband almost from the day of his landing. There were also other factors that helped make difficult the situation. He had come to the United States to do as he had

---

6. Samuel Hawk and Gardner Wetherbee, hotel owners.

7. Lalla Vandervelde, organizer of aid for the people of Belgium during World War I; the first wife of Emile Vandervelde, Belgian Socialist minister.

already done in Paris and London, to form a national committee of men and women prominent in public life, to raise money for the relief of sufferers in Poland, and to start a campaign of publicity and education that was at least as necessary in America as it had been in France and England. When he arrived he discovered that Madame Sembrich had already formed an organization for the raising of funds and that there were one or two others in operation. He felt, however, that none of this work was on a large enough or broad enough scale. He had been sent by the General Committee, the headquarters of which were then in Vevey, to organize the Polish Victims' Relief Fund in the United States, and he proceeded to do so. In the beginning there were more or less misunderstandings among the various people interested in Poland, but happily the wisdom of the course adopted by Mr. Paderewski soon became apparent, and harmony was restored.

As I have already said, from the very beginning Mr. Paderewski had the loyal support of the Polish Immigration. The vast majority of the more than four million Poles in America gave him their unquestioned confidence and trust, and through all the troubled years that have passed since then they have never wavered in their allegiance to him. An organization to raise funds for Poland had already been started in Chicago, with Mr. Smulski at its head. It was first called the Polish Central Relief Committee, then the Polish National Department, and finally the Polish National Committee. Ultimately, through this Polish National Committee the work among the Poles in America became systematized, and through its efforts millions of dollars were raised during the war and even after. Without its work the suffering in the young republic would have been infinitely more intense. Through it thousands of Poles were fed and clothed during the terrible first eighteen months following the liberation. Through it Haller's Army[8] came into being, and thus through it Poland was able properly to be represented at the peace conference.

From the beginning also, Mr. Paderewski had the unwavering support of the Polish clergy in America. This was most important. The Polish clergy in the United States, like the clergy in Poland itself, is made up of a superior class

8. Józef Haller (1873–1960), former Austrian officer, later one of the commanders of Polish units fighting on the side of Austria against Russia. After the signing of the Brest-Litovsk treaty, Haller renounced allegiance to the Central Powers and moved his forces into Ukraine. Eventually, under assumed identity, he made his way via Kiev, Moscow, Karelia, and Murmansk to France, where he arrived in July 1918. There he assumed command over the Polish divisions formed from former German prisoners of war and American Poles arriving from Canada.

of men. All of them are university graduates and for the most part are men of broad vision and wide sympathies. Their relations toward their parishioners are very intimate, for they are truly the shepherds of their flocks. The vast majority of Poles in America are of peasant stock, and for them the priest is not only a spiritual advisor but a friend and mentor to whom they go not only for spiritual advice but for common counsel in all matters affecting their life and welfare. The influence of the clergy is therefore very great and on the whole has been very wisely exerted.

Not only Mr. Paderewski but I myself have had much to do with the Polish clergy in America during the last five years, and it has indeed been seldom that we appealed to them in vain. But my first experience with the Church in America took me to Cardinal Farley.[9] During the winter the Pope had sent his blessing to the General Committee in Switzerland and had authorized it to appeal to the churches of the world for help. Armed with this, one day shortly after our arrival, I called on Cardinal Farley. Rarely have I met a man more sympathetic, more gentle, more cordial. I spent the better part of an hour with him, and when I left not only did he give me his check for a handsome sum but he promised to appoint a Sunday when a special collection for Poland should be taken in all the churches of his diocese. This collection raised more than $10,000. That was the beginning. A little later we received $7,000 from the bishop of Hartford, Connecticut.[10] Then came $3,000 from Cardinal Gibbons,[11] and collections became general throughout the country.

My personal experience with the Polish clergy came the autumn following our arrival. Among the first that I met was the late Father Strzelecki,[12] whose church was in Seventh Street. He was of invaluable service both to my husband and to myself and worked indefatigably for the cause up to the time of his death. Indirectly he was the means of my getting in touch with many of the clergy, and the following incident shows of what stuff the Polish clergy in America is made. He suggested to me one day that perhaps it would be well to ask to tea a few of the more prominent priests whose parishes were in and around New York, offering the services of his secretary to write the letters of invitation and setting the day for a week later. That evening his secretary

9. John Murphy Farley (1842–1918), Catholic archbishop of New York during 1902–1918; made cardinal in 1911.

10. John Joseph Nilan (1855–1934), Catholic bishop of Hartford during 1910–1934.

11. James Gibbons (1834–1921), Catholic archbishop of Baltimore during 1877–1921; made cardinal in 1886.

12. Monsignor Jan H. Strzelecki (1863–1918), pastor of St. Stanislaus parish in New York City.

brought me the letters to sign. I was very busy and did not pay much attention, except that it occurred to me later in the evening that I had signed a good many letters to ask a few men to tea. On the day appointed I was still at lunch when a priest entered and told me that he had come from Buffalo for the meeting.

"From Buffalo? For the meeting?" I asked, quite bewildered.

"Certainly," he replied, "in response to your invitation."

I was still trying to solve the mystery when another priest arrived, this one from Detroit, and to make a long story short, Father Strzelecki's secretary had sent out fifty letters to priests in New England and as far west as Detroit, and forty-six of these good men dropped their work and came to New York. I gave them tea, we talked the whole afternoon, and as a result the relief work received a most unexpected impetus.

One of our best friends was Father Manteuffel[13] of Passaic. In the course of the early summer, he asked my husband to visit his parish. This was the first time that Mr. Paderewski really met the Polish people in America, for up to then he had known only their leaders. We were greeted not only by the men and women of the parish but by all the schoolchildren, carrying flowers and banners and singing the songs of the old country. There were addresses and presentations, and Mr. Paderewski made his first speech for Poland to the American Poles. It was widely quoted through the Polish press and gave added speed to the work that had been begun.

But if good progress had been made among the Poles in America, the same could not be said of the work among the Americans themselves. From the very beginning, we had good, loyal friends who worked untiringly for us, Major Schelling and his wife, Herbert Satterlee,[14] James M. Beck,[15] Frank A. Vanderlip,[16] Miss Eleanor Blodgett,[17] and Ernest Urchs, to mention only a few. Mr. Vanderlip, for example, sent out an appeal to all the banks of the country. He had printed a very beautiful pamphlet for this purpose that must have cost a great deal of money. It was his own idea and was the result of an evening that

---

13. The Reverend Juliusz Manteuffel, pastor of St. Joseph parish in Passaic, New Jersey.

14. Herbert Satterlee (1863–1947), American lawyer, writer, and businessman; assistant secretary of the navy, 1908–1909; son-in-law of John Pierpont Morgan.

15. James M. Beck (1861–1936), American lawyer and politician from Philadelphia.

16. Frank A. Vanderlip (1864–1937), president of the National City Bank of New York, 1909–1919.

17. Eleanor Blodgett (1855–1930), New York philanthropist; godmother of Franklin Delano Roosevelt.

my husband and I dined with him at his home in Westchester County. It was our first meeting, Mr. Paderewski was "in the vein,"[18] and from that time on we counted Mr. Vanderlip among our warmest friends.

One of the first things Mr. Paderewski did was to send an appeal out through the country to the farmers, asking for gifts of seed grain, particularly wheat and rye, in order that the Polish farmers might have a chance to plant the lands that had been devastated by the fighting between the Russian and German armies. This came to little. The Rockefeller Foundation, to which he applied for aid, declined politely to be interested in Poland, although later it issued a report in which it praised most warmly the methods used by the General Committee in Switzerland and gave its unconditional approval to the work. The government in Washington looked on his efforts with suspicion because it feared that his was really a political mission, and I daresay that Washington felt that it was having enough trouble with Germany without risking friction with Russia, which then was all-powerful. For a time it seemed as if the task was hopeless. There were all kinds of hostile influences working against him, as well as the inertia that came from indifference. Few Americans who were not brought directly into contact with it realize how powerful were the German influences during the first year of the war. In addition to this, there was at least no sympathy to be had from the Russians, and as for the Jews, my husband constantly was made to feel the results of the campaign that had been carried on against him the year before. Moreover, ignorance of Poland and of all things Polish was just as pronounced in America as it had been in England and France, despite the statues that had been erected to Kosciuszko and Pulaski.

My husband was not long in discovering that it was one thing to be in a country as a great and admired artist and quite another to be there asking for favors. But while he was often deeply hurt by the attitude of some men who in other years had eagerly sought him out, he allowed neither his pride nor his injured feelings to interfere with his mission. There were instances when he was turned away from doors by servants, quite unable to see the man he sought. There were dozens of letters from him that were never acknowledged, and more than once when he received a refusal, verbal or written, it was put in curt, brusque terms that hurt even more than the refusal itself. Often the artist in him was cut to the quick, for this treatment that he received was something quite new in his experience, and it gave him some bitter moments, but the

18. This phrase does not translate well into English, but it most likely means something along the lines of "was inspired."

patriot in him was strong enough to enable him to set aside personal slights and to persevere in the work he had set out to accomplish.

As I look back to those first weeks in the United States, I feel that however real the rebuffs my husband received then seemed to him, he perhaps took them too seriously. Although he had been in America and knew the country and the people very well, he was being brought for the first time into contact with an aspect of American character unnoticed by him before and was experiencing for the first time that brusqueness of manner natural to them in business and affairs of importance that, at least until the last three years, has never been understood by the Europeans. We realize now, like most Europeans, that this is after all simply a manner, that under it are kindliness, sincerity, and warmhearted generosity, and it would ill become us, either as individuals or Poles, to criticize America or Americans, for their bounty to our country has been its salvation.

Another thing that perhaps impeded his progress was the general unwillingness of the Americans to accept him in any other role than that of an artist, very different in this respect from the treatment he had received in Paris and London. And truly, this idea persisted in America until the last few months of our stay there, until he had abandoned his art and devoted himself entirely to his work for Poland. I suppose even today that there are many who cannot understand how a pianist could ever have become a prime minister.

Notwithstanding the many disappointments and nerve-wracking delays, real progress was made with the committee, and before he left for the West, he had on its roll a very representative body of men and women. Its honorary president was ex-President Taft. Its vice presidents were Madame Marcella Sembrich, Cardinal Farley, Miss Anne Morgan,[19] Miss Blodgett, Madame Szumowska-Adamowska,[20] and James A. Patten.[21] James M. Beck was the chairman of the executive committee, Frank W. Vanderlip was the honorary treasurer, and Edward B. Lynam[22] was the executive secretary. Included in the

---

19. Anne Tracy Morgan (1873–1952), American philanthropist; daughter of John Pierpont Morgan.

20. Antonina Szumowska-Adamowska (1868–1938), Polish American pianist and student of Paderewski; taught at the New England Conservatory of Music in Boston; along with her husband, Joseph (cellist), and brother-in-law, Tim (violinist), made up the Adamowski Trio.

21. James A. Patten (1852–1928), American financier and grain merchant.

22. Edward B. Lynam, 1895 graduate of Yale University, journalist, and author of "The Jan and Halka Happy-Here Helpers," a booklet about the cloth dolls for the Polish Victims' Relief Fund (1916).

list of members were Cardinals Gibbons and O'Connell,[23] Archbishop Hanna[24] of San Francisco, Charles W. Eliot,[25] Harry Pratt Judson,[26] Mr. and Mrs. William H. Crocker,[27] Mr. and Mrs. Herbert L. Satterlee,[28] Mr. and Mrs. Bryan Lathrop,[29] Bishop Greer,[30] James J. Hill,[31] Henry W. Taft,[32] John Wanamaker,[33] Mr. and Mrs. Howard Van Sinderen,[34] Mr. and Mrs. Edward J. de Coppet, Bishop Lawrence,[35] Robert De Forest,[36] Thomas A. Edison,[37] H. H. Flagler,[38] Martin Ryerson,[39] Mrs. James B. Duke,[40] Mr. and Mrs. Edward Bok,[41] Mr. and Mrs. Cyrus H. K. Curtis,[42] Mr. and Mrs. Ernest Schelling, David R. Forgan,[43]

23. William Henry O'Connell (1859–1944), Catholic archbishop of Boston during 1907–1944; made cardinal in 1911.

24. Edward Joseph Hanna (1860–1944), Catholic archbishop of San Francisco during 1915–1935.

25. Charles William Eliot (1834–1926), president of Harvard University during 1869–1906.

26. Harry Pratt Judson (1847–1927), historian; president of the University of Chicago during 1907–1923.

27. William Henry Crocker (1861–1937), president of Crocker National Bank, and Mrs. Ethel Sperry Crocker (1861–1934).

28. Herbert Satterlee's spouse was Louise Pierpont Morgan (1866–1946), older sister of Anne Tracy Morgan.

29. Bryan Lathrop (1844–1916), Chicago real estate investor, art collector, and patron, and Mrs. Helen Lynde Aidis Lathrop (1849–1935).

30. David Hummell Greer (1844–1919), Episcopal bishop of New York during 1903–1919.

31. James J. Hill (1838–1916), Canadian American railroad executive, Great Northern Railway.

32. Henry W. Taft (1859–1945), antitrust lawyer, brother of President William Howard Taft.

33. John Wanamaker (1838–1922), American businessman, religious leader, and political figure; pioneer in modern advertising and marketing.

34. Howard Van Sinderen, New York lawyer.

35. William Lawrence (1850–1941), Episcopal bishop of Boston during 1893–1927; known as the "banker bishop" because of his successful fund-raising drives.

36. Robert De Forest (1845–1924), Connecticut politician, US congressman.

37. Thomas A. Edison (1847–1931), American inventor and businessman.

38. Harry Harkness Flagler (1871–1952), philanthropist; music promoter; president of the Symphony Society of New York.

39. Martin Ryerson, Jr. (1857–1932), Chicago philanthropist and art collector.

40. Mrs. James Buchanan Duke at that time was Nataline Holt Inman, the second wife of the tobacco and electric power industrialist and philanthropist; they married in 1907; he died in 1925.

41. Edward William Bok (1863–1930), Dutch-born American editor and Pulitzer Prize–winning author; editor of the *Ladies' Home Journal*.

42. Cyrus Hermann Kotzschmar Curtis (1850–1933), publisher of magazines and newspapers, including the *Ladies' Home Journal* and *Saturday Evening Post*; major philanthropist.

43. David R. Forgan (1862–1931), Scottish-born Chicago banker; president of Union National Bank and its successors; championship golfer.

Mrs. Emmons Blaine,[44] Mrs. Robert Patterson,[45] Mrs. John Borden,[46] Richard M. Tobin,[47] John B. Cassidy,[48] and John Parrott.[49] These men and women represented New York, Boston, Chicago, and San Francisco, and later in Chicago and San Francisco large local committees were formed to work in connection with the benefit concert that my husband gave the following season.

Within a few weeks of our arrival in America, it had become evident that return to Europe was out of the question, for the present at any rate. There was too much to do in America. Not only did my husband feel that it was his duty to stay there and continue personally to solicit funds for Poland but he was made to realize early in our stay that his presence was quite as necessary for the work among the American Poles themselves. Any lingering doubts about staying that he may have had in his mind were banished by the sinking of the *Lusitania*. From that day he was quite certain that America must enter the war, and he felt it his duty more than ever to be there when that event happened in order that he could look after the interest of Poland and the Poles.

Consequently, early in May we made out plans to stay on. When Mr. Paderewski arrived in America, he had no idea whatsoever of playing and had so said publicly on his arrival; but if he were to stay on, it was necessary to provide for means of existence. We had come to America on borrowed money, as our own was unavailable. Naturally, with our traveling and the secretariat my husband had to create, our expenses were very heavy so he decided that the next winter he would give a limited number of concerts and asked his American manager, Mr. Ellis[50] of Boston, to arrange these. We also decided to go for two months to Paso Robles, where Mr. Paderewski would have the time and quiet to prepare the necessary programs for his tour and also to gather and put into shape certain material he needed for some speeches he was planning

---

44. The wife of Emmons Blaine (1857–1892), son of the US secretary of state and presidential candidate; president of Baltimore and Ohio Railroad; she was born Anita McCormick (1866–1954).

45. Mrs. Robert Wilson Patterson (1853–1933), born Nellie Medill, widow of Patterson (d. 1910), Chicago newspaper publisher and editor; their daughter, Eleanor ("Cissy"), married a Polish count, Józef Giżycki.

46. Mrs. John Borden, born Ellen Waller, married to a Chicago socialite and financier.

47. Richard M. Tobin (1866–1952), San Francisco banker, philanthropist, and diplomat.

48. Unable to verify.

49. Probably John Parrott, Jr. (1859–1918) of San Mateo, who inherited his father's San Francisco financial and shipping empire.

50. Charles Ellis was Paderewski's manager since 1902; he also administered the Boston Symphony Orchestra during 1882–1918.

to make the following fall and winter. Among other things, he planned to give concerts for the benefit of the Polish war victims in certain of the larger cities and at these concerts devote half of the program to an address in which he could personally describe the plight of his country. He hoped in this way to get into closer contact with the American public, for truly money for the relief fund was coming in very slowly.

Before we left for the West, we went to Chicago for a great Polish mass meeting on Decoration Day. While my husband had been working on his committee, Bishop Rhode,[51] Father Zapała,[52] Mr. Smulski and his colleagues, Mr. Heliński,[53] Mr. Żychliński,[54] and others had made much progress in the work of organizing the Poles in the Middle West, and this great meeting had been planned as a formal inauguration of the campaign, with Mr. Paderewski as the principal speaker. It was to be given in Humboldt Park under the shadow of the Kościuszko monument.

The meeting was an extraordinary success. Mr. Smulski and his committee had done their work well. In Humboldt Park that day there was a crowd estimated at over one hundred thousand. There were twenty thousand Poles in the traditional military uniform of their country—a thing that my husband saw then for the first time in his life. It had been planned to have the speakers' stand at the base of the Kościuszko monument, but as it had rained for several days, and the turf was very soft, the authorities had moved the stand to another part of the park. Besides Mr. Paderewski, the speakers were Governor Dunne[55] of Illinois, Mayor Thompson[56] of Chicago, and the Reverend W. Zapała of the Polish clergy. My husband's was the principal address, and he showed then as he has so many times since his power to sway a crowd with his eloquence.

51. Paul Peter Rhode (1871–1945), Catholic bishop of Green Bay 1915–1945; first Polish-born American bishop.

52. Father Władysław (Ladislaus) Zapała (1874–1948), pastor of the St. Stanislaus Kostka parish in Chicago; later superior general of the Congregation of the Resurrection.

53. Teodor Heliński (1857–1921), banker and Polish American activist; during World War I he chaired the Military Commission of the National Department, responsible for organizing a Polish army in America.

54. Kazimierz Żychliński (1854–1927), president of the Polish National Alliance of Chicago in the years 1913–1927.

55. Edward Fitzsimmons Dunne (1853–1937), former mayor of Chicago, governor of Illinois during 1913–1917.

56. William Hale Thompson (1869–1944), the last Republican mayor of Chicago, 1915–1923 and 1927–1931.

How his music could be an aid to his speaking he tested on this day in a curious and interesting fashion. When he began to speak, he felt that while he was using sufficient voice, it was not reaching so far as it should have done. It "did not come back to him," as musicians say, for the final test of the acoustics of a hall or a theater is the way in which the sound returns to the performer, and if the performer is not able to feel this, especially a musician, his work will suffer accordingly. While conditions in open air must necessarily be very different from those in a building, where there are trees, a crowd, and nearby buildings to reflect and deflect the sound, the same rules of acoustics generally hold. In this particular instance, Mr. Paderewski, whose ear is very sensitive, experimented for three or four minutes until he found the direction from which the sound best came back to him, and he was told later that after his opening, when it was difficult for many to hear him, his words carried almost to the very outskirts of the crowd. The test was so conclusive to him that in all his subsequent speeches in large halls or in the open air, he always applied it always with the same results, and this undoubtedly has had much to do with his success as an orator.

It was at this meeting that the remarkable snapshot of him was taken by a reporter of the *Chicago Herald*. His head is thrown back, his coat is open, and he is seemingly in the very middle of an impassioned sentence. It is really a most unusual character study, which the photographer just happened to get by chance. The *Herald* copyrighted the picture and gave us ten thousand copies, which added a very handsome sum to our relief fund, for we sold those original ten thousand and many thousand more afterward.

When we left for Paso Robles toward the end of June, it was Mr. Paderewski's plan to stay there for six weeks or two months in which he could prepare for the concerts of the following season and at the same time gather material for the addresses that he was to make in the autumn. At that time he had no idea of playing any concerts in the West, but in Paso Robles we had the good fortune to meet Mrs. William B. Bourn[57] of San Francisco. We liked her, and she seemed to like us, and one day my husband spoke of his plan to give a few benefit concerts at which he should make an address on Poland and asked what she thought of it. She thought so well of it that she urged that the first one of these concerts be given in San Francisco, saying that she would make all arrangements.

---

57. Born Agnes Moody, she married William Bowers Bourn II (b. 1857), San Francisco entrepreneur; they built the Filoli country estate in San Mateo County, California, where both died and are buried (1936).

It will never be possible for us to express adequately our gratitude to the men and women of San Francisco. It was the year of the fair,[58] and busy as they all were, they found time to help us and our cause. One does not often meet such wholehearted sympathy and cooperation, such a beautiful spirit of helpfulness. Mrs. Bourn arranged for the concert that was to be given in Festival Hall, and, incidentally, she and her husband paid all the expenses. It was also arranged that my husband should play with the Exposition Orchestra under Max Bendix,[59] and to cap the climax, Mr. and Mrs. William H. Crocker offered to give a Polish fête at their place in Burlingame.

We had two very busy months at Paso Robles. A part of each day my husband devoted to his piano. He worked on the address he was to make later in San Francisco, Boston, New York, Philadelphia, and Chicago, and besides there was an enormous amount of correspondence to be taken care of. By this time the Poles in America were beginning to realize the needs of their countrymen, and wherever there were Poles they formed a society or organization to carry on relief work. In the beginning, naturally, things did not always move smoothly. There were conflicting ideas, conflicting opinions, and more or less friction, and it seemed that every question that arose was brought to Mr. Paderewski for solution. He had to pour much oil on troubled waters those first few months, and this alone was enough to keep him very busy without the other things. I shudder even now when I think of the thousands of dollars he had to pay for telegraph and cable tolls, but all in all they were very happy weeks. My husband felt that at last he was making progress, and he was confident that the next winter would bring real results.

In the meantime, during the summer much work had been done in San Francisco. A list of patrons and patronesses for the concert had been made that included the most prominent people of the city. At the head were Archbishop Hanna of San Francisco, Bishop Nichols[60] of California, Judge William W. Morrow,[61] Mayor Rolph,[62] President Wheeler of Berkeley,[63] Pres-

58. Panama-Pacific International Exhibition, celebrating the opening of the Panama Canal and the rebuilding of San Francisco after the earthquake of 1906.

59. Max Bendix (1866–1945), American composer, conductor, and violinist.

60. William Ford Nichols (1849–1924), Episcopal bishop of California.

61. William W. Morrow (1843–1929), served three terms as US representative from California; also served as a US judge.

62. James Rolph (1869–1934), mayor of San Francisco during 1912–1931.

63. Benjamin Ide Wheeler (1854–1927), philology professor; president of University of California during 1899–1919.

ident Branner of Stanford,[64] and C. C. Moore,[65] president of the Panama-Pacific International Exposition. The list of patronesses was headed by Mrs. William H. Crocker.

Mrs. Bourn had arranged that the benefit concert should be given on a Sunday afternoon, August 21,[66] and while we were in San Francisco we were her guests. The concert was a huge success. Extra prices had been charged, and the receipts amounted to $10,000, while the sale of programs, flowers, autographs, and the like brought in another $2,000. In the beginning my husband spoke for nearly an hour. He had carefully prepared and memorized the address for not only was it the first time he had ever made a formal speech in English but he wanted to leave nothing to chance—to the dangerous inspiration of the moment. In the hundreds of speeches that he has made since, in Polish, English, and French, he had memorized only a very few. As a rule, when he prepares one, he makes notes of the principal points he wishes to make and really composes the speech on the platform.

Both the public and critics have been good enough to speak most highly of this address, while his mastery of idiomatic English, his sympathetic understanding of the spirit of the language, surprised nearly everyone. Certainly, with this speech in which he spoke of Poland, described her plight, and pleaded her cause, he was able to move deeply five great audiences of Americans, to stir them as I have rarely seen any audiences stirred.

The speech was widely quoted throughout the United States. and I will here repeat only two short passages from the end, and these because they show the spirit that moved Mr. Paderewski in his work during those years in America.

I will accuse no one; I will make no complaints against any of the belligerents. We have been treated according to the logic of war, which is in itself a cruelty, an atrocity nowadays multiplied by science. . . . My errand is not of hatred but of love. I do not intend to excite passion but to awake compassion. If I have succeeded, pray speak about Poland to your kind, good friends. . . . Someone may be convinced by your arguments, touched by your words, moved by your voice; someone may try to help us. God will bless him as he will bless you.

64. John Casper Branner (1850–1922), geologist; president of Stanford University during 1913–1916.

65. Charles Caldwell Moore (1868–1932), prominent San Francisco businessman.

66. August 21, 1915, was a Saturday, not a Sunday.

Following the speech he played a short program, pieces by Chopin, of whom he had said a little before:

But it was given to a Polish poet to reveal the genius of our race, to express in an accessible way our pain and joy, our doubt and faith, our loss and hope; it was given to a Polish poet to carry far into the wide world the immortal message of beauty from his mother country, to reach every land, almost every home, almost every heart. This poet was Chopin, and you know him well.

At the end of his program, he played the national anthem of Poland, and the entire audience rose. It was the first time perhaps in history that a foreign audience had ever risen to the Polish hymn. It was the first time perhaps in history that the anthem had ever been played to a foreign audience. That, for us, for my husband and myself, was a moment of inexpressible emotion.

The following Sunday he appeared with the Exposition Orchestra, playing his own Concerto in A Minor, and during that week came the beautiful fête that Mr. and Mrs. William Crocker gave. With tickets at $5 each, with a bazaar for the sale of all kinds of articles, we raised from this more than $7,000. It was a charming affair, set in a most beautiful frame of lovely scenery. There was tea, dancing, and music and quantities of pretty women in pretty gowns.

There was but one unpleasant incident during our stay in San Francisco, and that was not of great moment except as it illustrated how the Jewish campaign carried on against my husband the previous year persisted. Just before his appearance, there was broadcast in San Francisco a circular emanating from an unknown source that urged all Jews to stay away from his concert because of his alleged connection with the anti-Jewish newspaper in Warsaw—the same old story that had caused him annoyance, particularly in San Francisco, the previous year. This circular was straightaway denounced by some of the leading Jews of the city, notably the bankers Mortimer and Herbert Fleishhacker,[67] and Mr. Paderewski himself sent a note to the papers in which he pointed out that on the General Committee in Switzerland, of which he was the second president and the official representative in America,

---

67. Mortimer (1866–1953) and Herbert (1872–1957) Fleishhacker, San Francisco bankers and philanthropists.

were such eminent Jews as Severin Bergson,[68] president of the Jewish community of the city of Warsaw; Philip Fruchtman,[69] director of the Bank of Lwów, and Professor Simon Askenazy,[70] the great historian. As happened the year before, nothing came of the threatened boycott, and the matter ended there.

We started for the East at the end of August, planning to spend a fortnight in Bar Harbor with the Schellings, who were there for the summer. On our arrival in New York I found waiting for me the first consignment of dolls that Miss Mickiewicz had sent from Paris. Mr. Paderewski had lent me ten thousand francs with which to start the work, and the dolls were my constant companions for nearly three years. Wherever we went, there went two or three great trunks filled with these dolls. We sold them at concerts. We sold them at bazaars. We organized special sales, and when I remember the sheer physical labor of packing and unpacking those dolls, I actually marvel that Aline, my maid who was always with me, and myself ever lived to tell the tale. There were big dolls and little dolls, dolls fragile and dolls unbreakable. Most of them smacked, I might say, of *l'art nouveau*, and everybody found them fascinating. More than once, I parted with some particular doll with real sorrow, so fond had I become of it, but I never allowed sentiment to interfere with business, and my sole complaint was that the Treasury Department refused to grant me the same privileges that had been given, for example, to Belgium and Serbia. I had to pay duty on every doll, and the duty was more than the actual cost of the dolls themselves.

When we left for Bar Harbor we took the dolls with us, and there I had my first sale. It was at a Polish fête given at the home of Mr. and Mrs. Ernesto Fabbri[71] by which the relief fund was richer by more than $3,000. It was at this fête that Mr. Paderewski made his debut, and those who were present were treated to quite a new sensation. Mr. Alessandro Fabbri[72] was a skilled amateur in moving pictures, and he had taken a series of pictures of Ernest Schelling and Fritz Kreisler[73] as they were playing, alone and together. My husband was

68. Although Paderewska uses the name "Severin" in her manuscript, she must have meant Michał Bergson. Michał Bergson (1831–1919), a banker, philanthropist, and civic leader, was president of the Warsaw Jewish community during 1896–1918.

69. Unable to verify.

70. Szymon Askenazy (1866–1935), historian, diplomat, and politician.

71. Ernesto G. Fabbri was an associate of J. Pierpont Moran; married to Edith Shepard, great-granddaughter of Commodore Cornelius Vanderbilt.

72. Alessandro Fabbri, younger brother of Ernesto.

73. Friedrich "Fritz" Kreisler (1875–1962), Austrian-born violinist and composer.

so enchanted with them that he was more than willing to have Mr. Fabbri take some of him. At the fête they were shown—with music—for the first and only time. The artist was placed behind the screen, and when he saw the picture, he played, carefully timing himself so that it was as if that longed-for goal of scientists had been reached, the perfect synchronization of the phonograph and cinema. First Major Schelling played Chopin's Polonaise in A-flat, then he and Kreisler played the Grieg Sonata, Kreisler playing his "Caprice Viennois," Schelling playing Dvorak's Humoresque, and then Mr. Paderewski played a Chopin Polonaise and Schumann's "Warum."

The illusion was absolutely perfect. It was as if the pictured artist was really playing. It was a huge success, for the program had to be repeated three times in order that all could hear it, and the performance lasted three and a half hours altogether. The sale of dolls was so successful, and the people, especially the women, were so taken with them, that I cabled Miss Mickiewicz in Paris saying that I could dispose of all she could send me.

Returning to New York, we had only a short time before the concerts began, and that time was filled to overflowing with work that had to do with Polish Relief. All thought of returning to Europe had vanished, and we settled down to stay in America until the end of the war.

CHAPTER SIX

September 1915—June 1916

With our return from Bar Harbor in September, there confronted my husband nine months of unbroken work that would have been almost drudgery had it not been for the spirit that filled him, for the cause that urged him on from day to day. Mr. Ellis had arranged about fifty concerts to be given between the early part of October and the end of March, these entailing close to twenty thousand miles of travel, for the tour extended from Boston in the east to Minneapolis in the north and Oklahoma in the south. In addition to these concerts were the score or more of Polish meetings in different cities of the country at which he made addresses. On top of all this came the routine work of correspondence. His daily post was huge. There was hardly a question affecting Polish Relief or Polish propaganda that was not referred to him for decision or advice. The Polish Victims' Relief Fund had established offices in the Aeolian Building,[1] offices which the Aeolian Company most generously donated to the work, and there much of the routine work was done, but our own apartments in the Gotham had also been transformed into offices. Day and night during the weeks we were in New York, we had typists at work in them, and there seemed to be not a room where one could rest quietly and collect one's thoughts. During this time I do not believe that Mr. Paderewski averaged five hours sleep in the twenty-four, because after midnight was practically the only time he could work without interruption.

His only recreation was an occasional game of bridge. After dinner, now and then, he would steal an hour or two from his work, if partners were available, for bridge gives him almost as much rest as sleep. He has always been fond of games requiring skill and science, such as bridge, chess, billiards, and the like, and plays all of them well. Gambling as such does not interest him in

---

1. The Aeolian Building, 689–691 Fifth Avenue, Manhattan, was built in 1925–1927, so what the author has in mind is the Aeolian Hall building at 33 West 42nd, across the street from Bryant Park; the building was built in 1912.

the least, for the gambling instinct is completely lacking in him. If this had not been so, perhaps to his other distinctions he might have added that of having broken the bank at Monte Carlo, for once he had a most extraordinary turn of luck there, and to the dismay of his friends and the disgust of all true gamblers there, he did not know how to take advantage of it.

We had been in Monte Carlo several times. Once or twice he had played, losing insignificant sums and thoroughly bored with the game. It was the year before the war, I think, that we were in Nice when one morning he told me that he felt an irresistible impulse to go to Monte Carlo and play, that he knew he was going to win. So to Monte Carlo we went, and in that afternoon, playing only numbers, he won thirty-seven times. He risked only five francs at a time, and his winnings came to seven thousand francs. The next day he felt the same call to the tables and won thirty-eight times, and on the third day, following his intuition, he returned and won thirty-four times, a run of luck that, we were told, was almost without precedent. Had he played as he was almost tearfully urged to play by the excited spectators, I do not know how much he would have won in those three days, perhaps a million, but he continued to play his little five francs, vastly amused, for it was the first and only time in his life, I believe, that he ever got something for nothing. The fourth day he did not feel the "call," but he went to see what would happen, and the tables took every five-franc piece he placed on them.

Luck, or chance, has played a very small role in his life. In fact, it almost seems that whenever there was an opportunity for luck to step in and help him, it has not only failed to do so but more often than not it has been actually antagonistic. For example, we had a dream of wealth from oil, which lasted two and a half years, and we missed it by perhaps only a few hundred feet. In the summer of '16, while we were in Paso Robles, my husband thought that there were indications of oil on his property there, and he asked Mr. Doheny,[2] the great oilman of Los Angeles, to send an expert to make an examination. He sent Mr. James O'Donnell,[3] who has become one of Mr. Paderewski's most devoted friends. There was no oil on the Paso Robles ranch, but the following summer my husband bought twenty-five-hundred acres in the Santa Maria oil fields on which experts told him that there was surely oil, but very deep, perhaps four thousand feet. A company was formed, and drilling began in

2. Edward L. Doheny (1856–1935), American oil tycoon based in Southern California.
3. James E. O'Donnell (b.1874), manager of American Oilfields Company of Edward Doheny and other Southern California oil companies.

the summer of 1919, and while we were in Warsaw the following winter, we received news from America that the papers in San Francisco were announcing that oil had been struck on his property. It was almost too good to be true—and was, for before we had time to get used to the idea of great wealth, we received official news that at a depth of 3,434 feet, in oil-bearing sand, the casing and tools of the well had been hopelessly lost and the work abandoned.

It was a very real blow to both of us, but my husband accepted it with his usual philosophy. It was again evident that he was not of those upon whom wealth is thrust. Everything that he has, or has had, he had been compelled to earn by hard work, and so it will probably be to the end. If his earnings in the past have been ample, few realize what sacrifices, what self-denial, what unremitting labor they cost. Even in his mid-twenties, when practically all artists who are to have success are in the full blossom of their prosperity, he was still in the midst of the drudgery of teaching, still preparing for his career. Difficult and discouraging as were those gray years of his youth and early manhood, to them perhaps more than to any other factor in his life, to the self-discipline that they taught him, to the completeness of preparation they gave him, he now attributes his career of success, which lasted unbroken from the time he was ready to ask the approval of the public in 1888 until he definitely retired from the concert stage in 1917.

Mr. Paderewski devoted the winter of 1915–16 almost entirely to what might be called missionary work, not only among the Americans but among the Poles. While the leaders of the Poles in America and the clergy had become very active, there was a vast amount of work still to be done to carry home to the minds of our people the true significance of the war and what it meant to Poland. It must not be forgotten that the great majority of Poles in America, citizens or not, belong to the laboring classes. As my husband once had occasion to say in an address he made to Americans, of the more than four million Poles in the United States, there was not a single millionaire.

The situation was difficult. In the United States there were three classes of Poles, those from Germany, those from Russia, and those from Galicia in Austria. The Poles who had come from Germany, refugees or the children of refugees from Bismarck's[4] *Kulturkampf* of the 1870s, were practically all American citizens and, naturally, thoroughly in sympathy with the Entente.

---

4. Otto von Bismarck's anti-Catholic *Kulturkampf* ("culture struggle") and anti-Polish measures alienated the Polish population of the country, contributing to emigration from German-occupied western Poland.

They comprise rather more than a third of the Polish population. There were perhaps a half-million Russian Poles, and these were easily inclined toward the Entente, at first by Russia's promise to give independence to Poland and later through the German victories that seemed for a time to doom Poland to German domination, a condition at least as deplorable as that which had existed under the Russian Empire. As for the Galician Poles, it was among them that the greatest amount of work had to be done. They were almost entirely laborers, and the majority of them dreamed of returning to Galicia after they had saved money enough to keep them in comfort at home. It must not be forgotten that the lot of the Galician Poles, politically, had for fifty years been fairly good. Galicia was a self-governing province, there were no restrictions of language or schools, and so long as the very heavy taxes were paid, Austria did not bother with it very much. To the Galician Pole of the last score years, Kaiser Franz Josef was a kindly, benevolent deity who let them alone. Moreover, there was the Polish Legions[5] of volunteers who were fighting the Russians under the black eagle of Austria. In the beginning, it cannot be denied that the sympathies of these Galician Poles, if not actively against France and Great Britain, were certainly for Austria as compared with Russia, and these Galicians composed over half of the Polish Immigration.

It was chiefly to these Poles that my husband devoted himself. During the whole winter, in addition to the concerts he gave, he went from city to city wherever there was a Polish population and talked to the people. While urging them, of course, to contribute funds for the immediate relief of their countrymen, to organize themselves so that this relief might be administered most efficiently, he unceasingly preached the gospel that only by the victory of the Entente could Poland hope to secure its liberation. Moreover, as the months wore on, he became more and more convinced that the United States must enter the war, and he felt it a most serious obligation to prepare the minds of the Poles for that event. It was a long pull, a hard pull, but in the end, as the next eighteen months were to show, he was completely successful, and what the Polish immigrants did for their adopted country as well as their fatherland will ever remain one of the brightest pages in the history of our race.

5. The Polish Legions were formed in August 1914 from Polish paramilitary organizations in Galicia as a separate unit of the Austro-Hungarian army. They fought against the Russians until April 1917, when most of them refused to swear allegiance to the Central Powers, which resulted in disarming, imprisonment of top officers (Józef Piłsudski), and internment of the rank and file.

While my husband had every minute of his time occupied, I, too, was as busy, and so were others. My son devoted himself entirely to the work of Polish Relief as he has done to the present day. Madame Sembrich worked unceasingly in her own organization and collected thousands of dollars. In the end she broke down physically and for weeks was desperately ill. In Boston, Madame Szumowska-Adamowska entirely abandoned her professional work to organize Polish Relief throughout New England and, practically unaided, collected, in the course of three years, a very large sum of money, over one hundred thousand dollars. And there were Sigismund Stojowski, the pianist, his mother, and Thaddeus Wroński,[6] the singer, who did invaluable work for the cause. It was Miss Elinor Comstock and the girls of her school who organized with such success the first Polish bazaar in New York, which was given in the Biltmore the first week of November. An orchestra under Arnold Volpe[7] performed a program of Polish music, with Wroński as soloist. A group of Polish dancers from Madame Pavlova's[8] troupe danced Polish dances, and dolls, autographs, photographs, and souvenirs were sold. In Chicago Mr. Smulski, Mr. Heliński, Father Zapala, Mrs. Smulski,[9] Mrs. Neumann,[10] Miss Napieralska,[11] and others were just as busy.

In September, my husband attended an important meeting of the Polish clergy in Pittsburgh, and a month later he made two addresses, one in Polish and the other in English, at a great meeting of Polish miners in Wilkes-Barre. In the meantime his concerts had begun, and on Sunday afternoon, October 10, he gave the first of the four Polish benefits he had planned for the East, in Boston. If any doubt had lingered in his mind after San Francisco regarding his ability to move an American audience with his work, the effect his address had on that Boston audience must have banished it. Symphony Hall was filled, and I have rarely seen a public more deeply stirred. The address was exactly the same as he had given in San Francisco in August, the same as he was later

6. Tadeusz Wroński (1887–1965), Polish basso opera singer; came to the United States in 1913; performed in Boston and later Detroit; dubbed "Father of Detroit Opera."

7. Arnold Volpe (1869–1940), Lithuanian-born American conductor and composer.

8. Anna Pavlova (1881–1931), Russian ballerina; performed with her Russian Ballet Company in the United States during 1914–1917.

9. Jadwiga (Harriet) Smulska, operatic singer in her youth; wife of John Smulski.

10. Anna Neumann (1860–1947), Polish American activist; president of the Chicago-based Polish Women's Alliance of America in the years 1902–1906 and 1909–1918.

11. Emilia Napieralska (1882–1943), Polish American activist; president of the Polish Women's Alliance of America in the years 1918–1935.

to repeat in New York, Philadelphia, and Chicago, and the same Chopin program followed it. After the concert I sold dolls, and my husband began what became the routine of autographing pictures for sale. Mr. Urchs, who during our whole stay in America was of such invaluable service to us, had suggested the sale of autographed photographs as another source of income for the relief fund, and during the next two years these brought in thousands of dollars. It is not the easiest thing in the world for an artist, after playing a recital of two hours and a half, to sign photographs for another hour, but no work was too tiring for Mr. Paderewski if it meant additional money for his beloved cause. This concert, adding to the admissions the money raised from the sale of dolls and photographs, brought ten thousand dollars to our fund.

It was shortly after this Boston concert that Mr. Paderewski met Colonel House for the first time. It is and always will be difficult for us to speak of Colonel House in measured, temperate terms, for of all the friends, old and new, that my husband has in America, there is none to whom he owes a greater debt of gratitude. He has been his staunch friend, the staunch friend of Poland, and Poland's debt to him is greater than is realized now. Although not until the autumn of the following year did Mr. Paderewski come to know him well, from the beginning he showed a very kindly interest and true spirit of helpfulness.

This first meeting had to do with the shipments of foodstuffs to Poland. Up to this time, all funds collected in America had been forwarded to the General Committee in Switzerland, of which Sienkiewicz was president, this committee buying foodstuffs in Europe with the money so received. Mr. Smulski and others of the National Polish Department in Chicago felt that more could be done with the money if the foodstuffs were bought in America and shipped directly to Poland, there to be distributed by the representatives of the General Committee. Guarantees had been secured from Germany that any such food would reach its destination safely, and the Poles in Chicago had subscribed funds with which to send a cargo of flour and the like in a ship specially chartered for the purpose. It was necessary, however, to get the consent of the British government, and after various efforts made to secure this had failed, my husband went to Colonel House and asked him to use his good offices with the government in Washington. This he did, but nothing came of it, for England refused definitely to consider the request.

The Polish benefit concert was given in Carnegie Hall, New York, a fortnight after the one in Boston, and from the sale of tickets, dolls, and souvenirs, about $12,000 was raised. A month later the same concert was given in Philadelphia with similar success. In addition to all these various activities, since the early part of October Mr. Paderewski had been giving two, three, and sometimes four concerts a week. Mr. Ellis has so arranged the schedule that all the concerts before the Christmas holidays should be in the East, within easy reach of New York so that we could keep our headquarters at the Gotham. Yet these concerts, the greater part of which were in New England, meant practically five thousand miles of railway travel, largely at night, and there were comparatively few places where he gave concerts that my husband was not called into consultation with local Polish residents. Consequently, the brief rest of a fortnight at Christmas time was very welcome to him.

The tour began in earnest immediately after the New Year. We put our possessions into the private railcar Commonwealth, which was to be our home for nearly two months and started for St. Paul and Minneapolis. For my husband, on the long tours that he has made in America, a private car has not been a luxury but a necessity. Giving three and four concerts a week in the West and the South, in places often several hundred miles distant from each other, it is only by traveling in this manner that he can get his needed rest and his meals at regular hours, nor is life at all uncomfortable in a car when one has adapted oneself to the confined quarters. It is infinitely more comfortable than dragging oneself from hotel to hotel, eating food that is not always what it should be, and catching trains at almost any hour of the day or night. On some of the tours a car has been our home for four months running, during which period we have not gone to hotels a half-dozen times. And it has really been our home, for year after year we used to have almost the same crew of servants, the Pullman Company always having been very thoughtful in this respect. I don't believe that Mr. Paderewski has a more devoted friend and partisan than Copper,[12] who was our cook for at least ten years.

We left New York in a very contented frame of mind. In the middle of December the Senate had unanimously passed the resolution of Senator Kern[13] of Indiana requesting the president to name a day during the holiday season on which contributions should be made throughout the country for the relief of Polish victims. The president had issued a proclamation naming January 1, 1916, as the day. Little really came of it, but it meant much to my husband since it was the first real recognition of the existence of Poland that the American government had given.

12. James Copper, Paderewskis' chef during their travels in Pullman Company cars.
13. John Worth Kern (1849–1917), senator from Indiana; Democratic majority leader during 1913–1917.

The Chicago benefit was given in the Auditorium on Sunday afternoon, February 6. The whole affair had been placed in the hands of the Chicago branch of the National American Committee of the Polish Victims' Relief Fund, of which James A. Patten was chairman and James B. Forgan[14] the treasurer. The Poles, too, had formed a committee to help, and the concert was a huge success. A few days before our arrival, Mrs. Bryan Lathrop had given a luncheon at which $2,500 had been pledged to start the fund. Mrs. John F. Smulski had recruited a bevy of the prettiest girls in the Polish colony, and dressed in their national costumes, they sold souvenir programs, photographs, and the like. I had a booth for my dolls in the lobby.

The Auditorium was filled to its utmost capacity. All sorts and classes were there, from the richest people of the city to Polish workmen from the stockyards, and when in the intermission following Mr. Paderewski's address Mr. Kellogg Fairbank[15] went on the stage and called for pledges and money for the fund, it was a truly affecting sight to see scores of these Polish workmen come down and give their money, some not more than a dollar, some as much as a hundred dollars, but every gift meaning a very real sacrifice. The money given and pledged at the concert that afternoon came to over twenty thousand dollars, and the total sum raised from the concert was a little less than $40,000.

While in Chicago this time I was able to see started a work that was very close to my heart and the fruits of which are only now beginning to be realized: the care of the unfortunate girls who were victims of the war. The human wreckage, the ruined lives left by the war in France and Belgium, terrible as they were, could not be compared with the devastation wrought among the girls and young women of Poland. Practically the whole of Russian Poland and the whole of Eastern Galicia were a battleground or were occupied by armies from August 1914 to the signing of the armistice. Three hostile armies had swept over this territory, the Russians, the Germans, and the Austrians, and of these the worst were the Hungarian troops of the Austrian army. That it was the inevitable logic of war made it nonetheless horrible.

Dr. Francis Fronczak[16] of Buffalo, who has played such an important role in Polish-American affairs, had talked to me about these conditions the pre-

14. James B. Forgan (1852–1924), older brother of David R. Forgan; president of the First National Bank of Chicago and later a director of the Chicago Reserve Bank.

15. Unable to verify; probably a relative of Nathaniel Kellogg Fairbank (1829–1903), industrialist and philanthropist.

16. Franciszek E. Fronczak (1874–1955), Polish American doctor from Buffalo; member of the Polish National Committee in Paris.

vious spring, and when we were in Chicago for the meeting on Decoration Day, I had spoken about it to Miss Napieralska, secretary of the Polish Women's Alliance. Following the concert, this organization gave a banquet for my husband, and in the course of it Miss Napieralska and Mrs. Neumann, the president of the alliance, told me that work had already started to raise money for this cause. Miss Napieralska had organized the Polish girls of Chicago into a society called "Polish Girls for Polish Girls," and already a considerable sum of money had been collected. Later an American committee was formed in New York, chiefly through the efforts of Mr. Stojowski, and, from one source and another, the sum of about $25,000 was raised with which last spring I bought a property outside of Warsaw where girls will be sheltered and taught useful occupations, such as poultry raising, agriculture, gardening, and the like.[17]

There seemed to be no limit to the work Mr. Paderewski was able to accomplish, and this despite the fact that his neuritis was troubling him more or less all the time. At one time in the season, the pain was so severe that he was compelled to postpone a concert that he was to have given in New York, but in March he found time to study a new work for piano and orchestra by Stojowski. He played this first in New York with the New York Symphony Orchestra under Walter Damrosch[18] at a special gala concert when Elgar's "Polonia" was played for the first time in America. A fortnight later he played it with the Boston Symphony Orchestra in Boston. This had been a labor of love for him. Stojowski had been his pupil, one of the three, the others being Mme. Szumowska-Adamowska and Ernest Schelling, and for years he had been a most loyal friend. Thus it was a very real joy to my husband to be able to show his love for his friend, and the joy was not lessened by the success the work had.

Earlier in the winter he had assisted in the concert given at Carnegie Hall for the benefit of the French Musicians' Fund, and when at the end of March came the news of the tragic death of Enrique Granados and his wife, he took a most active part in organizing the concert given at the Metropolitan Opera House for the benefit of the Granados children.

---

17. This was in Julin, northeast of Warsaw, near Łochów. The school for girls functioned in the Julin manor house until World War II. Recently, a plaque commemorating Helena Paderewska, the foundress of the Julin school, was mounted on the wall of the manor house, now an orphanage.

18. Walter Damrosch (1862–1950), German-born American conductor and composer.

This concert was given on May 7. The artists who took part were Maria Barrientos,[19] Julia Culp,[20] Pablo Casals,[21] Fritz Kreisler, John McCormack,[22] and my husband. I doubt whether artists ever gave themselves more sympathetically to a task than these gave to this concert. Few tragedies of the war were more pathetic. Granados, who had attained the summit of his ambition with the successful performance of his opera at the Metropolitan, was returning with his wife to his home in Spain. By one of those strange freaks of chance, he changed his sailing from New York at the last moment, taking an earlier steamer than he had intended. This change made him and his wife passengers from England to France on the *Sussex*, the ship that was torpedoed. I was told by one of the survivors that Granados had been rescued and was safe when he saw his wife struggling in the water. He jumped in to save her, and both were lost.

Early in April I had a most successful Polish "tag day" in New York, a "Lenten Offering" I called it, by which nearly $50,000 was raised.[23] In this I had the invaluable cooperation and help of Mrs. Phillips,[24] who for two and a half years was my secretary. It was the first day of the kind Poland had had, and it would not be gracious of me to fail to speak of the courtesy and kindly help I received from Mayor Mitchel,[25] the board of aldermen, and the New York authorities in general. All over the city were girls in Polish costumes and Falcons in the picturesque uniforms of their organization, and New York responded generously as it always does at such times.

If I have gone somewhat into detail regarding our activities during this winter, it has been to give an idea of how completely filled every minute of

19. Maria Barrientos (1883–1946), Spanish opera singer; one of the most eminent sopranos of her time.

20. Julia Culp (1880–1970), known as the "Dutch nightingale," she was an internationally celebrated mezzo-soprano.

21. Pablo Casals (1876–1973), Catalan cellist and conductor; considered one of the greatest cellists of all time.

22. John McCormack (1884–1945), world-famous Irish tenor.

23. "Tag day" is a charity fund-raising day where anyone who makes a contribution is given a tag.

24. Anna Mary Laise Phillips, principal and owner of the Laise-Phillips girls' boarding school in Washington, DC; Paderewska's close collaborator in the Polish Victims' Relief Fund and the Polish White Cross; American hooked-rug designer and collector; and owner of Hearthstone Studios of New York. Paderewska's personal secretary during those years was Mary Lee, later Mary Lee McMillan, mentioned in the introduction.

25. John Purroy Mitchel (1879–1918), mayor of New York, 1913–1917; killed in a training accident as an army air officer.

my husband's time was, for he limited himself by no means to his own personal work. He was interested in all that I did and was always ready with help and advice. For my sake or, rather, for the sake of our cause, he lent himself during the winter to many social affairs to which under normal conditions he could not have been induced to go, "lionizing" never having been a favorite diversion with him even at the beginning of his career, when the novelty of it might have made it endurable.

We left for Paso Robles in June, taking Mrs. Phillips with us. Rest was very necessary for him, and, besides, another even longer tour had been prepared for the following season. At that time he did not dream of what a vital role the next winter would play in his life. The entrance of the United States into the war seemed to be as distant as ever. The continual defeats of the Russian army seemed not to shake the security of the imperial throne in the slightest degree, and the liberation of Poland seemed still to be in the dim future.

CHAPTER SEVEN

July 1916–July 1917

The story of Mr. Paderewski's last two years in the United States might almost be called the story of the liberation of Poland, to so great an extent was he a part of all that happened. They brought him not only the fruition of the labors that had engrossed his mind and his soul since the beginning of the war, but they brought him the realization of the hopes, the dreams, and ambitions that had been his since childhood. All the more cheerfully did he accept the burden of responsibility that was put on his shoulders. The full extent of that responsibility may be gauged from a document that must always be one of his most treasured possessions.[1] On July 1, 1917, all the Polish societies of the United States and Canada, with a membership of over a half a million and representing at least 90 percent of the more than four millions of men, women, and children of Polish blood in America, made, constituted, and appointed him—so the document read—

> their true and lawful representative and plenipotentiary, authorizing him, in their name, place and stead . . . to represent them either in person or by written document or memorial, in all matters pertaining to the Polish question, in all departments of the United States Government and in the Embassies of the Governments allied with the United States, to perform any and all acts which may be necessary to be performed in the furtherance of the cause of Poland, giving and granting unto the said Ignacy Jan Paderewski, as such representative and plenipotentiary, full power and authority to perform everything and act whatsoever, requisite and necessary to be done in and about the premises as fully, to all intents and purposes, as the said organizations might do or could do by

---

1. The document was issued to Paderewski in connection with the US entry into the war against the German Empire on April 6, 1917.

their duly elected officers at the doing thereof, with full power of sub-
stitution and revocation, hereby ratifying and confirming all that said
representative and plenipotentiary or his duly authorized substitute,
shall lawfully do or cause to be done by virtue thereof.

The spirit in which he accepted this token of trust and confidence was that
which has guided him constantly since the beginning of his political career.
Never was a man more devoid of personal ambition. Never did a man care
less for personal glorification. Perhaps this would sound better coming from
another than from his wife, but it is the truth, and all who know him well,
all who were associated with him during these last half-dozen years know it
well. Had he been ambitious, the story of these last years might have been very
different. The work he has done, the high offices he has held, did not come of
his seeking, rather they were thrust on him. To accept them demanded a very
real courage, and he did so, believing at the time these different tasks developed that he was fitted to undertake them. His whole attitude in life has been
one of service. He was a servant of his art, and he became in the same way a
servant of the cause that was so dear to him, asking only to be able to give to
it the best that was in him.

It was no light thing for him to give up his music. It is difficult to say
for how many years longer he would have continued to play in public if the
war had not come. He had always said that when he felt that he had ceased
to advance in his art he would stop. An artist cannot stand still; either he
must go forward or backward. Up to the very end of his concert giving,
he had felt in himself a constant development, a constant advance. He felt
that never had he reached such a height as he did during his last two tours
in America. It must always be a mystery to me how he endured the weight
of these two seasons when to the great strain of giving many concerts was
added the burden of unending work and continual anxieties for the Polish
cause. It must have been as he says, that when he sat down at his instrument
to play a program, he had, in addition to the art impulse, which had always
moved him, the inspiration that he was playing for Poland. This he was
literally, for it was those concerts that enabled him to do his work for his
country. Without the money that they brought to him, I do not see how he
could have continued his other tasks. All the money that came from those
two very successful tours, with the exception of a very few thousand that
he invested in his property in California, was spent directly or indirectly
for Poland.

Although he had a very strong presentiment after his last appearance in the spring of 1917, at the concert given for Marshal Joffre[2] at the Metropolitan Opera House, that he would never play again, it was only a presentiment, and already plans had been made for an extensive tour the following season. Even when he sailed for Europe after the armistice, he was not at all certain that he would not resume his career, especially since the war had taken away most of his fortune, and there was the future to think of. Only when he reached Poland and was plunged into the midst of the rebuilding of his country did he finally realize that the chapter of his life that had to do with music was definitely closed.

We were in Paso Robles in the summer of 1916 until well into September. With us were my son and daughter-in-law, Mr. and Mrs. Górski,[3] Mrs. Thomas Krajewski,[4] and her daughter Leonida, now Mrs. Fudakowski[5] of Warsaw. Old friends of ours, both of these women had been indefatigable workers from the beginning, and, especially in the following year during the organization of the White Cross, they were of invaluable help. The concerts of the season began in San Francisco, and we gradually worked our way east, arriving in New York at the end of October. Mr. Ellis had arranged a rather longer tour than that of the previous year, and there was talk of concerts in Havana, where we had never been, but this excursion was not definitely arranged until some weeks later.

The country was in the midst of the presidential campaign, and little Polish work could be done outside of the Poles themselves. By the first of October, a total of $457,000 had been raised in the United States for Polish Relief. Of this sum, about $80,000 had come from Mr. Paderewski's special concerts and addresses and $210,000 from Polish citizens and residents. It was not much when one considers the wealth of the United States, even while admitting the many calls that were being made on American generosity, and when we left for

2. Joseph Joffre (1852–1931), French general most famous for stopping the Germans at the first battle of the Marne in 1914.

3. Wacław Górski, something of a ne'er-do-well and a gambler, was married twice, first to Belle Silviera, an aspiring Chicago portrait artist, and later to another American woman, this time from Indianapolis. In 1916, it was probably the second Mrs. Górski who was in Paso Robles. She was called "Mausunia," likely a diminutive nickname. She outlived her husband, whom she buried in Indianapolis.

4. Rose Schnell Krajewski (1859–1943), American-born widow of Tomasz Florian Krajewski (1851–1913), Polish-born inventor, industrialist, and music enthusiast.

5. Leonida Krajewski Fudakowski (1881–1941), piano student of Theodor Leschetizky; her marriage to Jerzy Fudakowski was the result of Paderewski's matchmaking. The couple lived in Poland during 1919–1921.

the East the chief task that confronted my husband was to give added impulse to the work of raising funds. This he was able to do in a measure but shortly after his arrival in New York, he found work even more important.

In every man's life there are certain days that stand out from all others as turning points in his career, days full of portent the full significance of which may not become evident until long after. Such a day was Mr. Paderewski's birthday, November 6, 1916. I must tell the story of it as I heard him tell Mr. Smulski a few days later, for it will ever remain one of the most memorable days in Polish history, the day on which President Wilson intimated for the first time his sympathy for Poland and his intention to demand her liberation.

The president was at his home in New Jersey, where he had gone to vote in the election on the following day, and for the afternoon of the sixth he had invited the presidents and executive secretaries of all the various war relief organizations to meet him, and Mr. Paderewski, as the head of the Polish Victims' Relief Fund, was among those to go. It happened that on the previous day, November 5, a proclamation by the German and Austrian emperors was published that declared that a part of the ancient Republic of Poland heretofore belonging to Russia was henceforth to be an independent kingdom. The proclamation applied specifically to what since the Congress of Vienna in 1815 has been known as the Congress Kingdom, of which the capital is Warsaw.

When the party arrived at the house of the president, his secretary asked them to enter a large room where Mr. Wilson would greet them. Mr. Paderewski, however, declined to accompany them but told the secretary that not only as the founder of the Polish Victims' Relief Fund in America but as the representative of the Polish people he requested a private audience with the president. It was less than a minute when the secretary returned, saying that Mr. Wilson would be glad to have a talk with him directly after the other guests had left.

They were by no means strangers to each other. We had been guests at the White House, had, in fact, dined there only the winter before, and Mr. Paderewski had played there at least one other time during the administration just ending. The interview was very long, and when I had heard what had taken place, I no longer wondered at the state of exaltation in which my husband returned to New York that evening. Almost the first words of the president were: "Before all, I wish to hear from you something about this declaration of the Central Empires."

Mr. Paderewski was exceedingly skeptical about the purpose and motives of the declaration, and he discussed the whole question at great length and most freely. He pointed out to the president that both monarchs had obviously issued this proclamation as supreme commanders of their armies. Moreover, the proclamation lacked the signatures of the chancellors of both empires, and this, in itself, under the provisions of the German constitution, made the document of doubtful value. He told the president that the strategic character of the proclamation was proved by the fact that while it assigned the new kingdom no king nor gave it definitive boundaries, it plainly called upon the subjects of the proposed new state to form a national army to fight for the Central Powers.

This proclamation, he said, meant nothing more than a new partition of Poland, which would bring in its train new miseries, new sufferings, and new sacrifices to a people who had already suffered more from the war than any other nation. He ended by saying that nothing would satisfy the Poles in Poland, the Poles in America, the Poles throughout the world except a Poland absolutely free, absolutely independent, a Poland with her ancient territories restored to her, with access to the sea, so that she might once more take her place among the nations of the world.

Mr. Wilson listened most attentively to Mr. Paderewski, and when he ended the president said, without any reservation whatsoever, "I am very glad to hear you confirm my own opinion, because I am personally for a free, independent, and united Poland."

It is not difficult to imagine the effect that this declaration had on my husband. Made voluntarily, without qualifications, by the president of the United States, it was as if a dazzling ray of sunshine had burst unexpectedly through a thick sky of dull, depressing gray clouds. It was the beginning of the end, the first step toward the realization of the dream that had persisted with our people through an agonizing century and a half. The conversation continued for some time after this, and as Mr. Paderewski was leaving, the president remarked: "Some people think and pretend that I am not sincere. Believe me that I am always sincere in everything I say or do."

Of course, Mr. Wilson did not know that it was my husband's birthday, but he had unwittingly given him a most precious birthday present. This came on the eve of the election on which such great issues hung, and thus it seemed doubly significant. My husband interpreted the president's declaration as meaning that whatever the result of the election on the morrow, he intended to speak for Poland. It would have been impossible at that time to have exaggerated the importance of this. Events were so shaping themselves that it seemed certain that whether the United States entered the war or not, hers would be a most influential voice when the time came for the making of peace, and with the president committed to a free Poland, the Poles had at last substantial hope to build it. The news of this interview, which naturally was spread abroad, immediately created a great tide of enthusiasm among the Poles for the president, which was heightened by the message to Congress in the following January in which Mr. Wilson publicly declared his support for a free and independent Poland, and this enthusiasm maintained itself until the end of the war and through the Peace Conference. The interview also gave a tremendous impetus to the work among the Poles. Money for the relief fund came in more rapidly and in larger sums, and everybody was doing his utmost to help the work. It was still necessary to send the money to the General Committee in Switzerland and to buy the foodstuffs at very high prices in Germany and Austria because it was impossible to get the consent of the British government to ship food directly from America.

Colonel House, whom Mr. Paderewski calls "Poland's providential man," had been most active in furthering Polish interests, and this generous and sympathetic attitude brought him and my husband together quite often. Even at that time, Mr. Paderewski's admiration and affection for him were very real. Not very long after the interview with the president, Colonel House asked my husband if he could write for him a memorandum on Poland, taking into consideration the political, geographical, and other conditions in which the country was at that moment. Although Mr. Paderewski did not know it at the time, it was the president who had asked for this information. Naturally, he accepted the commission most gladly but did not begin work at once. For one reason he was in the midst of the rush of concerts that preceded the Christmas holidays, and besides, he did not think that there was any great hurry about it. When the memorandum was written, it was done under terrific pressure and under conditions that were about as unfavorable as could be imagined.

Work has never frightened my husband, and he has shown many times his ability to concentrate on a given task, making himself oblivious to all else, but the writing of this memorandum tested his endurance to the very last degree. He says now that the memory of it is a sort of nightmare to him. To me, had I needed it, it would have been a final proof of that driving power, that complete self-discipline that have been such potent factors in his success.

His second New York recital of the season was to have been given at Carnegie Hall on Tuesday afternoon, January 9, 1917. A few days before, he had contracted a slight attack of influenza, which gave him two or three degrees of fever. In nursing him, I fancy I caught his influenza. At any rate, I was thoroughly exhausted from the work I had been doing since the early autumn, and the combination proved too much for me. On the Sunday before the concert, I had a complete collapse, and for a time it seemed as if the end had come. I had more than five degrees of fever, and as I look back at it now, I am certain that my life was saved only by the realization of how much there was to do, how quite impossible it was for me to die at that time.

Worry over me did not help my husband's illness, and he had before him the very important concert of Tuesday. As if this were not enough, on Monday morning Colonel House telephoned him, telling him that he must see him as soon as possible on most important business. Mr. Paderewski dropped everything and went at once, and when Colonel House asked him what progress he had made with the memorandum, he had to answer that he had not even started it. "I am going to Washington Thursday morning," said Colonel House, "and it is of the utmost importance that I have the memorandum to take with me."

Mr. Paderewski protested that it was impossible. He had his concert the next afternoon for which he must prepare, his wife was desperately ill, and he did not see how he could possibly do it. All of this, replied Colonel House, did not matter. The memorandum was of vital importance and must be written and must be in his hands Thursday morning before he left for Washington.

In view of this, there was nothing to do but to tell Colonel House that the memorandum would be ready at the required time. The task seemed appalling. He could not do any writing until after the concert, for he had already suffered severely from writer's cramp and dared not risk his hands before playing his recital. He spent the rest of Monday making his final preparation for his concert, for he was playing a new program and getting together such few books as he could find that contained the material he needed for his work.

He went to Carnegie Hall that Tuesday afternoon in a highly nervous condition. What with worrying about me and worrying about the memorandum, his fever returned, fortunately only slightly but enough to add a certain amount of physical discomfort to his mental strain. Yet all accounts have it that he fairly surpassed himself at this concert. He himself even says that he has never played better, and he has always been his own most severe critic. He was strung to the highest pitch of nervous tension, and after the performance of the printed program he played an unusual number of extra pieces.

It was after six when he returned to the hotel. Taking only time enough to change his clothes and to talk with me for a few minutes, without any dinner he sat down at his desk and began to work, and he was at his desk practically without intermission until midnight the next day. Then, as there remained only a few corrections to make, and he knew that the manuscript could be delivered in time, he slept for two hours. He was back at his desk at two o'clock and worked again until four. All day Wednesday and all Wednesday night, there were three typists copying, correcting, and recopying. The last page was finished at eight o'clock in the morning, and a special messenger gave the complete manuscript to Colonel House as he was leaving his home a half hour later to take the train to Washington.

He likes now to say that he could never have finished the work in the given time if it had not been for the encouragement I gave him. Toward the end he came to me and said that he did not see how he could possibly go on. He said that his brain was completely fagged, his nerves were on edge, and he must have sleep. Although I was very ill and could not speak above a whisper, I did my best to encourage him. I helped him, I know, but I know also that he would have finished it had I not been there. It is not his nature to fail in such tasks.

The memorandum, as he says now, was sound propaganda for Poland, addressed to an exceptionally distinguished mind. In it he had to take into account the atmosphere prevailing then among the people who held the fate of the country in their hands. He had also to consider certain principles that were raised at that time and that, however lofty and noble they were, do not now seem to be practical and, in fact, could not be always applied in the final settlement. It treated the whole subject of Poland most exhaustively from practically every angle.

A few days later my husband went to see Colonel House in response to a telephone message, and the latter told him that he had read the memorandum on his way to Washington. So deeply had it impressed him that he had reread it several times in order to become thoroughly imbued with its spirit and thus be properly able to present the case to the president. Mr. Wilson himself had said that he would read the memorandum carefully and furthermore had said that he intended to make some mention of Poland in his forthcoming message to Congress.

As Mr. Paderewski did not feel that he had done a particularly good piece of work because of the haste in which he had written it, it was all the more gratifying to him to hear the memorandum warmly praised by Colonel House, and when he asked him if the Poles could really expect anything of value to their cause and to their country, Colonel House smilingly replied: "I'm telling you to get ready, to prepare yourself for a shock. The first shot will be fired soon, and it will take your breath away."

We were at that time on the point of leaving New York for several weeks. Arrangements had been made for some concerts in Havana, and several were to be given on our way south. We were in Spartanburg, South Carolina, on Monday, January 22, when my husband read the famous message in which the president made his formal declaration that Poland should be free and independent. I leave to the reader's imagination the effect this message had on him, the effect it had on all the Poles in America and in the whole world. A new day had dawned for all of us, and to the end of time we Poles can never discharge our debt of gratitude to President Wilson and to Colonel House, for they are the men who made the liberation of Poland not only possible but a fact. I include the name of Colonel House, for without him, without his interest, the paragraph in the message referring to Poland, if it had been written at all, is likely to have been different, and when at the Peace Conference little by little of that which had been assigned to Poland in the message was being taken from her, it was Colonel House who was her constant and indefatigable champion.

It was most characteristic of the man that he requested that nothing be said of the part he had taken in presenting the cause of Poland to the president, in fact that nothing whatever be said regarding this interest and intervention in the Polish question. He said that it was his rule to avoid publicity as much as possible. Whatever he did, he did because he felt it his duty, and in the case of Poland he felt very deeply that anything he might do to help towards its liberation would be working toward the attainment of a righteous cause.

Mr. Paderewski naturally had to consent to this request, but he did so with a certain amount of unwillingness. He felt that his own debt and that of all the Poles to Colonel House was so great that it should be in some manner publicly acknowledged. Besides, several of the Polish leaders in America, knowing of the memorandum, had not much difficulty in guessing the role that Colonel House had played, and they were eager to show their appreciation. A year later, Mr. Paderewski went to Colonel House and asked to be released from his promise of silence. He said that his Polish friends, not understanding, were suspecting him (my husband) of ingratitude, and the situation was becoming embarrassing. Colonel House told him in that case to do what he thought best but please to make as little fuss as possible. The result was a quiet dinner at which several of the leading Poles in America met Colonel House and thanked him personally for what he had done.

All this had been in addition to a very heavy concert tour and, incidentally, a most successful one. And there were numerous meetings in various cities at which addresses had to be made. The great meeting at the Metropolitan Opera

House in Philadelphia took place in December at which Mr. Paderewski made two speeches, one in English and one in Polish. This meeting was largely due to the work of Judge von Moschziesker[6] who, like his wife, was an indefatigable worker in the cause, and one of the principal addresses was made by the Honorable James M. Beck, one of Poland's most enthusiastic champions.

I, too, had been very busy. In November I organized a Polish Day at the Inter-Allied Bazaar. Aside from the very real success of the day, it meant much to us, for it was the first time Poland had been admitted to one of these bazaars as a nation. To many, such a fact may seem trivial, but to us who were struggling so hard to get recognition, every little incident of this kind helped enormously. I also organized a Christmas Tree Bazaar at the Gotham, which was held for two days the week before Christmas. That was real work, Aline, my maid, herself making hundreds of tiny Christmas trees, which we sold; but the feature of the bazaar was a Polish *szopka*, which was the contribution of Mr. Wroński.

At Christmas time in Poland there is a quaint custom that has come down from earliest times. In the cities, in the towns, and in villages in the country districts, puppet shows called *szopka* are held. Groups of men and boys go about the country from house to house, carrying the little theaters in which the shows are played on their backs, and in a very primitive and naive manner, not unlike the old English and French morality plays, the play tells the story of the Nativity. One sees the star of Bethlehem leading the shepherds to the crèche, the visit of the Three Kings, the Three Wise Men, a foolish and comic Herod and an ugly and wicked Herodias, to say nothing of a most horrific devil, who in the end carries away the king and his wife. There are other quaint medieval figures and fancies, curiously mixed with modern ideas, and through the plays run continuously some most lovely old Polish Christmas songs that every Pole knows from childhood.

Mr. Wroński built the theater, made the puppets, arranged the music, and practically gave the whole show himself. To us Poles it was inexpressibly affecting, if only because it had been a very vital part of our childhood, and I was curious to see how it would appeal to Americans, to whom it all would be strange and who had not the tradition that made it so real to a Pole. I have never seen audiences more fascinated, more enthusiastic. Mr. Wroński was forced to give the performance several times each afternoon and evening, and it was even proposed that a performance should be given in a theater where

---

6. Robert von Moschziesker (1870–1939), chief justice of the Pennsylvania Supreme Court.

the general public could see it, but a theater was not available at that time, other things occupied our minds, and it was never done.

Directly after the bazaar we went to Boston, where Mr. Paderewski was to play on Friday and Saturday with the Boston Symphony Orchestra. With the exception of a special concert given the next month in New York, these concerts were to be the last that my husband was to play with Major Higginson's[7] great orchestra. Indeed, his performances with the Boston Symphony were to be his last with any orchestra, and I have always felt that there was a certain fitness in this. Since his first visit, there had hardly been a tour in which he had not been soloist with the orchestra in Boston and many other cities. There were several years when it was the only orchestra with which he played in the East. He had played under Gericke,[8] Nikisch,[9] Paur,[10] Fiedler,[11] and Muck.[12] Years ago, in the spring of 1892, during his first tour, he proposed giving a concert in aid of the Washington Arch Fund in New York,[13] and Major Higginson voluntarily offered him the assistance of the orchestra, which was then under Arthur Nikisch. He had played in Boston at the orchestra's Pension Fund Concerts. Since 1902, Mr. Ellis, the manager of the orchestra, had had charge of all his tours in America. His relations with the orchestra had been so intimate that he really felt himself almost an integral part of it, and when he finished his symphony in 1908, he made a special trip to the United States in order that it might first be played by the Boston Symphony. I speak of this now because it is a part of the musical history of America, because it belongs to the old order that has passed away forever. Major Higginson is dead, Mr. Ellis has retired from active work, and my husband seldom touches the piano.

What lovely and fragrant memories my husband has of the years he traveled in America! Daniel Mayer,[14] his agent in England at the beginning of his

7. Henry Lee Higginson (1834–1919), businessman, philanthropist, and founder of the Boston Symphony Orchestra.

8. Wilhelm Gericke (1845–1925), Austrian-born conductor and composer.

9. Arthur Nikisch (1855–1922), Hungarian conductor.

10. Emil Paur (1855–1932), Austrian-born conductor.

11. Max Fiedler (1859–1939), German conductor.

12. Karl Muck (1859–1940), German-born conductor.

13. The Washington Arch Fund collected funds for the building of a triumphal arch in New York City's Greenwich Village to celebrate the centennial of George Washington's inauguration as president of the United States (1789). The marble arch was dedicated in 1895.

14. Daniel Mayer represented Paderewski until about 1901. He was responsible for the unfortunate advertising for the 1890 London tour of Paderewski as the "Lion of Paris," which cost the pianist some public ridicule.

career, arranged for his first American tour with Charles Tretbar[15] of Steinway and Sons. That season he gave 120 concerts in six months, sometimes playing twice a day, Mr. Tretbar pushing him to the utmost limit of his strength. Once he had to prepare three new orchestral programs in a fortnight in addition to giving six recitals, each with a different program. He tells how when he was preparing for these, he used to practice all day at the Windsor Hotel and then go down to Steinway Hall on Fourteenth Street to work most of the night, while Hugo Goerlitz,[16] who was traveling with him in those days, slept on the top of a neighboring piano and the night watchman on another. He says that he worked an average of seventeen hours a day during those two weeks.

Mr. Tretbar is dead these many years, and so is John C. Frye,[17] who succeeded him in the management of the American tours. When, after our marriage, I accompanied him to America, his business generally was in the hands of our beloved "Governor," as we called him, William Adlington of London, who was with us during several tours in America and accompanied us to Australia. From 1902 to the end, all of Mr. Paderewski's American business was in the hands of Mr. Ellis. When Mr. Adlington retired from active work, he was succeeded by L. G. Sharpe, who was with us on several tours in America and accompanied us to South America and South Africa. The facility that my husband has always had of making devoted friends of those with whom he has business relations has held true with his managers to a remarkable degree and with all the other men who had something to do with him: Herman Schaad, Rudolph Heck,[18] Joubert,[19] Fischer,[20] Brennan,[21] and Walter.[22] These men were as loyal and devoted to his interests as they could have been to their own, and it was one of his great joys in returning to America to know that he would be surrounded year after year by men whom he could trust implicitly.

15. Charles F. Tretbar (1832–1909), German-born concert organizer and executive at Steinway and Sons for some forty years.

16. Hugo Goerlitz (b. 1854), German-born international music agent, who was Paderewski's secretary for several years in the 1890s.

17. John C. Frye, likely a Steinway executive.

18. Unable to verify.

19. Eldon Joubert, Paderewski's (Weber and later Steinway) piano tuner and travel companion for more than three decades beginning in 1906.

20. Emil C. Fischer, Paderewski's "piano doctor" who traveled with him during several seasons.

21. W. C. Brennan, from Boston, one of Paderewski's US managers.

22. Unable to identify.

The concert in Boston on Friday afternoon was very successful. The concert on Saturday evening was sensational. There were but two works on the program, Liszt's Faust Symphony and, after the intermission, Schumann's Concerto in A Minor. Everything seemed to conspire to make the performance memorable. The orchestra, Muck, the conductor, my husband, and the audience itself seemed to be under the spell of a great inspiration. The very atmosphere seemed to be tense with electricity. All artists know that, now and then in their career, such conditions exist when they are carried out beyond themselves. So it was in Boston that evening, and at the end of the concerto hardly a person in the audience left his seat, not one in the orchestra, and for another hour Mr. Paderewski played, one piece after another, the audience leaving only when the lights were turned out. If it was to be his farewell to Boston and the Boston Symphony, it was a glorious one.

We were in Cuba at the end of January and the early part of February. Mr. Paderewski gave three concerts in Havana but did not stay as long as he had planned, for the weather was cold and dreary and generally unpleasant, and, moreover, he was restless and uneasy, eager to return to the States. There was no question now in his mind that the United States was to enter the war at an early date, and he felt that the time had finally come when he could work seriously on his most treasured plan, the creation of a Polish army. There was much to be done, for it was necessary to start at once a strong propaganda among the Poles—the unnaturalized Poles—in favor of creating a military force.

The Russian Revolution, which came in March, confirmed him in his belief that the time was ripe for a Polish army. One of the early acts of the provisional government of Russia had been to declare that Poland should be free and independent. The fact that this declaration in favor of Poland had its inspiration in Mr. Balfour and the British government made it appear that, unlike the proclamation of September 1914, which had been signed by the Grand Duke Nicholas, unlike the decree of the Central Empires of the preceding November, it could be taken seriously. Containing no qualifications or conditions, it seemed to be a straightforward and honest document.

No one who lived through the spring of 1917 can easily forget the impression made on the world by the overthrow of the Romanov dynasty and, with it, the overthrow of that vast mechanism of despotism that had been built to make the imperial throne secure. The wildest hopes were raised in the breasts of lovers of liberty. Staid, sober men prophesied that the first real step had been taken toward the millennium. But those who knew Russia and the Russians were far from certain that the millennium was at hand. They hoped that the new government would be able to carry on and gradually build a substantial structure, but they could not help being more or less skeptical. I remember that Mr. Paderewski at this time continually warned his American friends not to expect too much. No one could foresee the desolation and horrors of Bolshevism, but he, in common with most observers familiar with Russia, predicted that there would be a long period of unsettlement and disorder before a stable government could be established. Few of his friends to whom he talked about Russia would believe him, thinking him hopelessly prejudiced against all things Russian. Nonetheless he persisted in his belief, which was shortly to get its first confirmation in the rise of Kerensky[23] and the collapse of the Russian army.

That spring, it will be remembered, after the declaration of war, two important missions came to America, one from France headed by Marshal Joffre, the other from England with Mr. Balfour as its chief. Each of these gave rise to interesting incidents. At the gala concert given at the Metropolitan Opera House in honor of Marshal Joffre, my husband was a soloist—in fact, he was playing when the marshal entered the auditorium. This was his last appearance in public as a pianist. When he finished his performance, he told me that he had a strange feeling, an almost intuition, that it was the end of his career, but neither he nor I thought much of it until more than a year later when he finally decided that he could never go back to his instrument again. That he should have made his farewell appearance under such conditions as these has always been a source of satisfaction to him. He was assisting in a tribute to a great soldier and, through that great soldier to France, all this in a city and a country that for years had treated him with such generous devotion—what more ideal conditions for a farewell could have been chosen?

The other incident was of a quite different character. With the British Mission came a copy of Professor Dietrich Schäfer's[24] famous geography in which the learned author, with an extravagant use of fantastic figures in his statistics and of red ink on his maps, sought to demonstrate the right of Germany to control the British Channel through "Teutonic" Belgium and tried to prove that a German protectorate over Central Europe was fully justified. Naturally,

---

23. Alexander Kerensky (1881–1970), Russian lawyer and politician; prime minister of the provisional government overthrown by the Bolsheviks in November 1917.

24. Dietrich Schäfer (1849–1929), German political scientist; a copy of Paderewski's response to Schäfer is in the Yale University Library's Karl Weigl Papers.

one of the things that Professor Schäfer sought to show was the unimportance of the Polish race, its numerical insignificance, and how, generally speaking, it was unfit to have a country of its own, especially when its great and good neighbor Germany was at hand, ready to guide its faltering footsteps into the paths that lead to "Kultur."

The appearance of this map with its statistics caused a little uneasiness and apprehension among the Americans who were working for Poland, particularly since it was difficult to secure at the time data with which to refute Schäfer's assertions. Wherefore Mr. Paderewski was asked to write an answer, which he did, and his "A Few Remarks upon Professor Schäfer's Map," a memorandum of about three thousand words, produced a very satisfactory effect.

Early in June we left for Paso Robles. Before going, however, we went to New Haven, where Mr. Paderewski received the degree of doctor of music from Yale University. He was one of a group of distinguished foreigners who received honorary degrees at that time, the others being Andrew Tardieu[25] of the French Mission, Sir Ernest Rutherford,[26] the physicist, and the Reverend John Kelman[27] of Edinburgh, a member of the British Mission.

25. Andre Tardieu (1876–1945), French politician; later prime minister.

26. Ernest Rutherford, 1st baron Rutherford of Nelson (1871–1937), New Zealand–born British physicist and chemist; dubbed "father of nuclear physics."

27. John Kelman (1864–1929), English-born Presbyterian minister; pastor in New York City.

CHAPTER EIGHT

1917

I do not propose telling in detail the story of the Polish army that—raised in the United States, trained in Canada, and transported to France—fought so gallantly in the engagements to which it was assigned. That story, written by someone far more competent than I, will make a book in itself, for it is one of the most remarkable incidents of a remarkable war. It was the final factor in the liberation of Poland, and the time is not yet come when the whole history of that liberation can be told. But this army was the creation of Mr. Paderewski, the offspring of his imagination, the realization of his dreams, and to him must go the responsibility and credit for its coming into being.

Yet he could have accomplished nothing had he not had the loyal and devoted support of the vast majority of the Poles in America and the Polish National Department of Chicago. In a certain sense, I think that the last eighteen months we spent in America were among the happiest of his life. Although it was a period of constant anxiety and worry, this worry and anxiety entirely lacked the doubt and uncertainty that had been with him almost continuously since the beginning of the war. At last he had before him a definitely marked goal. With the entrance of the United States into the war, there was no longer any possible doubt as to its ultimate result. The collapse of Russia, growing more complete month by month, although serious for the Entente, removed a great obstacle from the ambition of Poland be free once more. With Russia emerging from the war still a powerful empire, the future of Poland, despite the declarations and wishes of President Wilson, would have been far from certain. Thus with the goal actually in sight, he felt that his task now was to make the position of the Poles in the eyes of the Allies as strong as possible so that when the day of final reckoning should come, they could go before the Peace Conference as an allied nation.

The trust and confidence, the unfailing cooperation that the Polish Immigration gave to him during these last months, were of themselves a great reward for all his work. Massed solidly behind him in all that he did, in all that he planned, in all that he asked, were the National Department of Chicago, the Polish National Alliance, the Polish Falcons' Alliance, the Polish Roman Catholic Union, the Polish Women's Alliance, and the other principal societies and organizations of our people. Their leaders, Smulski, Żychliński, Father Zapała, Starzyński,[1] Heliński, and Piotrowski,[2] to mention only a few, worked indefatigably to realize and carry out his plans and ideas. I wonder if Poland will ever understand what she owes to these men and to their colleagues and to the four million Polish patriots in America whom they represented.

Following our return from Cuba, Mr. Paderewski plunged at once into the work of laying the foundations of a Polish army. I have already spoken of the idea that had been in his mind from the very beginning of the war, the formation of an army of Poles to fight in the armies of the Entente as Poles, under the Polish flag. I have referred to his energetic opposition in Europe before we went to America to the various plans made to form Polish legions to fight under foreign flags. History had taught him only too well the futility of this, so far as any benefit was to come from it to Poland. For over a hundred years, Polish legions had fought in foreign armies, Polish youth had bled and died for foreign causes, and that had been the end of it. The one meager reward that had come from all these sacrifices had been the Duchy of Warsaw of Napoleon I, which had vanished with Waterloo.

Early in the war one battalion of Polish legionnaires had been formed in France, with headquarters at Bayonne, but this was the only organization of the kind in the armies of the Entente on the western front. To organize a Polish legion of thousands would have been difficult at any time during the first years of the war, and, in fact, the French army contained many thousand Poles who had enlisted voluntarily. The Poles are notoriously good fighters, sturdy and docile soldiers, and a legion of forty or fifty thousand of them would not have been unwelcome on the western front. But Mr. Paderewski was convinced that it was best to wait for a more favorable moment.

Arriving in America he found quite an influential body of American Poles who at that time honestly believed that the future of their country was bound up in the fortunes of the Central Empires, their legitimate hatred of Russia

---

1. Teofil Antoni Starzyński (1878–1952), first Polish American doctor in Pittsburgh; principal organizer and national leader of the Falcon (Sokół) organization promoting physical education and traditional values in the Polish American community.

2. Nikodem L. Piotrowski (b. 1863), Chicago city attorney, 1911–1915; in 1918 elected president of the Polish Roman-Catholic Union of America.

blinding them to all else. Not a small part of the missionary work that he did during the first two years of his stay had been to convert these men from their fixed belief in Germany and Austria.

There was also another element, very much larger and very much more influential, that was most eager to support the Entente in an active way. These Poles were keen to form a legion that might fight in the armies of France. Early in the war, while we were still in Switzerland, a telegram had been sent to the Polish National Alliance from Paris to the effect that France had proclaimed the independence of Poland and urging that men and money be sent by the American Poles. Among other names that were signed to it was that of Mr. Paderewski. Of course, he knew nothing about it, and the telegram itself was wholly unauthorized, but it stirred most strongly the imagination of the younger Poles in America, and when we arrived there, the movement to give active aid to the Entente had gained considerable headway.

The same reasons that had led Mr. Paderewski to disapprove of the formation of Polish legions in Europe held good in America. There was also another and very important reason why the Poles in America should take no such action. The United States at the time was a neutral country, and if any such thing had been attempted, serious complications might have resulted. Therefore, almost immediately after his arrival and for nearly two years, Mr. Paderewski was forced to oppose with all the strength of his persuasion and logic this idea of sending men to Europe.

The situation in February, when he returned from the South, was entirely different. Diplomatic relations between the United States and Germany had been broken, and no one believed that the actual declaration of war could be delayed more than a few weeks. With this in view, he went to Chicago and laid before the leaders of the National Department and the Polish National Alliance the plans he had formed in his own mind, with the result that in March the first definite step toward the organization of the Polish army was taken. A preliminary course for officers was established in the Polish College at Cambridge Springs, Pennsylvania. The beginning was very modest, but nonetheless it was a beginning, and great results came from it, which are felt even now. Some of the most efficient officers in Poland's army of today are graduates of this school or of its successors in Canada and France.

The plan of which this school was the first step had been developing in Mr. Paderewski's mind during the months he had been in America to be put into effect when and if the United States entered the war. If a Polish legion could not fight to advantage under the flags of France, Britain, or any other of the Allies, a Polish army certainly could do so under the flag of the United States. The conditions were quite different. Over four million Poles had accepted the United States as their adopted country. Of these, a considerable part had not yet been naturalized chiefly because they hoped that someday Poland might be free and that then they might return; this hope, however, not making them the less loyal Americans. Moreover, if the United States entered the war, it would do so from disinterested motives, and, most important of all, its president had publicly declared for a free and independent Poland.

Why not, then, organize an army in the United States composed entirely of Poles residing there who had not yet been naturalized, and officered partly by Polish officers trained in America but chiefly by Polish officers in the Russian army, the whole to be under the general American command, fighting under the flag of the United States as well as under that of Poland? He felt the Poles could well offer such an army to the American government as a token of their gratitude for the hospitality that had been so generously given to them as exiles, and as a final tribute he proposed that this should be called the "Kosciuszko Army" in memory of Poland's great hero and most beloved leader, who had given his services to the struggling colonies in their war of the revolution.

From the beginning he had the hearty support of the Polish leaders in America in this project, but before he took any decided steps, he consulted with many of his American friends, including many men prominent in business and politics. There were no technical difficulties in the way. The supply of men eager to volunteer in such an army was ample. The problem of officers was most easy to solve. In addition to such as could be trained in the United States, the breakup of the Russian army would make available the services of an almost unlimited supply of officers of all grades, commissioned and noncommissioned, who had received their training in the hard campaigns of the eastern front, and these were only too willing to embark on such an adventure.

Practically all the men whom he consulted looked upon the idea as not only feasible but as something that would be of real advantage to the United States. From all sides he received much encouragement, the greatest of all, perhaps, being the patriotic spirit of the Falcons' Alliance. Mr. Paderewski had nothing but the warmest praise for the indefatigable manner in which Dr. Starzyński, its president, had always fostered that spirit among the youth. A special convention of the Falcons was called to meet in Pittsburgh in the early days of April and take action.

It was a meeting of unexampled fervor. All lines of demarcation between differing factions disappeared. Love of the fatherland and loyal devotion to the adopted country swept away all opposing opinions, however antagonistic they had been in the past. Mr. Paderewski was received tumultuously. His words to the men, in which he urged them to make their arms ready for the great day when they would fight for America and, fighting for America, would fight for Poland, were answered by full-throated shouts that left no doubt about the sentiments of the American Poles.

As a result of this convention, a telegram was sent to President Wilson, signed by Dr. Starzyński, offering an army of one hundred thousand Poles, fully trained and officered, to fight in the American army under the American and Polish flags. Simply as a Pole, not as the wife of the man whose idea this was, I feel that I can say that this was a magnificent offer, magnificently made, with none but the purest motives and impulses behind it.

Even in those stirring days that immediately preceded the declaration of war, the news of this offer created a sensation among the Americans. It was viewed in different ways. Some took it lightly as a wild scheme, the emanation of the brain of an irresponsible artist. Others took it as an unusually clever piece of publicity for Poland and the Poles. The majority, however, I believe took the offer seriously, even while many thought the idea impractical and, perhaps, undesirable. As for the Poles, there was no question as to their sentiment regarding it. They were for it heart and soul.

Several days passed before an answer came from Washington. In the meantime certain infallible signs appeared in the press showing that the hostile, secret, and powerful influences that have consistently opposed the interests of Poland were hard at work. Conscious of this, the courteous declination of the offer that finally came from Washington caused him no great surprise. Nonetheless it was a crushing disappointment for him. It ended for the time being his hope of a Polish army, which he regarded more than ever as time passed as essential to the complete restoration of Polish liberty.

Despite the unfavorable turn of affairs, the officers' school at Cambridge Springs continued its work, and the enthusiasm of the Poles in America did not abate one whit. With the declaration of war, they swarmed to the recruiting booths, volunteering for the regular army and the National Guard; citizens or noncitizens, it made no difference. The one thing they wanted was to serve. In Paris in the summer of 1919[3] an American staff officer told me

3. The original manuscript cited 1917 as the year, which must be a typing error because the Paderewskis were in Paso Robles that summer.

that he believed that close to 10 percent of the enlisted men in the American Expeditionary Force were of Polish blood or extraction.

When they entered the army, thousands of these Polish recruits could speak little or no English, yet they made, I have been told by American officers, most efficient and capable soldiers. Nor is this surprising. Most of these men, in addition to being natural fighters, the inheritors of a warlike tradition, had had more or less military training before they entered the American army. Those of them who had not left Europe until early manhood had served their time in the Russian, Austrian, and German armies. Of the younger men, a very considerable part belonged to the Falcons, the American branch of which since 1912 had made military training an important part of their routine, and at the Falcons' convention in Buffalo in 1914, two generals of the American army had reviewed five thousand of them, complimenting them highly on the proficiency of their drill.

All the efforts made directly or indirectly to secure a reversal of this decision came to naught, and the prospect of forming a Polish army would have been hopelessly discouraging but for one thing. During the years he had been in America Mr. Paderewski had seen much of Mr. Jusserand,[4] the French ambassador in Washington, for whom he had the highest regard. Their relations had been social as well as having to do with Polish interests in France. Directly following the refusal of the American government to act in the matter of the Polish army, advances were made to the French government both through the medium of Mr. Jusserand and that of certain influential Poles in Paris. Conditions in Paris were found to be much more favorable toward the creation of a Polish army, and negotiations were pursued most vigorously, with the result that in June a completely new turn was given to the situation. On the fourth of that month Mr. Poincaré, president of the French Republic, issued a decree countersigned by Mr. Painlevé,[5] president of the Council of Ministers, authorizing the formation in France of an autonomous and independent Polish army, which should take its place on the western front on an equal footing with the armies of the Allies. In this move France had the cordial support of Great Britain, and it was agreed that while France should furnish the funds

---

4. Jean Jules Jusserand (1855–1932), author and diplomat; French ambassador to the United States, 1902–1925; participated in the drafting of the Treaty of Versailles and the diplomatic mission to Warsaw during the Polish-Soviet war in 1920.

5. Paul Painlevé (1863–1933), French mathematician and politician; prime minister in the fall of 1917.

necessary for the support and equipment of these troops, England would furnish training grounds in Canada, officers for training purposes, and, when the time came, ships in which to transport the army to Europe.

Immediately after the decree of President Poincaré, steps were taken to secure the consent of Washington to the enlistment of Polish noncitizens, but without success. Again the dark, malign influences were at work, with their usual success. Finally, in August, the first Polish military mission arrived in America, comprised of Lieutenant Gąsiorowski,[6] Lieutenant Prince Poniatowski[7] (whose mother is an American), Second Lieutenant Szaniawski,[8] and Messrs. Rejer[9] and Mazurek.[10] At the same time came Mr. Franklin-Bouillon,[11] on behalf of the French government, to discuss and settle certain matters with Washington and with the Polish leaders. Colonel Martin,[12] a most distinguished member of the French general staff, came as the commandant of the new army under a direct commission from the French Ministry of War. As a result of the arrival of these missions, the State Department gave permission for the holding of meetings on behalf of an army among the Poles, but not for recruiting purposes—only, so to say, for propaganda. It was not until the early part of October that permission was finally given to recruit for this army among the Poles in the United States who had not been naturalized.

At this time, in August, we were in Paso Robles. We had gone there in the early part of July to rest and to enable Mr. Paderewski to prepare for his next tour. He was very tired. Between September and March he had played seventy-three concerts. This in itself in former years would have been thought a very respectable season's work, but in addition to these concerts, he had all his other work to do, had suffered from innumerable anxieties and worries, and when we left for the West he was thoroughly fagged. For the season of '17-'18, Mr. Ellis had arranged an even more extensive tour for him than

6. Wacław Gąsiorowski (1869–1939), Polish novelist and journalist.

7. Stanislas Poniatowski (1895–1970), the son of Prince André and Elizabeth Sperry Poniatowski.

8. Identified as either Waldemar or Wlodzimierz Szaniawski.

9. Stefan Rejer (1874–1940), union organizer of Polish coal miners in Westphalia and northern France.

10. *Dziennik Związkowy* [Alliance Daily] (September 10, 1917) reported on the greeting received by the French Mission in Chicago's Humboldt Park on September 9. The members of the mission are listed as Lieutenant Gąsiorowski; Prince Poniatowski; Sergeants Mazurek, Ziechecki, and Szaniawski; and one civilian, Stefan Rejer.

11. Henry Franklin-Bouillon (1870–1937), French politician.

12. Colonel James Martin, chief of the French military mission to Washington, DC.

the one he had just finished. Business had been extraordinarily good, and Mr. Ellis, whose loyalty had always made my husband's interests paramount, was ambitious to surpass the record of the past season. Concerts were to begin in the northwest in September and continue until May. It had been arranged that a break should be made in the middle of the winter by a trip to the West Indies, a conditional contract having been made by Mr. Ellis to give concerts in some of the islands, in Venezuela, and in Central America. It all sounded most attractive and desirable.

Although Mr. Paderewski had told Mr. Ellis in the spring, when they were talking over this tour, that there was a possibility that he could not give these concerts, it was only a possibility, and neither he nor I nor Mr. Ellis really thought the tour would not be made, at least in part. But when we reached Paso Robles, I observed that Mr. Paderewski was uneasy, unsettled, and worried and that he was actually unable to work at his piano. It was the first time since I had known him, perhaps the first time in his life, that he could not go to his instrument at anytime, in any place, and concentrate himself on his work no matter what the surrounding conditions might be. But that summer it was impossible. His other work so absorbed him, so completely engrossed his mind, that he had no time for his piano, no desire for it.

I did not wholly realize then that he was facing a very great decision. I am not sure that he himself understood the full significance of it. Toward the end of August the calls for him to return East and resume his work became more and more imperious. The arrival of Mr. Bouillon and Colonel Martin and the Polish military mission made his presence in the East most necessary, and he was particularly needed in Washington to look personally after a multitude of affairs that were constantly arising in connection with the new Polish army. There was a chance, too, that he might have to go to France.

At any rate, as time went on, it became more and more evident to him that music, at least for the present, was out of the question, and a few days before he was to start on his tour, he decided definitely to cancel it. It meant not only the loss of the very great sum of money that the concerts were certain to bring to him but also the expenditure of a very considerable amount against the expenses that had already been incurred. He did not, however, think of this. It was entirely beside the question. So it was that on September 18, 1917, he sent the following telegram to Mr. Ellis in Boston:

As foreseen and foretold in the spring, I have to leave Tuesday next for instructions. I may go to Europe or to Washington, and stay there. To my deepest regret the tour to which you so beautifully planned must be cancelled. Awfully sorry to give you so much additional trouble. Kindest regards.

I have quoted this telegram in full because it strikes me as having historic value from more than one point of view. Whether or not he realized it at the time, it marked the definite end of the career of Paderewski the pianist. It marked the end of a lifetime's labor and effort on behalf of his beloved art, the end of nearly thirty years of unbroken success. It took from music a man whose credo is found in a response he made to a toast a few years ago at a dinner given for him by the Bohemians[13] of New York. Then he said, in part:

I tell you frankly, I am not modest. Instead of being falsely modest, I am most sincerely humble, conscious of enjoying great privileges beyond my value; conscious of the duty to guard jealously the high character, the noble purpose, and, above all, the dignity of my profession. I try always to hold high the character of my art, to hold it pure, whatever other people may tell you. I will confess to you that I am a hard, persistent worker, one who had a deep respect for the masters, who stands with humility before God and Art. . . . Success, my friends, does not last. Public favor is easily lost, soon forgotten. The only thing that does last with a man, especially in public life, is the respect he has gained of his peers.

Since then he has never played in public; in fact, he has hardly touched his piano. Once in the wardroom of the British cruiser *Concord*, going from England to Gdańsk in December of the following year, he played for the officers of the ship. Once in Warsaw, in the summer of 1919 on my birthday, he played for me. At Riond-Bosson this spring he sat down to his piano several times for five or six minutes, but to all intents and purposes he closed his career at the concert given in New York for Marshal Joffre in May 1917.

This has been his great sacrifice for Poland. How great it is only an artist can realize and appreciate. The time, the labor, the fortune that he has devoted to his country may be accepted as a matter of course, but when he also gave his art, freely, willingly, cheerfully, he gave that which after his country itself

13. The Bohemians was another name for the New York Musicians Club. The dinner honoring Paderewski was held on May 2, 1914, in the Ritz-Carlton Hotel.

was dearest to him, that which was an integral part of his being, that which could never be replaced, the very memory of which must always sadden him.

The immediate purpose of our going to Chicago directly from California was a great meeting held there in honor of the Polish Military Commission, at which my husband was to make an address and, incidentally, present a flag to the first contingent of Polish soldiers. At this meeting also his "war song"[14] was heard for the first time, which he had composed for the occasion. After the meeting we returned immediately to California for the purpose of staying six weeks to clear up some business there, but we had hardly reached Paso Robles when we turned again to the east and to Washington, which was to be our second home during the winter.

The principal reason for our going to Washington at this time was that the task of convincing the government of the wisdom of allowing the recruitment for the new army of alien Poles over and under draft age fell to Mr. Paderewski. Day after day he was at the State Department in consultation with high officials. He had to fight the most powerful and persistent influences, but in the end he triumphed, and in the early part of October the State Department ruled that alien Poles under twenty-one years and over thirty-one could be recruited for service in the new Polish army, whose formation had been authorized by France.

To attempt here more than the briefest of sketches of the organization and training of the Polish army is impossible. The idea was Mr. Paderewski's, but the working out of it naturally was done by others. Directly after the consent of the State Department had been received, the Polish Falcons' Alliance sent out a call for volunteers. Earlier in the year a Polish-American commission had been organized, comprising Dr. Starzyński and Messrs. Heliński and Znamiecki.[15] Throughout the United States forty-two recruiting centers were established. Early in the summer the officers' training school had been removed from Cambridge Springs to Silver Lake near Toronto, where its work was greatly enlarged with Canadian, French, and English instructors.

The Canadian government gave the new army its cantonment at Niagara-on-the-Lake to use as a training camp. I remember very well that in

14. *Hej, Orle Biały!* (Hey, White Eagle!) was Paderewski's 1917 battle hymn for the Polish army in America, his last composition. Paderewski wrote both the music for a brass band and the words for a male chorus.

15. Alexander Znamiecki, in charge of Russia Division of the Foreign Trade Department of the National City Bank of New York in 1916; later worked as secretary of the American Relief Administration mission in Poland.

the beginning, there was considerable opposition on the part of the people of that town to the establishment of a Polish training camp there. They were very uneasy about bringing so many "Polaks" into their midst, a fact all the more notable because it was with positive grief that these good people saw the last of the army depart for France. In securing this camp, in fact during all the varied negotiations with the Canadian government, Mr. Paderewski received much valuable aid from Jan Horodyski,[16] a Pole who had become a British subject and had important government connections in London.

This camp was under the command of Colonel LePan[17] of the Canadian army from the beginning to the end, and too much cannot be said of the devotion which he, Major Young,[18] and the other officers gave to their task. Altogether, twenty-five thousand men were trained here. The first detachment was shipped from St. John's on the last day of 1917; the last ship carrying Polish troops sailed the following April, and, in all, 24,602 men were sent from America to France.

Arriving in France, the troops received additional training, and in August these American Poles were a part of the great offensive in Champagne to the east of Reims, under the command of General Haller, who had finally arrived in France from Russia after a journey that had taken months. These original divisions formed a nucleus around which a much larger army was built, which was organized in France from the thousands of Polish war prisoners who were in England, France, and Italy. They joined the new army with the same eagerness as their brothers in America had shown, and in the end, when the armistice was signed, Haller's Army, as it came to be known, counted more than seventy thousand men. During the spring of 1919, these troops were transported across Germany to Poland under the escort of American officers and immediately entered the campaign against the Bolsheviks, where they were of invaluable service. A year later the work began of sending back to America those soldiers of the original army who wanted to return.

16. Jan Horodyski (1881–1948), count and former Austrian subject; active in the Polish independence movement and émigré affairs, while also serving as a British intelligence agent.

17. Arthur D'Orr LePan (1885–1976), camp commandant.

18. Major Young was the camp adjutant.

CHAPTER NINE

1917–1918

Having definitely given up his concerts and his music, Mr. Paderewski was able for the rest of our stay in America to devote himself and his time wholly to Polish affairs. The speed with which everything moved that last winter left us all but breathless. As I look back at it, it seems like a huge phantasmagoria, with the sleeping cars of the Pennsylvania Railway as chief actors. Our home was nominally in the Hotel Gotham, but in reality I think we slept more nights going from New York to Washington and from Washington to New York than we did in our beds in the hotels of either city. From the time of our arrival in the East from California in October to the next September, when we left again to go to Paso Robles, I believe we must have averaged almost four nights a week in a sleeper.

Our traveling was by no means confined to the short distance between New York and Washington. There were at least a dozen trips to Chicago for meetings and for conferences with the National Department. There were trips to other cities to attend various Polish meetings, and many calls were made on my husband to speak to Americans. These he never refused except in cases where acceptance was quite impossible. He felt that if the Americans were good enough to invite him to talk to them, it was the least he could do in return for all the kindness he had received from them. To speak in English was no longer an effort for him, nor did the prospect of it cause him any of the trepidation he had felt in the beginning. The experience of two years had shown him that he could hold an American audience with his words as easily as he could with his music.

There was an enormous amount of detail work that he had to attend to personally as the representative of all the Polish interests in America, and as the year wore on this work continually increased. While for the most part it was interesting and engrossing, there was much real drudgery connected with it, as there must always be in such cases. Fortunately, in the early fall he found a man to assist him, Sigismund Iwanowski,[1] the artist. A native of Poland, after studying in Petrograd and Paris, Mr. Iwanowski had married an American and, moving to America, had lived there for upwards of twenty years. In that time he had won very considerable success as a painter and was considered one of the foremost illustrators in the United States. He had become completely out of touch with Poland and the Poles, and it was not until he went to the Polish benefit in Carnegie Hall in the fall of '15 and heard my husband's address that he went to my son and told him that he would like to do something to help Poland. At that time we thought it simply another of the many casual offers we were constantly receiving, and nothing came of it.

While we were in Washington in the early fall of 1917, his card was brought to our rooms with a request that he might have an interview with Mr. Paderewski. The latter was just leaving the hotel and sent word to Mr. Iwanowski to meet him in the lobby and walk with him to the State Department, where he was going. He did so, and almost from that moment he was my husband's constant companion and most trusted aide. He abandoned his own work, closed his beautiful home in New Jersey, and came with his wife to New York to live so that they might be near us, Mrs. Iwanowska[2] having been, I might add, as devoted as he. He joined the Polish army, ultimately receiving the commission of major, and when we went to Europe, he and his wife accompanied us. All the time we were in Warsaw, they were with us, and he left the army only when Mr. Paderewski retired from the government.

In the meantime I had started what was to become the White Cross of Poland. This has been my chief contribution to my country, and I must ask the reader to indulge me in my delight to tell something about it. It was, besides, a very direct result of my husband's work in America, for without him, there would have been no White Cross, no occasion for it. And if a further excuse is needed, it is that the White Cross was organized in the United States, it has been chiefly supported by the people of the United States, and this book gives me an excellent opportunity to tell my benefactors a little of what has been done.

During the winter preceding the declaration of war by the United States, Father Strzelecki had organized a charitable society in his parish in New

---

1. Zygmunt Iwanowski (or Sigismund de Ivanowski) (1876–1944), Polish-born American painter and graphic artist; military aide to Paderewski with the rank of major.

2. Helena Iwanowska (1882–1941), maiden name Moser, Florida-born American singer and wife of Zygmunt Iwanowski.

York, giving it my name. Later this developed into a sewing club, and it was so successful that before many months, there were several hundred Helena Paderewska societies scattered over the United States, for the organization of which Mrs. H. Piotrowska,[3] a graduate of Columbia University, was chiefly responsible. When the Polish army came into being in the fall of 1917, taking these societies as a basis, I organized the Polish Soldiers' Comfort Committee.

Its work was to care for the comfort and welfare of the soldiers in the training camps in Canada and also to look out for the families that they had left in the States. Before the beginning of the winter, in every city of the United States and Canada that had a Polish colony, the women formed committees, sewing clubs, and the like; collected money; and generally worked indefatigably for the cause. In the organization and work of this committee and afterwards of the White Cross, I personally had as chief assistants Mrs. Krajewski; her daughter, Mrs. Iwanowski; my daughter-in-law, Mrs. Górski; and Mrs. Ehlers,[4] the latter an American who gave practically her entire time to the work for over a year.

Toward the end of the year Count Orłowski[5] came from Paris with the idea of forming a Polish Red Cross in the United States to function with the Secours aux Blessés[6] of France, which had undertaken to look after the wounded Polish soldiers in that country. I was fully in sympathy with the idea because the work was already becoming too large for the committee, and it would have been of great advantage to have the prestige of the Red Cross. Before he could do anything himself, he was called back to France and left the matter in my hands. I made an application to the international organization for permission to form a Polish Red Cross, but it was refused on the grounds that Poland, not being an independent nation, could not, under the regulations of the society, have a Red Cross. Then I applied to the American Red Cross, asking leave to turn my organization, the Polish Soldiers' Comfort Committee, into a Polish auxiliary of the American Red Cross, but this was not feasible. So, to make a long story short, I organized the White Cross of Poland, calling it "White" because all the other colors seemed to be in use for other purposes. My idea then was to confine its work to the American Polish army. I could not foresee

3. Unable to verify.
4. Nellie S. Ehlers, formerly with the American Red Cross.
5. Mieczysław Orłowski (b. 1865), from Jarmolince in Podolia, married to an American, Mabel Ledyard Stevens (b. 1872).
6. Société Française de Secours aux Blessés Militaires (abbreviated SBM), French Society for the Help to Wounded Servicemen.

that within a year and a half its activities would cover practically the whole of Poland.

The White Cross did the usual welfare work for the soldiers in the training camps in Canada and during the influenza scourge provided a hospital with all the necessary supplies, as well as White Cross nurses. It established a training school for nurses in New York, and in the great procession of welfare societies that marched up Fifth Avenue were a thousand White Cross women workers.

It sent to France a military unit of forty-three graduate nurses trained in New York by Dr. Łapowski,[7] twelve ambulances, and two automobiles for use in the Polish army, its activities lasting in France from March 1, 1918, to June 1 of the following year. General Haller detailed Captain Kamieński[8] of Buffalo to the work of the White Cross, and the great burden of detail in France and afterward in Poland fell on him. He was of invaluable assistance to me, putting the machinery of the society in the latter country into smooth running order.

When I reached Poland in January 1919, I found several societies doing welfare work, but it was very limited through lack of experience, lack of material, and funds. Using some of these societies as a foundation, I organized the White Cross there, and it grew like the traditional beanstalk. By early summer its activities covered the length and breadth of the country.

The first charge of the Polish White Cross was the army. By the end of the summer, it had established over fifty regimental canteens, canteens at the principal railway stations, one hospital of eighty beds, and a wholesale store where soldiers could purchase much-needed articles of clothing and the like at minimal prices. It also supplied the army hospitals with great quantities of medicines, linen, surgical dressing, and blankets. Its work among the civilian population has also been most important. Through it, thousands have received clothing. Great quantities of supplies of all kinds have been given to hospitals, and many crèches and schools have been organized, especially among the typhus-ridden refugees. Not the least of its achievements, to my mind, has been the very difficult and delicate task of giving aid and relief to the many of the "intellectual" class who lost everything during the war, the "new poor" of whom one hears so much nowadays and of whom Poland has many.

---

7. Dr. Boleslaw Łapowski, dermatologist in the New York Good Samaritan Dispensary.

8. B. S. Kamieński, journalist; before joining Haller's Army, Kamieński was the editor of Buffalo's *Dziennik dla Wszystkich* [Everybody's Daily]; in Haller's Army, he edited the *Biuletyn Wojskowy* [Military Bulletin] and served as a liaison officer with the Polish White Cross.

The chief source of support for the White Cross has been the American Poles who have worked for it under the general direction of the women's section of the Polish National Department of Chicago. Literally shiploads of clothing, food, and supplies, as well as money, have come from them. Its second great support has been the American Red Cross, which has given it thousands of boxes of linens, socks, blankets, food, and medicines. There was never a time last year that I appealed in vain to the representatives of the American Red Cross in Warsaw. We also received splendid gifts from the Canadian Red Cross, the Jewish Distribution Committee, and from Australia.

It has been doing and still is doing a very necessary work, of which, I confess, I am proud. I am its president, and I can see for it as well as for the Polish Red Cross ample opportunity for a long period of useful work, for it will be years before Poland can repair the ravages of its wars.

During the summer of 1917 while we were in California, Mr. Paderewski received a telegram from Roman Dmowski in Paris, announcing the formation there of the Polish National Committee. Up to this time the only formal organization of Poles in Europe in touch with the Entente had been the General Committee in Switzerland, of which Sienkiewicz had been its president until his death in November 1916. The work had been devoted exclusively to relief, and in the early years of the war it was all that Poland needed, because she had no other interests that must be guarded. But with the virtual recognition of her right to independence by the United States and the authorization of a Polish army by France and Great Britain, it became at once most necessary that there should be some properly accredited person or body in Paris that could represent her officially.

Poland at this time was entirely in the hands of the enemy; communication with the outside world was cut off, except that which the German government might admit by way of Berlin. Travel between Poland and the West was impossible. Therefore this National Committee had to be formed of Poles who happened to be in Paris or London, and the telegram announcing its formation asked Mr. Paderewski to be a member and to represent it in America.

He hesitated a long time. In examining the membership of the committee, he found that it contained almost exclusively men of moderate or conservative political opinions and that the element of the Left, the Radical or Socialist element, was entirely excluded. This he felt was an error. It was not that the members of the committee were reactionary or anything of that kind; on the contrary most of them were decidedly progressive, but with the Socialist element so strong in Poland, he felt it most necessary that it should be represented, and he so presented his views to the committee. He even suggested certain names that he thought would be well to have on the list.

As events proved, his suggestion was very sound, and had it been possible to form the committee that way, the history of the next two and a half years might have been quite different. But it was not possible. It so happened that all the men he had suggested were in Poland, and either they could not leave the country, except at great personal risk, or they would not be admitted into France on account of their supposed sympathies with the Central Empires. In the end, seeing that it was physically impossible to form such a committee as he thought would be best for the country, he joined it as organized in Paris and became its representative in America. Shortly afterwards, it was recognized by France, Great Britain, and Italy and its recognition by the United States followed later.

There is one point concerning this committee that he has always emphasized in all his discussions concerning it. It never at any time pretended to be the government of Poland. Its functions were simply to represent Polish interests in foreign countries, which it did as if it had been, so to say, an ex-territorial foreign office.

During this winter a series of violent attacks on the American Poles in general and the new Polish army in particular appeared in certain American newspapers and periodicals. Nor was Mr. Paderewski spared. The similarity of character, purpose, and spirit found in all of them would naturally lead one to the conclusion that they all had the same inspiration, even if the publications were not conscious of it. These articles accused the American Poles of lack of patriotism, of lack of gratitude to their adopted country—for many of them, their native country—of sacrificing the interests of the United States for the interest of a country that did not exist and that really ought never to exist. They were particularly bitter about the new army, perhaps for the reason that led one prominent German to say that he would rather see three hundred thousand Poles in an American army than thirty thousand in one Polish army.

In view of this very hostile campaign, which was most vigorously carried on, he thought it well that the Poles in America, citizens as well as aliens, should give a formal expression of their views and aims and put an end once and for all to the slanders that were being uttered against them. To this end, a diet was called to meet in Detroit in August 1918, composed of about one thousand delegates representing practically the entire Polish population of the United States and Canada in all its various shades of political and religious opinion. It was the final step in the work that had been going on for over two years to unite and solidify the Polish Immigration in America. Among the delegates were Republicans, Democrats, and Socialists, clergymen of the Roman Catholic Church, of the Polish National Church, and of the Lutheran and Evangelical churches. Mr. Dmowski came from Paris to attend the meeting and explain the work of the National Committee, for, in the end, the entire campaign for the liberation of Poland was in the hands of the Poles in America. They were supplying the men and the money without which nothing could be done. They were even maintaining the National Committee in Paris.

The sessions of this diet were marked by an enthusiasm that had not been seen since the meeting of the Falcons in Pittsburgh the year before. It was during this meeting that Bishop Rhode of Green Bay, Wisconsin, made his memorable address appealing to the Poles to sink all their religious differences, to forget the particular creed to which they subscribed, and be only Poles. At the opening of the convention, Mr. Paderewski spoke for two hours, in the course of which he reviewed all that had been done and suggested the policy that should be followed in the future. At his request it was agreed that ten million dollars should be raised for the benefit of Poland. Nor were duty and the sentiments of these Poles toward the United States forgotten. There were no signs of the "separatism" and the like of which they had been accused in the hostile press, and, in fact, a very perceptible diminution of this criticism followed this meeting.

During the spring and summer Mr. Paderewski had accepted many invitations to address American audiences. It is a great grief to me now that more of his speeches have not been preserved. We have nothing of some of the most important ones because he spoke from scanty notes, and no stenographic reports were made. I shall always regret that neither he nor I kept a more careful record of the three and a half years we spent in America. In Paris in 1915, I started a diary, chiefly for my own amusement, thinking that it would be pleasant to go back to in the future, but like most diaries, after the first week or so, it began to dwindle, and by the time we reached London, it was buried in the depths of a trunk and all but completely forgotten. At that time I had no idea of the real significance of all that my husband was doing, and even in America many things that at the time they occurred seemed to be unimportant later assumed an extraordinary significance. It was a great mistake, for history was being made, and there is no record whatever except treacherous memory of many events that should have been recorded.

I should like to have, for example, the address he made to the officers at Camp Sherman near Chicago, when he discussed the importance of the eastern front and how unless the war was won in the East as well as in the West, Germany would never be thoroughly beaten. Another address, which I ought to have, he made at the University Club in Chicago in which he discussed the same subject from another point of view, showing how Germany, with Russia to develop and draw on, would be in an infinitely better position than she would have been possessing her gateway to the East through Constantinople and her colonies throughout the world, and Russia still an empire. The speeches are now of unusual interest because they showed how in 1918, months before the end of the war, Mr. Paderewski's vision enabled him to predict much of what has actually happened and seems to be happening today.

In March, in Chicago, he addressed a huge meeting held by the National Security League,[9] of which his speech was the principal feature. Perhaps, however, the most important of his addresses, the one that made the deepest impression, was that which he made in Columbus, Ohio, on the Fourth of July. The occasion was "Americanization Day,"[10] and he was asked by Governor Cox[11] to discuss the measures then proposed in the United States to suppress all foreign languages.

It was a subject on which he felt very deeply, one to which he had given much study. He differed entirely from those who believed that it was necessary or even desirable to abolish the teaching of the mother tongue of immigrants in private schools, to forbid its use in churches. He said:

The patriotism of the older civilized nations is based chiefly upon attachment to native soil, to mother tongue, to the ancestral faith and glory. It represents the sentiment of a people mostly belonging to the

9. The National Security League was an American patriotic organization most influential during World War I; it supported military preparedness, assimilation of immigrants, and rejection of foreign influences, especially German and Bolshevik. The league strongly supported the administration of President Woodrow Wilson.

10. Americanization Day, a local patriotic holiday reaffirming American political traditions and heritage, originally celebrated on July 4; later it was known as Loyalty Day and celebrated on May 1.

11. James M. Cox (1870–1957), US congressman during 1909–1913; governor of Ohio during 1913–1915 and 1917–1921; Democratic candidate for president in 1920.

same race, living for generations in the same country, following the same flag, obeying the same laws, using the same conventional symbols of values, the same currency, having common interests, a common past and present, hoping for and aspiring to a happier common future. This sentiment regulates the people's relation to the mother country and to their countrymen. It dictates their conduct, it inspires their action, and it leads them to life or death, to victory or defeat, to enjoyment or to sacrifice. The patriotism of those older nations is almost instinctive. It is the product of a slow biological and chemical process in which the ashes of generations have been the chief substance. It is a noble and beautiful flower growing on soil fertilized by the bones of the forefathers.

While possibly including all these characteristics, American patriotism is of a somewhat different and decidedly more spiritual nature. Its lofty and glorious temple, built upon the noblest of principles, dedicated to the purest and immortal ideals, is open to everyone and to every heart striving for the uplifting and betterment of mankind. Americanism is something more than the sentiments of a particular human breed. It is a creed, a belief; it is the political religion of many freely and so happily united races.

In the course of his remarks he pointed out how the Republic of Switzerland recognized four different languages and yet prospered, how in France four different languages are spoken. He pleaded that national unity meant before all else unity of spirit, of principles, of ideals. He questioned whether an immigrant who was willing at once to abandon his mother tongue would be in the end an altogether desirable citizen, but I think he made his greatest impression when he took up the demand that had been made by some that an immigrant who could not learn English in five years should be shipped back to the country from which he came. Mr. Paderewski remarked that there were in Europe, in France and Italy especially, thousands of Americans of wealth and culture who had lived for years in these countries without learning to speak the language. If this was so, how could it be expected that simple peasants and laborers, as such a great proportion of the immigrants to America were, could learn to speak English fluently in five years?

I think, however, the invitation that gratified him the most was that given him to be one of the speakers at the great Allied meeting held in honor of France in Madison Square Garden on Bastille Day, July 14, 1918. Here he was the only representative of the minor nations, the other speakers, as I remember, having been Secretary Daniels,[12] Judge Charles E. Hughes,[13] Lord Reading,[14] Mr. Jusserand, and Samuel Gompers.[15]

It was not until the end of September that we left for California, for not only had we to wait for the meeting of the Polish diet in Detroit in August but Mr. Paderewski had promised to be the principal speaker at the meeting of the Oppressed Nationalities, which was held in Carnegie Hall on the evening of September 18. I remember well how at the end of his speech Professor Masaryk[16] wept on his shoulder and proclaimed him the true champion not only of Poland but of Czecho-Slovakia and all other oppressed nations.

We went to California expecting to stay for six weeks or two months, but we had hardly settled down to rest and quiet when the air was filled with the rumors of peace. Even while we were there came a false report that peace had been signed, and there was a huge celebration among the natives. Whistles were blown, and all night long we were kept awake by dynamite explosions. Although there was absolutely no foundation for the report, it was evident that peace was in the air, and Mr. Paderewski felt that he must return to the East, for if peace really came, he must be prepared to sail for Europe immediately. We had not been there more than a fortnight when a telegram came summoning him to Chicago and so the trunks were packed again, and we started east. We spent a few days in Chicago and then went on to New York, reaching there in time to see that celebration of the Thursday when the false news of the signing of the armistice was received.

My husband was one of the very few men in America who did not receive the news of the signing of the armistice with rejoicing. I remember how when the whistles began to blow early that Monday morning, November 11, he said that he feared a terrible mistake had been made, and all day long he was in

12. Josephus Daniels (1862–1948), North Carolina politician and publisher; secretary of the navy during 1913–1921.

13. Charles Evans Hughes (1862–1942), New York politician and lawyer; governor of New York, 1907–1910; associate justice of the US Supreme Court, 1910–1916; secretary of state, 1921–1925; judge on the Court of International Justice, 1928–1930; chief justice of the US Supreme Court, 1930–1941.

14. Rufus Isaacks, 1st Marquess of Reading (1860–1935), English lawyer and politician; lord chief justice of England 1913–1921; later secretary for foreign affairs.

15. Samuel Gompers (1850–1924), English-born American labor leader; founder and president of the American Federation of Labor (AFL).

16. Thomas Garrigue Masaryk (1850–1937), Czech sociologist and philosopher; founder and first president of Czechoslovakia.

a most depressed state of mind. Nor had he ever changed his belief that the ending of the war at that time was unfortunate for the Allies and all the nations that depended on them. He had occasion many times in Paris the next spring so to express himself.

With the signing of the armistice and the announcement that President Wilson intended to go to Paris to attend the Peace Conference, my husband's work in America came to an end. He thought that France would henceforth be the center of all Polish interests, so he planned to leave as soon as possible, with the intention of spending the next few months in Paris. After consultation with his colleagues in America, it was decided that it would be best for him to go first to London and there discuss matters with the British Foreign Office. Consequently, we sailed from New York on November 23 on the *Megantic*. Major and Mrs. Iwanowski and Edward Piotrowski[17] of Warsaw, who had been acting as Mr. Paderewski's secretary for the past several months, went with us.

It was not without a heartache that we parted from America. It had been our home for more than three and a half years. If it had been dear to my husband in the past, it was doubly so now. His own personal debt to it was very large and the debt of his country beyond calculation. He had come to know Americans as they really are, as he never had done during his artistic career. He had lived with them through those wonderful days when, inspired by a great ideal, they had cast all aside to plunge into a terrible war. It was the home of those millions of his countrymen who, while devoted to the United States and its interests, had yet room in their hearts for a love of the fatherland, which impelled them to great and unending sacrifices. He had been accepted by them as a leader to be trusted in all things. Moreover, at heart Mr. Paderewski is very much American himself. He believes in American ideals, he sympathizes with American ambitions and aims, and he had great faith in the ability of the Americans to attain them.

17. Unable to verify.

CHAPTER TEN

December 1918 – January 1919

The conditions surrounding our arrival in England were not such as could raise our spirits unduly. The crossing had been stormy and disagreeable, typical of the season. There were not many passengers, which was fortunate, for the ship was still in the service of transporting troops and contained few of the comforts that Atlantic travel of the last ten or fifteen years has taught one to expect. It was after dark when we reached the landing stage in Liverpool, and, of course, it was raining. Mr. Sharpe had come down from London to meet us and brought the cheerful news that he had been unable to find quarters for us, that so far as he could discover, there was no such thing as a vacant room in the whole city. The town was full to overflowing, and rank, position, and wealth, so far as lodgings were concerned, meant nothing. I had cabled the Ritz from New York, and when Mr. Sharpe told me that there was nothing there for us, I just simply refused to believe him.

If there is anything more depressing than to arrive at Paddington Station, London, on a midnight in December, in a pouring rain, with no cabs in sight and not knowing where shelter is to be found, I have yet to experience it. Even in London I never had seen it rain harder and more persistently than it did on the night of our arrival. Although the streets were not so completely black as they had been during the war, in the first few weeks after the armistice they were far from being lighted in a normal fashion, and the all-pervading gloom did not add to our happiness. I can still see my husband and myself standing in the station, surrounded by a huge barricade of trunks and bags, while the others feverishly hunted for cabs for a full half hour. At last they appeared with two most disreputable looking four-wheelers, and we started with our luggage for the Ritz.

Mr. Sharpe was right. The Ritz had had no vacancies for weeks and could not take us in, nor did they know where any lodgings were to be hired at any price. They had been trying to get something for us all the evening and had failed. The situation was desperate. We were completely fagged, fairly famished, and faced the prospect of sitting up the rest of the night. Then I had an inspiration. If Miss Alma-Tadema was in town, she would rescue us. She and her sister lived in the great house in St. John's Wood built by their father. It was several miles from the Ritz, there was no telephone, and the only thing left was to drive out there on the chance that they might be in London; so off we started at one in the morning on this new quest, leaving Mrs. Iwanowska at the Ritz, where a good-hearted woman had taken pity and had offered to share her room with her.

The drive to St. John's Wood seemed interminable. We seemed to be going through countless miles of black, silent streets, fearing every moment that the wretched animal that was drawing our cab might decide to lie down and rest for the remainder of the night, but we finally reached the house. It sits in a garden back from the street, and for fifteen minutes, at least, we rang the bell at the gate and were about to give up in despair, thinking that nobody was there, when finally the old caretaker appeared, very much frightened, asking if the house was on fire. We assured him that it was not, and he let us in, and at the house we were met by Miss Tadema and her sister, who had come, candle in hand, to discover what all the noise meant. They did not know that we had left America, and to find us there on their doorstep, after midnight, begging a night's lodging, was something of a shock. It just chanced that they were in town for a few days and were, so to say, camping in the house, but they did all they could for us, gave us food, their own room to sleep in, and made us very comfortable and happy. We stayed with them for two nights, until we found one small room in a second-rate hotel, where for ten days my husband, myself, and the parrot[1] lived in thankfulness that we had a roof over our heads.

Only those who were in Europe in the months following the end of the war have any idea of the general discomfort of living and traveling. Even now, a year and a half later, travel has little to recommend it, for if one cannot use the few deluxe trains that are running, it means trials and tribulations and, in many parts of the Continent, actual hardship. But immediately after the war, travel under the best conditions tried the courage and patience of the strongest. The journey from London to Paris, for example, was a very real undertaking, and even when one was able to use government trains and boats, as we did, comfort was noticeable chiefly through its absence.

1. The Paderewskis had a parrot named Cockey Roberts, which accompanied them in most of their travels. The bird was famous for his love of piano music and foul vocabulary.

Mr. Paderewski had consultations with the British Foreign Office beginning almost at once. It seems that the British government was greatly concerned over conditions in Poland. The country, directly after the departure
of the Germans, had fallen into the hands of the Radical Socialist element,
and over the Zamek, the old Royal Palace, the red flag was floating. Generally
speaking, chaos ruled. It was then suggested to him that he go to Warsaw and
try to bring about some semblance of order. If Poland was to be represented
at the Peace Conference, it was most necessary that something approaching
a stable government be established at once, and the Foreign Office told him
that it thought that he was the man to undertake the mission. He had never
mixed in the local politics of Poland, he belonged to no faction, and he was
known to be entirely disinterested, wherefore the motives that sent him there
would be beyond suspicion.

Although the task was neither pleasant nor easy and might involve considerable personal risk, Mr. Paderewski said that he was willing to undertake it if
the Polish National Committee in Paris approved. So we went to Paris for two
days in order that he might discuss the project with Mr. Dmowski and the other
members of the committee. We arrived there in time to see the greeting given to
President Wilson. I doubt that anything in his life made such a deep impression
on my husband as this—in fact, no one who was in Paris that day could have
failed to be lifted out of himself by the spontaneous tribute given by the people
of Paris to the president of the United States. And it was all the more moving
to my husband since the presence of Wilson in Paris seemed to be practically
a guarantee that Poland would have a powerful champion at the conference.

The National Committee approved most heartily the plan proposed by the
British Foreign Office, and we returned to London to make final preparations
for our journey. Before we went to Paris, the best method for us to reach
Poland had been discussed. It was proposed, for example, that we go by air-
plane, in a big machine such as is now used to fly between Paris and London.
Mr. Paderewski was rather taken with the idea, but I would not listen to it. It
was then decided that we should go by way of Gdańsk—in a British cruiser,
escorted by a destroyer. This arrangement pleased my husband immensely if
only because it had been his ambition to return to Poland by way of Gdańsk,
which for centuries had been the seaport of his country and which he hoped
to see once more under Polish rule.

We sailed on the *Concord* from Harwich the week before Christmas; I think
it was the nineteenth. There were three in our party, Mr. Paderewski, Major
Iwanowski, and myself. Some trouble about Mrs. Iwanowski's passport pre-

vented her from going with us, and we had to leave her behind in London quite alone, without luggage, because her trunks were with ours.

In the *Concord* the admiralty had given us one of their newest ships, a light cruiser, built during the war and the last word in naval architecture of her kind. She was bright with new paint, spotlessly clean, but nonetheless my respect for the stuff on which the British navy is made grew tremendously in the five days we were on her. How even strong, hardy men can live, thrive, and seem to enjoy themselves in such positive physical discomfort as is found on a warship under war conditions in the North Sea in December will always be a mystery to me. It was awful weather, rough, cold, foggy, with endless rain and snowstorms, and the inside walls of the ship simply oozed moisture, but everybody seemed to be cheerful and happy, men and officers alike, and a more attractive, charming set of men than the officers I have never met. They did everything to make us comfortable. Captain Paton[2] gave us his cabin, consisting of a sitting room and tiny bedroom, but do all they or we could, it was impossible to keep warm or even half comfortable, and Mr. Paderewski caught a very heavy cold from which he did not recover until weeks later. This did not prevent him from going down into the wardroom one evening and playing for the officers. It was an interesting picture, the low-ceiled wardroom, thick with tobacco smoke, the group of fresh-faced, nice-looking young Englishmen and my husband seated at a little decrepit cottage piano that not only had one pedal missing and several broken keys but was most shockingly out of tune. The officers were most apologetic about the state of the instrument and were particularly worried about the pedal. Later they had it appropriately engraved and sent it to Mr. Paderewski as a souvenir.

I think we were in Copenhagen for two days, delayed by a continuous succession of snowstorms, which made it impossible to attempt to go through the great minefield that lay between Copenhagen and Gdańsk. We finally got away on Christmas Eve, our party having been increased in the meantime by four men, Colonel Wade[3] of the British army, Commander Rawlings[4] of the British navy, Mr. Langford,[5] his secretary, and Sylwin Strakacz,[6] who almost

2. William Douglas Paton, first captain of HMS *Concord*, 1916–1919.

3. Harry A. L. H. Wade (1873–1959), lieutenant colonel in 1918; later with the League of Nations and the World Court.

4. (Henry) Bernard (Hughes) Rawlings (1889–1962), Royal Navy officer and later admiral.

5. Mr. Langford, British Foreign Office employee.

6. Sylwin Strakacz (1892–1973), Polish diplomat; Paderewski's personal secretary and political aide during 1919–1941.

from that time has been Mr. Paderewski's private secretary. He was in Copenhagen on a mission from Poland and had received permission to return on
the *Concord* with us.

Our entrance into Gdańsk gave my husband a forewarning of what awaited
him in Poznań and Warsaw. The ship arrived early in the morning, but we
did not land until nine o'clock or so, when we were met by what seemed to be
the entire Polish population of the city, with several hundred sulky-looking
Germans on the outskirts of the crowd. It is one of the most picturesque towns
in northern Europe, and it made us feel all the more at home to see, overtop-
ping all else, the golden statute of King Sigismund Augustus of Poland, which
stands on the high tower of the *Rathaus*.[7]

The greeting we received was full of joy and happiness. A schedule had
been worked out that would keep us occupied up to the hour of our departure for Poznań the next day, and the program for this first day, Christmas,
was fairly heavy. There was a dinner in the afternoon, then a reception, then
a supper, and finally a concert. The Christmas dinner was interesting from
several points of view. Then I became acquainted with some of the *ersatz*[8] food
products of which we had been hearing so much in America, which someone
has called the finest products of Germany's chemical imagination. They may
have been the finest, and they certainly demanded a strong imagination or a
ravenous appetite to enjoy them. Ersatz ice cream, for example, once eaten will
not soon be forgotten. Fortunately, however, our hosts were not entirely dependent on these awful substitutes. Mrs. Chelchowska,[9] who has a large estate
near Poznań, had arrived in Gdańsk the day before, laden with great hampers
of good things to eat that at that time could be got only in the country, and
the joy of our Gdańsk hosts when they tasted them showed only too well on
what short rations they had been for months.

We left for Poznań by a special train on the afternoon of the twenty-sixth,
not without, I will confess, a certain feeling of relief on my part. The dour,
hostile attitude of the Germans, not only of the military but of the civilians,
had begun to get on my nerves. Their hatred of the Poles was so intense and
so bitter, and their resentment against the idea that Poland was again to be a
nation was so fierce, that it was far from unreasonable for me to fear that some

---

7. German word for "city hall."
8. German word for "replacement" or "substitute."
9. Possibly the correct spelling of the name is Chełkowska, a member of a prominent
landowning family in the area south of Gdańsk.

one of them might make an attempt on the life of the man who was on his way to organize the country. The Germans who had charge of the train were just as unpleasant as those in Gdańsk—in other words, the feeling against us Poles was universal in the nation. Nor did it make me any less uneasy when in the course of the day a German officer went to my husband and most politely informed him that he had been instructed by the German general commanding Poznań to request Mr. Paderewski to go directly through to Warsaw without stopping in Poznań. When my husband replied that it was quite impossible to grant this request, as he intended to stop in Poznań, the officer, formally in the name of his commander, announced that the German authorities in this case could not hold themselves responsible for anything unpleasant that might happen. Whereupon I remember that Colonel Wade informed the officer that he was going to Poznań under orders and that the British government would hold the Germans responsible for anything unpleasant that might happen. The officer saluted and withdrew, the incident ending there, leaving me a little more nervous than ever.

But all this was forgotten in the excitement of approaching Poznań. Like all trains during the war and immediately after, in fact like most trains in Europe today, our progress was slow, and we stopped at many stations. At all of these as we neared Poznań in the evening were crowds of townspeople, village folk, and peasants. Being the second Christmas Day—in Poland we celebrate the twenty-sixth as well as the twenty-fifth—it was a holiday, and everybody was free to join in the festivities. It was a most striking and impressive sight to stop at a station in a small village and be surrounded immediately by hundreds of peasants, all in the bravery of their holiday dress, carrying torches, lanterns of every size, shape, and age imaginable, burning red lights, with the village band playing its loudest in a futile effort to make itself heard above the cheering and singing of the crowds. Wherever the train stopped, a committee would come into our carriage, bringing flowers and the traditional bread and salt of welcome. My husband felt that at least he was once more among his own people for whom he had labored so long and so hard. He had expected to find joy among the Poles, but he was a little dazed by the ardor of the welcome given him everywhere. He was getting further hints of what was being prepared for him in Poznań and Warsaw, and he was a little fearful of it.

A beloved king returning from long years of exile, a national hero, sung and storied, could not have received a more impressive, a more affectionate welcome than that which the people of Poznań gave Mr. Paderewski, but had he been ever so vainglorious he could not have accepted it merely as a personal tribute to himself. It was so much more than that. It was a tribute to all he represented in the minds of these people—liberation, freedom, a nation reborn. He was for them the symbol of the new Poland, the sign that at last after nearly a hundred and fifty years of waiting, the rule of the detested Prussian had come to an end. Added to this was the grateful recognition of his labors for them in Europe and America, the expectation and hope of what his future labors would bring them. And, finally, they seemed to regard him almost as a personal messenger from that great nation beyond the seas whose president had declared for their freedom.

Only those who saw this demonstration in Poznań and the one that followed in Warsaw with their own eyes and those who have been so unfortunate as to belong to a race that for generations had been held in virtual captivity can understand what an emotional outpouring it was. The Slavs are naturally an emotional people, and when the feelings and sentiments that had been pent up for years in the bosoms of the Poles finally burst their bounds, it was as if a tidal wave swept over the entire nation.

Arriving in Poznań in the evening, we found the city full to overflowing. There were thousands of young Poles who had been serving in the German army who, without waiting for formal demobilization, had simply discharged themselves. People had flocked in from the neighboring towns and cities, while, it seemed, all the landed proprietors from miles around had brought their families in for the festivities. The city was veritably covered with garlands, flags, and Polish colors. All the windows were illuminated, while in the streets there were thousands of red smoking torches, which lent an almost savage tone to the reception. We were taken to the Bazar Hotel through the streets that were black with people, a sturdy band of soldiers making a way for the carriages through the densely packed crowd, and as we went, listening to the cheers and to the singing of the national hymn, I was greatly impressed by the lack of boisterousness, the lack of all roughness. Never was there a more orderly crowd. The emotion of the moment was too deep; tears were too near the surface for any "mafficking"[10] to take place.

At the hotel we were received by the mayor and all the notables of the city. There was a dinner, a reception, and many speeches, and finally in the small hours of the morning we got to bed, but even then, as I looked out of the window, I saw the same great crowd standing quietly in front of the hotel, and

10. The verb was formed from Mafikeng, a British garrison town in South Africa; its successful relief from the Boers in May 1900 was boisterously celebrated in London.

all the days we were there, except when the fighting was going on, the streets about the hotel were continually filled with people.

The day following our arrival brought the beginning of the street fighting between the German troops and the Poles, and for three days we were virtually prisoners in the hotel. The arrangements of the day provided for a parade of schoolchildren in the morning. This was to be followed by a dinner given in the hotel by the landed proprietors of the province, after which was to come a reception. The cold that Mr. Paderewski had taken on board the *Concord* had increased, and on this day he was so ill that I insisted that he remain in bed, and I took his place in the reviewing stand when the children—there must have been ten thousand of them—marched past.

The dinner was most lavish. Our hosts had brought their own food in from the country, and we really had the most wonderful things to eat. I remember that Colonel Wade looked on this dinner most critically, not understanding how such lavishness could be found in a country that was supposed to be suffering from lack of the most necessary articles of food, but three days later, when we had used up all that had been brought in and were reduced to hotel fare, he was convinced that the feast had been the result of many sacrifices.

At the reception that followed were many of the wealthier peasants from the neighboring country, and most of them came dressed in the national costumes, which made it in its way one of the most gorgeous affairs I have ever seen. The costumes worn in this part of Poland are very picturesque, and many of those worn at the reception were worthy of places in a museum. Such marvels of needlework and embroidery I had never seen. Many of them were heirlooms that had been handed down from generation to generation, each new owner adding a little to the work that had been done by her predecessor.

In the middle of the afternoon, during the reception, we were suddenly disturbed by the sound of firing. Someone rushed in, crying that the Germans were coming. I went to Mr. Paderewski's room to rouse him, telling him that he must dress and go to another part of the hotel where there was less danger. He answered that he was very comfortable and sleepy and thought he would stay where he was. The uproar in the street outside our rooms increased, and finally I succeeded in getting him out of bed. I remember how leisurely he was and how I thought on that particular day that he would never get his cravat tied to suit him, but while he was standing in front of the mirror working on it, a bullet struck the wall just above his head and about three inches to the right. Another came and then others, and we fled. Our windows faced the park at the other end of which the Germans had placed machine guns, and we were directly in the line of fire. After it was all over, we found that seven bullets had entered the room, and when we were in Poznań a year later, the marks of the bullets were still there.

The story of this affair makes but another count in the long indictment against the Prussians of Poznania.[11] That it ended most disastrously for the Germans, inasmuch as it hastened probably by weeks and possibly by months the deliverance of the entire province from Prussian rule, merely emphasizes its horrible brutality. It seems to have been a well-planned plot on the part of the German military forces left in Poznań to start a riot during these festivities and then place the blame of the whole affair on the disorderly Poles. The Supreme Council had warned all peoples who were waiting a change of government to be quiet and peaceful at the peril of incurring the displeasure of the Peace Conference. It would have pleased the Germans greatly to have been able to protest to the Supreme Council over the turbulence of the unruly Poles.

On the day of the children's parade, a counter demonstration was organized by the Germans. There was a small clash, and immediately a battalion of Prussian troops, composed, as it was since proved, almost entirely of officers, took machine guns to the end of the square opposite the Bazar Hotel and began to shoot into the dense crowd. Several were killed, and many were wounded, and for a minute it seemed as if the Germans were going to gain their end. But they had not taken into account the thousands of Polish youths who had just left their army.

Bands of these youths rushed to the German barracks, overcame the guards there, and took possession of all the arms and munitions, rifles, machine guns, and an unlimited supply of cartridges. Quite without leadership, they returned to the center of the city and made the Bazar their headquarters, with machine guns at the entrance and one in nearly every window facing the square. For nearly three days we lived in rooms on the courtyard side of the hotel, with the rattle of the machine guns constantly in our ears, but at no time were we seriously disturbed. Thanks to the people who had brought food in from the country we had plenty to eat, and the reports we were receiving constantly of the fighting showed that the young Poles were steadily driving the Germans away.

As it turned out, the Germans had once more overreached themselves, and the disorders they started resulted in their being thrown headlong out of

---

11. By Poznania, Paderewska means the whole former Prussian province of Posen, not only its capital city of Poznań.

Poznania weeks before they would have left under normal conditions, with the loss of all their great stores of arms, munitions, and clothing for soldiers, these stores enabling Poznania to arm and equip her own troops and to make them from the beginning the most efficient part of the Polish army. The revolutionary movement, for such it really was, spread through the province like wildfire. In the beginning the older heads attempted to check it, fearing that it might compromise the good name of Poland at the Peace Conference, but the youth were entirely out of hand and started systematically to rid the country of German soldiery. The extraordinary feature about the movement was that it was altogether spontaneous, entirely without formal organization, the fighting being done practically by leaderless bands. The day following the outbreak in Poznań, Gniezno was taken, and each succeeding day brought the news of some other town or district being rid of Prussian rule.[12]

In three days Poznań was quiet again, entirely in the hands of the Poles. The Germans had gone, but reports came that they had not finished with the city, as they were about to bomb it from planes; so on the last day of the year, it was decided that we should start for Warsaw that night by special train. At midnight at the hotel we brought in the New Year with appropriate ceremonies, and at three o'clock in the morning we left for the station in automobiles, a very large party, for in addition to those who had come to Poznań with us were a dozen or more gentlemen who intended to accompany us as far as Kalisz. There had been more or less uneasiness about the frontier, which was still in the hands of the Germans, but just as we were leaving the hotel, word was brought to us that the Polish bands had captured Ostrów at ten o'clock that evening and that the way to Warsaw was quite clear.

We drove to the station through a black, silent city with no one in the streets except the soldiers on guard. The password, I remember, was "Warszawa," and it gave us a thrill to hear this word flung from sentinel to sentinel as we rode through the streets. Despite the hour, peasantry and townsfolk were at every station to greet the train as it passed, and when we reached Ostrów at six o'clock, a great crowd of soldiers and people were at the station, and Mr. Paderewski had to make a speech to them. The next step brought us to the ruined city of Kalisz, destroyed by the Germans in the very first weeks

12. The Greater Poland Uprising (Powstanie Wielkopolskie) of 1918–1919 was largely a spontaneous uprising of the predominantly Polish former Prussian province of Posen against the Germans. The insurgents' success in restoring Polish sovereignty to most of the province was confirmed in the territorial provisions of the Treaty of Versailles.

of the war. There the gentlemen who had been with us left the train, and I was tremendously impressed when one showed me under his *bekesza*, the fur-lined coat that Polish gentlemen wear in the country, a veritable arsenal: two pistols and a short, wicked-looking saber. All of the men were similarly armed, having made themselves bodyguards for Mr. Paderewski to protect him if need arose.

Kalisz, where a tremendous demonstration was awaiting us, gave us our first view of the ruins that nearly five years of war had left in Poland. A large, prosperous manufacturing town before the war, the first town of importance east of the German frontier, it had been as completely destroyed as any of the larger towns in northern France. There we changed our train and rode the remainder of the way to Warsaw in the private carriage of General von Beseler,[13] who had been governor of Russian Poland in the last years of the war.

Our progress was slow and was in every respect a repetition of our journey from Gdańsk to Poznań. At every town, at every village, the train was met by people who brought flowers, bread, and salt. Everywhere along the way, there were signs of the ruin that had been wrought by the hard fighting of the first year of the war: roofless houses, factories with only a melancholy chimney standing to show what they had been, old trenches, and graves.

It was one in the morning when we finally reached Warsaw. Not until nine o'clock in the evening had they received news that we would really arrive that night, but all day long the crowds had waited, and when we finally arrived everything was in readiness. The reception was like that of Poznań only on a much greater scale, for while Poznań is a city of less than two hundred thousand, Warsaw at this time had over a million inhabitants. And as I look back to our progress from the Vienna station to the Hotel Bristol, I think that all of that million must have been in the streets. Never in my life have I seen so many people. It is a long mile from the station to the hotel, and it seemed to require an endless time for us to make the distance. The horses had been taken out of our carriage, which was pulled through the streets by Wilanow peasants in all the bravery of their national costumes. One unending cheer accompanied us, and when our carriage finally drew near to the Bristol, it seemed impossible that it could ever get through the densely packed masses that filled the surrounding streets. But it was great fun, tremendously moving, an experience that comes into the lives of very few.

13. Hans Hartwig von Beseler (1850–1921), German general; governor of German-occupied Russian Poland from 1915 until October 1918.

I have rarely seen my husband so deeply moved. In fact, from the time we left Gdańsk, he had been under a most severe emotional strain. It was not merely the greeting that had been given to him personally, although that had been very wonderful, and no man, no matter who, could have failed to be greatly stirred by it. But even at the risk of being boring, I must repeat again that he thought of himself least of all. He regarded himself as he had always done, simply as a servant of his people, and his attitude toward the work he was now doing was exactly the same as his attitude toward his art, which he had described in his address to the Bohemians of New York years before.

When he sailed from New York, he regarded his work as all but completed, that he had done his share as best he could, and now it was for others to carry it on. When he sailed from Harwich for Gdańsk, he planned to spend but six weeks in Poland. He stayed there fourteen months, including the time he spent in Paris at the Peace Conference.

When I say that he was deeply moved that night on our arrival in Warsaw, I do not mean that he was in an exalted frame of mind. Quite the contrary. He was very serious, for the days he had spent in Poznań had been sufficient to tell him what a huge task lay before him if he was to bring order out of the chaos that then reigned in Poland. I do not believe that any man could have felt more keenly the weight of responsibility lying on him. The joy with which his coming was greeted simply meant to him how much the people expected of him, which was enough to sober the lightest mind.

CHAPTER ELEVEN

January 1919

A greater contrast could hardly be found than that between the Warsaw that I had known before the war and the Warsaw that I saw seven weeks after the signing of the armistice. No city could have been brighter or gayer than the former, both for those who lived there and for those who chanced to be visitors. It was a city of which one might say that it knew no difference between day and night. With its theatres, operas, concerts and balls, its restaurants and cabarets, all infused with the spirit of hospitality for which the Poles have ever been famous, it justly had the reputation of being one of the most attractive capitals of Europe.

Five years of war, especially the years of German occupation, had left their mark on the town and on its people. A stroll through any of the streets was sufficient to show how Poland and the Poles had suffered. It is not pleasant to see on a bitterly cold January day a majority of the children without shoes or stockings, their feet wrapped in rags. Nor is it pleasant to see a majority of the people insufficiently clad and bearing all the signs of having been for months insufficiently fed. I treasure as a curiosity a piece of bread such as all but the very rich were compelled to eat. It seems to contain no grain at all, the principal components being moss and various kinds of herbs. It was horrid to the taste and not only lacked nearly every element of nourishment but was positively unwholesome.

Even the joy of freedom was unable to offset the very real misery of nearly all classes, and added to this physical discomfort was the mental unrest caused by the unsettled state of affairs and by the general dissatisfaction with the government that was then in power. The outlook was sufficiently discouraging to depress the spirits of the most optimistic, for, in addition to its internal troubles, the new country seemed to be surrounded on all sides by enemies seeking its destruction. To the north and east were the Russian Bolsheviks with whom Poland has been continually at war almost from the day it became a free nation. In the southeast the Ukrainian Bolsheviks had overrun

Eastern Galicia and were besieging Lwów. In the southwest the attitude of the Czechs was becoming more aggressive and more threatening each week, while fighting was continuous between the Poles and the Germans along the whole length of the frontier of Posnania.

There was no army in the proper sense of the word, for at that time it was impossible to transport to Poland Haller's well-trained and well-equipped troops that were in France. Following the events of Christmas week, Poznania quickly organized and equipped troops of its own to protect its frontiers against the Germans, being able to do so because not only had it a large supply of men who had been trained in the German armies but it had taken for its own use the large stores of arms and equipment that the Germans had left in the province. In Russian Poland, the conditions were lamentable. Joseph Piłsudski, who, returning from Germany after the armistice had assumed the position of chief of state, had organized a volunteer militia as a basis for a new army, but the feeling ran so high between these men and the members of the Citizens' Guard that had been organized in Warsaw to protect the city that hardly a day passed that there was not street fighting between the members of these two organizations, with many casualties. But even if there had been an army, Poland had at that time no means of equipping it. It had neither arms nor munitions, uniforms nor shoes, and such hospitals as there were had no surgical dressings, no antiseptics or disinfectants, no medicines. When a soldier was wounded or fell sick, the chances were all against him.

As I look back at those first months of the Polish Republic, I cannot help marveling at the restraint shown by the people. They had every incentive to revolt, and they were surrounded by what seemed like successful revolutions. Bolshevism in Russia, Lithuania, the Baltic states, and Hungary, Spartacism in Germany, and their own country filled with revolutionary agents who had unlimited means with which to spread their propaganda. Yet there was very little real or serious disturbance. Such was the primitive patriotism of the people that Poland was able to endure those months of trial, emerging from them a state that won and compelled the respect of her neighbors.

The most interesting spot in Warsaw in those early months of 1919 was the Hotel Bristol, especially the lobby. It was the political, social, and, if I may so put it, international center of the country. Our apartments and Mr. Paderewski's offices were there until we moved to the Zamek in July. General Szeptycki,[1]

1. Count Stanisław Maria Szeptycki (1867–1950), Austro-Hungarian army officer and later Polish general; chief of staff, 1918–1919; later an opponent of Piłsudski.

the chief of staff, lived there, as did many other Polish leaders. Later in the winter, when the various missions began to arrive, they made the Bristol their headquarters. For months it housed the American legation until Hugh Gibson,[2] the minister, secured the Blue Palace of Count Zamoyski[3] as a home. It used to be said that if anyone wanted to see anyone of importance in Poland, it was necessary to spend only an hour or so in the lobby of the Bristol, and he would appear.

I don't know how many governments and factions of governments had their secret agents in Warsaw at that time, but the number of mysterious men and mysterious women one saw sitting in the corners of the lobby and reading room, whispering to each other and trying to hear what was being whispered by others, led me to believe that most of those who had been released by the armistice from service in Bern, Copenhagen, and Stockholm had come to Poland. It was quite impossible to stop and talk with anyone—about the weather or any subject equally innocent—without having one or more of these persons at one's shoulder listening to what was being said. I am frank to confess, however, that after having observed for several months the character and caliber of the male and female agents sent to Warsaw, in the future I shall read tales of international spies with more skeptical reserve than I have in the past. Perhaps I am unfair to the craft. Perhaps Poland did not receive its most distinguished members.

It is not my purpose to attempt a detailed account of the eleven months during which my husband was prime minister of Poland.[4] As a woman and as his wife, I hear that I lack the judicial frame of mind necessary to the writing of such a history, and, besides, there is much of which I do not pretend to know. Furthermore, such a story, I think, would have little attraction for any but the publicist and those who have a vital interest in Poland. I can only tell it from my own point of view, however prejudiced it may seem to be, as I saw it develop from day to day, as it is known to scores of men connected with it

---

2. Hugh Simons Gibson (1883–1954), American diplomat; US minister plenipotentiary to Poland (1919–1924); close associate and friend of Herbert Hoover; author of voluminous correspondence and diaries.

3. Count Maurycy Klemens Zamoyski (1871–1939), conservative politician and diplomat; member of the Polish National Committee in Paris; Poland's ambassador to France during 1919–1924; perhaps the biggest landowner in Poland, and the Blue Palace was his Warsaw residence.

4. During 1919, Paderewski's title was president of the Council of Ministers and foreign minister, hence his closes associates addressed him as "Mr. President."

or interested in it, directly or indirectly, adding here and there more intimate sidelights, perhaps, on incidents that have not yet been made clear to the public at large. The one thing above all others that I wish to avoid in this book is cause for any controversy, and for this reason naturally I shall limit myself to obvious facts, all or most of which have already been related and commented on in the newspapers.

In considering his course of action before and during his term of office as prime minister, it should always be kept in mind that Mr. Paderewski went to Poland to perform a specific task given him by the British government, as I have already related. It was to secure the establishment of a stable government that could be recognized by the Allied nations and thus give Poland a voice in the Peace Conference then about to begin in Paris. The commission, flattering though it was, brought him no joy, and he accepted it only through his deep sense of duty to his country. In London, when he consented to go, he realized in a measure how thankless the task before him would be, but only in a measure compared with the realization that was brought home to him after his arrival in Poland. And as for the premiership, I doubt if any man ever accepted a high office more unwillingly. But it had to be, although he knew then as well as he knows now that little of the credit for things accomplished and all the blame for things unaccomplished would be his, however great the former or small the latter.

In January 1919, Warsaw fairly seethed with political unrest. Following the evacuation of the country by the Germans, an interim government had been formed by Piłsudski that was expected to remain in power until a general election of a diet could be held, it being planned for February. The government was of the extreme Radical Socialist type, containing no representatives of the moderate or conservative elements, and discontent with it was general. It had not been recognized by any of the Allied Powers, nor was there any possibility of such recognition coming to it. Under it, Poland had neither money nor credit nor the possibility of securing either. The air was filled constantly with rumors and reports of revolutions, conspiracies, corruption, and treason, and conditions, bad as they were, seemed continually to grow worse, matters culminating in the spectacular but futile coup d'état of Saturday, January 5.[5]

5. There is no consensus as to who was the architect of the failed bloodless coup of January 4–5, 1919, led by Colonel Marian Żegota-Januszajtis. Its main effect was the resignation of the unpopular leftist government of Jędrzej Moraczewski but the strengthening of its former sponsor, Józef Piłsudski, the temporary chief of state. Piłsudski came out of this affair as the

My husband was not in Warsaw when this occurred, nor had he any suspicion that it was being planned. Almost from the moment of his arrival, he had been besieged by an unending stream of callers, men of every shade of political opinion, all of them desperately seeking some remedy for the sickness that held the new republic in its grasp. That something must be done, and done speedily, to be rid of the government seemed to be the opinion of everybody, without exception, but there seemed equally to be no agreement as to the best means of bringing this about.

It so happened that just at this time the fate of the city of Lwów was causing great anxiety. It had been beset by the Ukrainian Bolsheviks for several weeks, and while so far it had been able to resist successfully all attempts to take it, its stock of munitions was very low, and unless something was done to renew this, it would be only a matter of a short time before it must fall. General Szeptycki spent much time with Mr. Paderewski, talking of the necessity of organizing and training an army if Poland was to protect herself against the enemies within as well as without her borders, and he used to use Lwów as a moral, how easy it would be to relieve the city if only there were even a small body of trained troops at his disposal.[6]

The situation weighed heavily on my husband. It was not merely a question of saving for Poland one of the principal cities of the ancient kingdom, the capital of Galicia, but it was a question of saving the people of Lwów from the horrors of Ukrainian Bolshevism that in sheer savagery surpassed anything that Russia had known in the worst days of the Terror. Finally, on the morning of January 5, General Szeptycki brought the news that a dispatch had just come from Lwów to the effect that the city was down to its last round practically, and something must be done at once. What could it be? At that time only

---

unquestioned political arbiter who selected the very popular Paderewski for the difficult task of forming a new government.

6. The Polish-Ukrainian conflict over Lwów (Lviv in Ukrainian, Lemberg in German) was an ethnic conflict, as the city was mostly Polish and a historic Polish cultural center, and the surrounding territory of Eastern Galicia was mostly Ukrainian. The Ukrainian side was represented by the West Ukrainian People's Republic, which was nationalist and agrarian socialist—enough for Mrs. Paderewska to call it "Bolshevik." The conflict began on November 1, 1918, when Ukrainian soldiers of the Austrian army attempted to occupy Lwów but were repelled by the local Poles. By the end of November, Polish regular forces advancing from the west managed to capture and hold the rail connection between Poland and Lwów. Fighting on the periphery of the city and along its vital rail supply line continued until the spring of 1919, when units of General Haller's Army, just arrived from France, were used to defeat the Ukrainian forces and lift the siege of Lwów.

munitions were needed, for the citizens of the town, men and women, boys and girls—even the girls fought in the trenches—were so well organized and were so well led that they had shown themselves amply able to defend the city if they had the means of doing it.

Mr. Paderewski could see only one possible solution for the difficulty. In Budapest there was a very considerable force of French troops that had been moved there from Thessaloniki, and in that city there also was a great stock of munitions, the only one available in that part of Europe. On less than an hour's notice, he decided to start himself and try to get through to Budapest, and, once there, he felt confident he could persuade the French authorities to send a trainload of these supplies to Lwów. We left for Kraków as soon as a special train could be made up, our departure being made with greatest secrecy because it was quite essential that the errand should not become known.

During the night we had a nerve-wracking experience that I have always attributed to an attempt to blow up the car in which we were riding. As we were passing through the town of Ząbkowice, there was a tremendous crash as if from an explosion. The car was lifted into the air, we were all thrown from our berths, and our luggage and belongings went flying in every direction. Fortunately, the car was built of steel, and it settled back on the rails without overturning, as I had feared for a minute that it might, with no worse results than giving us all a severe shaking. I was thoroughly frightened, but Mr. Paderewski took it as calmly and as philosophically as he had the fighting in Poznań and as he took other incidents that were more or less disturbing to me.

Although it was early morning when we arrived in Kraków, and although our coming was supposed to be very secret, the news of it had become known, and a great crowd was at the station to greet my husband. They escorted him to the Grunwald monument and then to the hotel, where all day long there was an uninterrupted reception. Immediately upon his arrival, he learned that it would be impossible for him to get to Budapest because the Czechs and Hungarians were fighting on their frontier between Kraków and that city, and it would be useless to attempt to get through. Rather than return immediately to Warsaw, he decided to remain over in Kraków until the next day and go back leisurely and in comfort.

At three o'clock the next morning, Sunday, he was awakened by a great pounding at his door. General Szeptycki had just arrived by motorcar from Warsaw with a message from Piłsudski, asking him to return posthaste—there had been a revolution, and the government had disappeared, literally. Beyond this, Szeptycki professed to know little, for he had left Warsaw very early in the morning. Our car was attached to a locomotive, and, leaving Kraków before seven o'clock, we reached Warsaw that evening, only to find that the members of the government had been discovered and rescued and that the famous coup d'état had been a complete failure.

The story is well known. A group of men, most of them men of standing and influence in the army and in civil life, decided that the time had come to get rid of the government then in power and made plans to do it themselves. During the night of January 5–6, they kidnapped all the members of the civil government, whom they confined in a building in Warsaw. The plans also called for the arrest of Piłsudski and Szeptycki, but the men to whom this was delegated failed utterly in their task, and the conspiracy ended almost before it began. The members of the government were found and released early the next morning, and when we arrived in Warsaw, nothing remained of the "revolution" except the sensation it had caused.

But returning to Lwów for a moment—not long after the city got its trainload of munitions from Budapest, which enabled it to hold out for many weeks until, through the efforts of Mr. Paderewski, Poznania sent troops to relieve it and rid it of the Ukrainian peril, I hope once and for all. Commander Rawlings of the British navy, who had joined our party in Copenhagen when we were on our way to Poland, was the man who succeeded in getting the train through, an exploit as thrilling and as romantic as any incident that happened during the great war.

If the attempt of January 5 to overthrow the government by violent means had failed, it nonetheless made the position of the cabinet untenable, and less than a fortnight later its members handed in their resignations to Piłsudski, who requested my husband to form a government, with himself as president of the council and prime minister. He did not accept at once, and in fact he consented to serve only after great and continual pressure had been brought to bear on him from all sides. He was told that he was the only man in the country available for the post, that he not only had the confidence of the Poles but he was known personally and had the confidence of the statesmen and the governments of the United States, France, and Great Britain and therefore was better fitted to deal with them than any other man who could be appointed to the place. And finally, he was persuaded that the only possible way in which he could perform the mission that had brought him to Poland, to establish a stable government that could secure the recognition of the Allied Powers, was to form such a one himself.

The scene when he finally decided to accept the task of forming a government is stamped indelibly upon my mind. It was in the reception room of our apartment in the Bristol at five o'clock on the morning of January 17. With him were Major Iwanowski; Mr. Strakacz, his secretary; Lieutenant Świrski[7] and Mr. Car[8] of General Piłsudski's staff; and myself. As he signed his name to his acceptance, he remarked: "This is the greatest sacrifice a man can make for his country. I know, at this moment I am certain, that the price of this office will be the love of my countrymen and, perhaps, my good name."

I myself was afraid that the price might be even greater than that, for I lived in continual fear of an attempt on his life, and an incident that happened almost immediately after his signing his acceptance gave me good ground for uneasiness. Mr. Car had left for the Belvedere with the letter of acceptance, but the rest of us were still in the room talking when a man entered suddenly from another door, having slipped by the sentry stationed at the entrance of our apartment and got in through an adjoining room. Very excitedly, he demanded a private interview with Mr. Paderewski, and the latter, despite my urgent objections, took him into the next room, which happened to be my bedroom, leaving the door open so that we could see them but could not hear their conversation. They were sitting side by side on the bed talking most earnestly when suddenly my husband jumped up, seized the man by the shoulders, and, shaking him as if he were a child, fairly shouted: "Look in my eyes! Can't you see that I am an honest man?"

There was more talk that we could not hear, and then they came out together, my husband escorting him into the hall to the stairway. When he returned, he told us that a committee of some forty Radicals and Communists had gone to Piłsudski two or three hours earlier to demand that he refuse to accept Paderewski as premier, and when Piłsudski had refused to do so, this man, one of the leaders, had come to Paderewski himself to tell him that he, the caller, would kill him if he took the position of prime minister; in fact, he was prepared to kill him then unless he promised to resign. In the end he was stricken with remorse and so far lost his desire to become an assassin that he begged my husband not to tell me about his errand and to see that he got safely by the sentry at the door without being arrested, and it had been in response to this last petition that Mr. Paderewski had escorted him out of the room. When

---

7. Czesław Świrski (1885–1973), aide and associate of Piłsudski going back to pre–World War I anti-tsarist underground; aide to Paderewski during the Paris Peace Conference.

8. Stanisław Car (1882–1938), Warsaw lawyer and politician very close to Piłsudski.

I remonstrated with him for having taken such a risk as going alone into the room with this man, he simply remarked again, as he had many times before, that there is no place in politics for a man who is afraid of death.

The formation of the cabinet brought with it many serious and complicated problems, the solution of which was not made the easier for him by his long absence from the country, with its resultant loss of personal contact with men and affairs in it. He was compelled to rely greatly on others, and disinterested advice is no more common in Polish politics than it is anywhere else in the world. It was agreed that the government should be "nonpartisan," that its members should be as far as possible "specialists," each man being chosen on account of his particular fitness for his bureau without regard to his political opinions or connections, an idea that I have been led to believe usually works out more successfully in theory than in practice. The conferences lasted for days and for as many nights. From the very beginning, he found opposition and obstruction, oftentimes most unexpectedly, and the cabinet, when it was finally formed, by no means represented his wishes, by no means represented his judgment. One little illustration. Mr. Skulski,[9] formerly mayor of Łódź, was one of his friends and advisors during this period. He had a very high opinion of him and was certain that he would be quite the best man for the Ministry of the Interior. For the greater part of one night, he argued with Piłsudski in favor of this appointment, but Piłsudski would not listen to the proposition, insisting on the appointment of one of his own men, Wojciechowski,[10] and Wojciechowski was appointed. But when the Paderewski government retired in the early part of the following December, it was Skulski whom Piłsudski was compelled to summon to form the new ministry.

But the chief thing was that despite its unsatisfactory character, a new government had been formed that could be trusted to carry on the affairs of the country until a diet was elected, one that was likely to banish all dangers of turmoil, to say nothing of revolution, and one that fulfilled, to a large degree, the mission that had brought Paderewski to Poland. There were reasonable grounds for hope that the Allies would soon grant it recognition, and Poland would thus be able to take her place in the Peace Conference in Paris. When he took the post of premier, he sent telegrams announcing that fact to all the

9. Leopold Skulski (1878–1940), mayor of Łódź during 1917–1919; succeeded Paderewski for a few months as prime minister, 1919–1920; interior minister during 1920–1921.

10. Stanisław Wojciechowski (1869–1953), Polish politician and scientist; interior minister, 1919–1920; president of Poland during 1922–1926.

Allies, and the congratulatory messages that came back were published in the Polish papers, sometimes in special editions. They seemed to signify that at last Poland was on the way, and the joy of the people was very great; but the day on which the telegram came from Secretary of State Lansing[11] in which the United States recognized Poland as a nation was one of universal rejoicing. To my husband it meant even more than it could to anyone else. That the United States was the first to admit Poland into the family of nations and to recognize her government seemed to him to be the final reward for the work he had done during the war. The promise virtually given him by President Wilson on November 6, 1916, had finally been redeemed.

11. Robert Lansing (1864–1928), American lawyer and politician; secretary of state during 1915–1920.

CHAPTER TWELVE

January 1919 – March 1919

Although the new government was a vast improvement over the one that preceded it and thus had won the speedy recognition of the United States, it was still only an interim government. No such ministry could be truly representative of the wishes of the people; therefore, Mr. Paderewski deemed it necessary to hold the general elections as soon as possible so that the diet might be convened and the government be one of the people in fact as well as in name. Plans had already been made to hold the elections in February, and the machinery for them was so advanced that one of the first things he did on taking office was to order that these elections be held a month earlier than had been planned, and he set the day for January 26 in the face of, it is true, very considerable opposition.

Election Day was really a festival for the people of Poland. Suffrage was universal for men and women[1]—several of the candidates for the diet being women—and the Poles on that day for the first time since the partitions were to vote for men and women of their own choice, undisturbed by outside influences. And once again, as so often happened, the women of Poland showed the stuff of which they were made and how worthy they were of the franchise that had been given them. Before the elections, there had to be a great campaign of education, and in this work they took first place. They organized clubs and meetings, "stumped" the entire country, and made a house-to-house canvass the length and breadth of the land. The day passed as quietly and as uneventfully as any election day in the United States, the people seeming to worry only about their vote. At hundreds of voting places throughout the country, men and women stood patiently in line all the preceding night in order that there might be no chance of their missing the great privilege that freedom had

---

1. Poland granted the unrestricted right to vote to women in 1918, and eight women were elected to the Polish parliament (Sejm) in 1919.

brought them. Mr. Paderewski's name was on the tenth list, and he was elected both from Warsaw and Lublin, accepting the former.

The task that faced him as prime minister was sufficient to daunt the most courageous man. The whole governmental edifice had to be built from its lowest foundations, and there was, practically speaking, no trained material for the purpose, especially in Russian Poland, where for over a hundred years Poles had had no opportunity to receive training in executive work. To illustrate, for weeks after he had assumed the post of foreign minister, he was compelled to write all his own dispatches, even his telegrams, because he had no one with him capable of doing the work. Moreover, he was constantly hampered by hostile influences, which acted often in the most petty but nonetheless exasperating fashions. Often his telegrams were not sent or were subjected to inexplicable delays. Just as often, telegrams sent to him were never delivered. I recall two particular instances. The morning that he became premier, the Warsaw papers published the report of the death of Colonel House. The news almost prostrated him, although he could not bring himself to believe it, and it was several days before he was able to learn that the report had been manufactured in Bern out of whole cloth—he was quite unable to get a wire though to Paris.

The other instance was more important, for it had to do with the very safety of the country. It was when the Czechs issued a fraudulent proclamation to the effect that the Supreme Council had declared that all Polish troops should be removed from the Cieszyn district of Austrian Silesia and that this territory, with its great Polish population and its valuable coal deposits, was to be under the control of Czecho-Slovakia. They had sent their troops into Cieszyn, had acted very badly, and would have succeeded in their undertaking had it not been that General Latinik,[2] commanding the small Polish forces there, had refused to accept the proclamation as genuine and had resisted their advance. During this time it was quite impossible for Mr. Paderewski to get any first-hand news from Cieszyn or even to get into communication with Paris.

One evening during this period, we had dining with us Commander Rawlings and Lieutenant Foster,[3] the latter an American officer who had just come

2. Franciszek Latinik (1864–1949), colonel of Austrian-Hungarian infantry during World War I; later Polish general commanding the military district of Cieszyn; military governor of the Polish capital during the Battle of Warsaw of August 1920.

3. Lieutenant R. C. Foster, a 1911 Harvard graduate, reported to Professor A. C. Coolidge's committee in Vienna. The committee, a unit of the US Peace Commission, studied the political, social, and economic situation in East Central Europe. Foster interviewed Piłsudski, Paderewski, and others.

to Warsaw with the American Food Commission, and my husband was commenting on the situation when Foster, turning to Rawlings, said: "What do you say, Rawlings, to starting for Cieszyn tonight and finding out what is really going on there?"

It was no sooner said than done. In a half hour they were on the train accompanied by Jan Ciechanowski,[4] then the head of the British section of the Foreign Ministry and later Mr. Paderewski's chief aide in the Paris Peace Delegation. They investigated on the spot, then went on to Prague while Mr. Ciechanowski returned to Warsaw, and thus it was only through two foreigners, an American and an English officer, that the prime minister of Poland was able to get authentic information of important events practically within the borders of his own country.

The opening of the first Polish Diet since 1792 came on February 7, and it was the occasion of great public rejoicing. There were impressive ceremonies in the cathedral over which the archbishop presided, and the first session had as its marshal Prince Ferdinand Radziwiłł,[5] following the ancient custom whereby the oldest member in years is the presiding officer. But this was not permanent, for shortly afterwards Mr. Trąmpczyński[6] was elected marshal of the diet, an office weighty in dignity and power under the present fashion of doing things. One of the first measures of the new diet was to confirm the appointment of Piłsudski as chief of state until such time as a constitution could be made and new elections held, while it also confirmed Paderewski as president of the council and approved the nominations of the various ministers. At last Poland had a real government.

A few days later my husband appeared before the diet to make his first exposé in which he outlined the policies of his government, his plans, and his hopes for the future. The chief point in his address, the one on which he laid the greatest accent, was an urgent demand that the diet at once take measures to create a regular army capable of defending the frontiers of the country against foreign aggression. I emphasize this in particular because the creation of the Polish army is one of the several achievements the credit for which his detractors have tried to take from him. It was a most inspiring session. There

4. Jan Ciechanowski (1887–1973), Polish diplomat; his last posting was as ambassador to the United States during 1941–1945.

5. Ferdynand Radziwiłł (1834–1926), Polish aristocrat and one of the leaders of the Polish minority in the German Empire.

6. Wojciech Trąmpczyński (1860–1953), Polish lawyer and National Democratic politician from the Poznań area.

had not been time for development of factional quarrels, pure patriotism was the order of the day, and all the deputies were filled with the keenest desire to do their uttermost to bring happiness and prosperity to the country. For the first two or three weeks, it seemed almost as if the legislative millennium had arrived. The future looked very bright.

But if the future seemed to be bright, the present held some very terrible problems. Food was fearfully scarce. Clothing was out of the reach of all but the very rich, and even for them boots and shoes were unobtainable. All the factories were idle either because of lack of raw materials or because the Germans had removed the machinery—and often it was both causes—and the country was full to overflowing with the unemployed. The sending to Poland of the American Food Commission under Colonel Grove[7] in early February proved to be a veritable godsend. Coming to investigate the food conditions, it found them so palpably bad that it was followed shortly by the arrival in Gdańsk of a ship laden with flour, fats, and other foodstuffs, and although this cargo was only an infinitesimal part of what was needed, it gave the people new courage. Mr. Paderewski was wont to say that if there was any real danger of Bolshevism in Poland, it disappeared with the arrival of that ship.

In the early part of the session of the diet, while the Inter-Allied Commission[8] was in Warsaw, an incident occurred that illustrated the temper of the people and how easy it would have been to stir up serious trouble. One afternoon, just as he was about to start for the diet, a great crowd of twenty-five or twenty-six thousand men and women gathered in front of the Bristol, where they were being harangued by several agitators, obviously Jewish. The crowd massed itself under the window of our apartments and cried to Paderewski to give them bread, to give them work, to give them better wages. He decided that he would go down and talk with them, I going with him to talk to the women. Everything became quiet immediately, and in a few minutes we got into the automobile to go to the diet, but the crowd pressed so closely that it was impossible to move, and we returned into the hotel. Directly after we left, the

7. William H. Grove, US army colonel who headed US government relief efforts in Poland during 1919–1921.

8. Later known as the Inter-Allied Mission in Poland, and made up of two representatives each from France, the United States, Great Britain, and Italy, it was created by the Allies' Supreme War Council to gather information on the situation in Poland. Its members, accompanied by dozens of military and civilian experts, visited Poland during February and March 1919.

agitators began to talk again, and the cries were renewed, so Mr. Paderewski went out on the balcony to address the people. He had just started to speak when one of the agitators began to hurl abusive names at him and ended by whistling at him with the most unearthly shrillness. That turned out to be a most unfortunate move, for if there is one thing in the world my husband cannot endure, it is the sound of whistling. It drives him nearly frantic. He had paid no attention to the abuse, but when the fellow began to whistle, he cried to the crowd: "He's a Bolshevik! The devil is whistling in him. Put him out!" With splendid unanimity, the crowd fell on the man, rolled him in the mud, gave him a sound beating, and then cheered Paderewski to the echo. A diversion had been most unexpectedly created, the danger was past, and the people were once more thoroughly in good humor.

But in the meantime, rumors had reached the diet that a mob was attacking the Bristol and that we were in danger. The members of the mission were there, and, hearing the news, Mr. Noulens[9] and General Carton de Wiart[10] jumped into a motorcar to come to our rescue, but when they arrived there was only a peaceful, cheerful crowd that meant harm to no one. We returned with them to the diet in their car, and on our way Mr. Paderewski remarked laughingly that with France on one side of him and Great Britain on the other, he felt quite safe.

France, Great Britain, and Italy had withheld their recognition of Poland until they made their own investigation of conditions, and in the late winter they sent the great Inter-Allied Mission, whose coming was the signal for festivities the like of which Warsaw had not seen in years. It was headed by Mr. Noulens, who until the preceding summer had been the French ambassador in Petrograd. He had been there through the war, through the revolution, and through the early months of Bolshevik rule, only leaving because his life was in danger, and he had been compelled to return to France by way of Archangelsk and the Arctic Ocean. A most gifted diplomat, the possessor of great personal charm and attractiveness, he has always been a very good friend of my country. With him came his wife, to whom fell the distinction of being the first woman to accompany a diplomatic mission to the new republic, and she was made much of accordingly. The military attaché of the

9. Joseph Noulens (1864–1944), French diplomat and politician; ambassador to Russia during 1917–1918.

10. Adrian Carton de Wiart (1880–1962), British officer and war hero; member of the British military mission to Poland.

French Mission was General Niessel.[11] At the head of the British Mission was Sir Esme Howard,[12] a most distinguished member of the British Diplomatic Corps, and associated with him was that most interesting man General Carton de Wiart, who has remained in Warsaw ever since. General de Wiart wears, along with at least a dozen decorations, the V.C.,[13] and has, if I remember rightly, nine wound stripes, which include the loss of an eye and an arm. The Italian representatives were Mr. Montagna[14] and General Romei Longhena.[15] The United States—I suppose because it had already recognized Poland—had no diplomatic mission, its representative being Brigadier General Kernan.[16]

Mr. Paderewski had seen to it personally that the mission should have a reception becoming to its importance. All the troops that Warsaw boasted, horse, foot, and guns, had been ordered out, and by far the greater part of the population came, with the soldiers. The broad boulevard on which the Vienna station stands was black with people, and all the streets leading to the Bristol were equally crowded. In the first motorcar rode Mr. Noulens with Mr. Paderewski, and Mrs. Noulens[17] was in the second motorcar with me. In the beginning they were all the least bit nervous, having heard direful tales of Warsaw, of anarchists, and of Bolsheviks, to say nothing of hunger-maddened people that kept the city in turmoil all the time, no story concerning Poland in those days having been thought too wild to be refused publication in the newspapers of western Europe. And when they saw this mass of people, among whom, after we left the station, were neither soldiers nor police, they were all a little apprehensive. The motorcars were compelled to move at a snail's pace between ranks of people massed so thickly that they brushed against them. Suddenly the first cars, including the one I was in, were taken possession of by bands of boys in their teens who formed a bodyguard and never left us until we reached the hotel. It made a tremendous impression on all the visitors.

11. Henri Albert Niessel (1866–1955), led French military mission to Russia in 1917; oversaw the withdrawal of German *Freikorps* from the Baltic area.

12. Esme Howard, 1st Baron Howard of Penrith (1863–1939), British diplomat; his final posting was as ambassador to the United States during 1924–1930.

13. Victoria Cross (VC), the highest British military decoration for valor.

14. Giulio-Cesare Montagna (1874–1953), Italian diplomat.

15. Giovanni Romei Longhena, Italian general who was in Russia in 1917.

16. Francis J. Kernan (1859–1949), general; technical military advisor to the US Commission to Negotiate Peace during 1918–1919. The second US representative to the Inter-Allied Commission for Poland was Harvard professor Robert Howard Lord (1885–1954), a specialist on Polish history.

17. Unable to verify.

As first impressions are always the most important, we were naturally anxious to have everything work smoothly, but almost at the very beginning there was a slip that, if not of vital importance, was rather embarrassing. Shortly after we reached the Bristol, a servant came to me in great trouble, saying that one of the members of the mission was very angry. I went out to find General Kernan pacing up and down the corridor, decidedly out of temper and with considerable cause. His luggage had gone astray, and no room had been prepared for him. There was no question about his being decidedly put out, nor could I blame him, for it was a most stupid mistake and I felt it particularly because if there was one country whose representative we wanted to make happy, it was the United States.

I went immediately to my husband and told him what had happened. It would be some little time before the blunder could be straightened out, and in the meantime he decided that there was only one thing to do—give General Kernan and the Americans with him the very best supper that could be devised on such short notice. This we did. We had all eighteen of the American members of the mission, Mr. Paderewski himself mixed the cocktails, and the supper was excellent. We kept them until two in the morning, by which time a fine room had been found for the general, his trunks were in it, and he was quite happy; and as he bade me goodnight, he remarked that I had shown myself a most excellent diplomat, which made me happy too. At any rate, during the time he remained in Poland we were the best of friends.

The stay of the mission brought great social activity. There were dinners innumerable, receptions, and gala performances at the opera. A reception and dinner we gave I like always to remember. The reception was the first official function that Poland had had in over a century. Most of our entertainment was done at the Bristol, but for this Mr. Paderewski thought a hotel would hardly be suitable. Next to the Bristol is the magnificent old Namiestnikowski Palace, once the property of the Radziwiłł family but for many years the government offices for the Russian administration of Warsaw.[18] It had fallen into decay and was cluttered up with trash and dirt, and its beautiful salons had been cut up into small office rooms.

It was an ideal place for such a reception, and I determined, if possible in any way, to have it there. When I went to the proper authorities to get permission to use the palace, they readily granted it but assured me that while they were willing to do all they could, it would be out of the question to undertake

18. The palace serves now as the official residence of the president of Poland.

to clean it in the five days allowed them. But I was not convinced. My heart was set on my original plan, and, to make a long story short, I succeeded in imparting some of my enthusiasm to the men in charge of the palace, and when the night of the reception came, one would never have recognized it. The old salons were restored to their former beauty; the magnificent old floors had been cleaned and polished; tapestries, furniture, and pictures had been assembled from I don't know where; and electric lights and lusters had been installed—it was as if the palace had never been used for anything but functions of this kind. The reception itself was interesting from every point of view. Fifteen hundred invitations had been issued, and everybody who was anybody in social and official life was there, including all the members of the diet, which was then in session. It was particularly interesting for the Poles, because few if any of them had ever been inside the palace before. During their lifetime it had been Russian, and no Pole ever went of his own accord under a roof that was Russian.

The dinner was at the Bristol, a men's affair entirely. It was the first diplomatic dinner Poland had had, and Mr. Paderewski personally looked after all the arrangements. As I remember it, there were about three hundred guests: the members of the various missions, the principal members of the government and diet, and representatives of the aristocracy and the clergy. The rooms were decorated in the colors of the Allied nations, as to flags and banners, but the flowers were the red and white of Poland. Mr. Paderewski began the speaking, and then as each country was toasted, the band played its national hymn, and the responses to the speeches of the different representatives were made by Poles in the language of the country toasted. I had seen many brilliant and successful official dinners but none more so than this.

Before leaving Poland the mission spent several days in Poznań. While it was still there, Mr. Paderewski returned from the diet one evening desperately worried over the situation in Lwów. Thanks to Commander Rawlings and the trainload of munitions he had piloted through from Budapest in January, the city had been able to continue its defense against the Ukrainians with a dogged courage unsurpassed in history, but the end had been reached. It had no food, it had no water, it had no light, to say nothing of heat, and the stock of munitions that had come from Budapest was practically exhausted. The mayor of the city had managed to get word through the cordon of the enemy that surrounded it that unless help came at once in the shape of troops, Lwów would be compelled to surrender and endure all the horrors that the fiendish ingenuity of the Ukrainian Bolsheviks would invent.

For one reason and another, which cannot be gone into here, Warsaw and the national government could do nothing to help the city. As a last resort, therefore, my husband decided to go to Poznań and beg the Poznanian army to send aid. He left late that evening by special train, and the greater part of the next day he spent with the Poznań general staff trying to devise some means by which reinforcements might be sent to Lwów at once. It was neither easy nor safe for Poznań to send even a small body of troops so far away. Her means were very limited, fighting was continual along the German border—although the world at large heard very little of it—there were continual threats of incursions from Silesia, and every man of the little army was needed at home. I really think it was our friend General Kernan who turned the balance. He made a most impassioned appeal to Poznań to send help, and finally it was agreed that something more than a regiment should be sent to the relief of Lwów, with it going a considerable supply of munitions. The story has often been told how these troops leaving Poznań that night fought their way through the Ukrainians into the city and, joining with the citizens, gave the Ukrainians such a beating that Lwów was saved.

While they were in Poznań, the members of the mission were entertained in that vast, unspeakably ugly castle that Wilhelm II had built to the glory of the Hohenzollerns and to the permanence of Prussian rule in Poznania. We lunched there with the mission, and really it gave us Poles a weird, almost uncanny impression to walk through those endless salons and corridors, sumptuously furnished in typical German taste, its walls hung with pictures or covered with frescoes celebrating the great deeds and high mission of the House of Hohenzollern. It was only a few years ago that it was finished at a cost of millions, and today it stands more than anything as a monument to the uncertainty of life and fortune.

When Mr. Paderewski formed his government in January, he had taken the portfolio of foreign affairs in addition to assuming the post of president of the council. He had done this because the work was peculiarly agreeable and because from his experience in the past he believed himself peculiarly fitted for the work. The diet had appointed him and Roman Dmowski delegates to the Peace Conference in Paris, and until April Mr. Dmowski, who was a fixture in Paris, had had sole charge of Polish interests there. But as the spring wore on, Polish questions were rapidly assuming great importance, and it became evident that Mr. Paderewski's presence there was most necessary. When the Inter-Allied Mission was leaving Poland, Mr. Noulens very courteously offered to take him on its special train, an invitation he gladly accepted, a private car being provided for him. It really meant much because in those days, so far as railway travel was concerned, Poland was enjoying a "splendid isolation." There were only three trains a week between Paris and Warsaw, the famous "Entente" trains known so well to travelers of that period, and these, wandering amiably through Switzerland, the Tyrol, Vienna, and Czecho-Slovakia, required from three to four or more days to make a journey that before the war had needed but thirty-two hours.

We went by way of Kraków, where we picked up the members of the mission who had preceded us there, and then we had two days in Vienna, two really ghastly days, for at that time Vienna was actually starving, and all the time we were there, our train was surrounded by pale, wan little children who climbed on the platforms of the cars, knocked at the windows, wailing for bread, just a little piece of bread. I exhausted the available supply of bread and chocolate we had on the train, and one good American bought at an extortionate price the entire contents of a nearby bakeshop that I might have more, and when we left—more affecting still—the mothers came to the train to thank us and bless us for our goodness to the little ones. Later in the spring, when I returned to Warsaw I filled half the luggage van with bread and chocolate to distribute among these children, but we passed through Vienna by another route and saw none of them.

Our party consisted, in addition to Mr. Paderewski and myself, of Mr. Ciechanowski, Major Iwanowski, Mr. Strakacz, Lieutenant Świrski of General Piłsudski's staff, and Lieutenant Szebeko.[19] In the Gare l'Est in Paris, we were met by Mr. William Martin,[20] that remarkable man who as head of the protocol of the French government had charge of all the ceremonies and decided all questions of precedence during the conference, by members of the Polish National Committee, and by the Polish Peace Delegation, while a company of French *poilus*[21] acted as guard of honor. We went to the Hotel Wagram, which the French with their usual skill and tact had made all ready for us. Polish soldiers from Haller's Army were there as orderlies and guards, and in the Tuileries Gardens opposite, a Polish military band was playing Polish airs.

19. Probably Lieutenant Witold Szebeko (b. 1889), aide to General Dowbór-Muśnicki of the Poznań-area forces.
20. William Martin, chief of protocol of the French Ministry of Foreign Affairs during the Peace Conference.
21. Literally "the hairy ones," popular name for French infantrymen.

CHAPTER THIRTEEN

April 1919—July 1919

For the greater part of the next seven months, we were in Paris. Arriving there the first week of April, we spent Easter at Riond-Bosson, which we had not seen since January 1915, and returned to Warsaw in May for a fortnight. We went to Warsaw again the middle of July, but on the first of September the Austrian treaty called my husband back to France, and it was not until well into October that Paris saw the last of him. The situation was one of great difficulty for him. As president of the Council of Ministers and premier, he was undoubtedly sorely needed in Poland during those first months of the new republic, but on the other hand the negotiations going on in Paris before the conference unquestionably demanded his presence there.

It would not have been nearly so embarrassing had Poland not been in a state of practical isolation from the rest of the world. During those spring months, so far as communication between Warsaw and Paris was concerned, it was as if the clock had been turned back at least a half century. At best, there were only three trains a week, those in charge of the French, trains that wandered amiably through Switzerland, the Tyrol, and Vienna, taking nominally sixty-four hours for a journey which before the war had required but thirty-two, and rarely making the trip in less than three full days. As for the telegraph, it was as slow as the post and much more uncertain than when one could send one's letters in a diplomatic pouch. The wireless had usually something the matter with it, and such telegrams as were sent by wire were dependent entirely on the convenience of Poland's neighbors, for whom it was seldom convenient to forward them promptly.

It was necessary for Mr. Paderewski to decide where the need for him was greater. That he chose wisely in going to Paris has never been questioned, however desirable his presence in Poland at that time may have been. It was in Paris that Poland was being made. It was in Paris and in Paris only that her hopes and ambitions could be realized, and it was in Paris that her most formidable enemies, open and secret, were striving their utmost to thwart and hinder those who would help her come to this realization. Already when we arrived in April, the great questions involving the future of her ancient provinces, East and West Prussia, Upper Silesia and Cieszyn, and, above all, Gdańsk and her road to the sea, were being threshed out, and in the autumn came the disposition of Eastern Galicia and Lwów.

Mr. Paderewski believed that for the moment the future of Poland lay in Paris. Until all these vital problems had been solved, the country must, as it were, mark time. The great work of reconstruction could not begin until it was known what was to be reconstructed, and he felt that with his knowledge of conditions and with the acquaintances and friendships he had made in the past years, he could at this time better serve Poland in Paris than in Warsaw.

Arriving in Paris, he plunged at once into the work, which completely absorbed him all the months he was there. Mr. Dmowski and he were at the head of the Polish delegation, which numbered in all about forty men, vice-delegates, secretaries, and technical experts. His headquarters were at the Hotel Wagram, where he had offices for his personal staff from the Foreign Ministry, and work went on day and night, broken only by the luncheons, dinners, receptions, and other functions belonging to the necessary social routine.

I don't believe that the world at large has yet any idea of the mental and physical strain endured by the men who were actively engaged in the Peace Conference. There was a general feeling—and perhaps still is—that the members of the conference had a very good time in Paris and incidentally wrote the Treaty of Versailles, but I know, as does every woman whose husband was connected with the work there, that this was anything but true. Never were men harder pressed for time—with a steady grind of seven days a week and thirteen, fourteen, and fifteen hours a day. Undoubtedly there were men in subordinate positions who found more time for play than was really good for them, but it was not so with those on whom great responsibility rested. My husband, as I have already said, is a man of exceptional physical strength, of most uncommon endurance, but many were the times he went to bed so completely exhausted that he could not sleep—and his was only one case among many.

My own position in Paris was rather more than that of an interested observer, although there was so much of enthralling interest to observe that this alone would have kept me fairly busy. But it is impossible for me to be idle, and I found enough to do to make me welcome the trips between Paris and Warsaw almost as divinely granted opportunities for rest. In Warsaw, as I have already told, I had organized the White Cross, and there was a great amount of work to be done for it in Paris, such as the purchase of supplies and arranging for their transportation to Poland. When we went to Warsaw in May, I took with me Captain Kamieński and twelve White Cross nurses who had come from America with the Polish troops. When we went in July, I took Dr. Violette Berger,[1] an American physician who had been with the French army and chaperoned eight Red Cross nurses who had been assigned to the Polish government for typhus work. Dr. Berger was in Warsaw all the following winter, acting as an inspector of hospitals and as liaison officer between the White Cross and the American Red Cross. I have never met any woman of more untiring energy, of more wholehearted enthusiasm for her work, and she accomplished some things that seemed to me to be little short of miracles; and, incidentally, she became a sort of physician-in-chief to the entire American colony. Several times I visited prison camps containing Polish prisoners,[2] one of them an American camp near Tours, and I shall not soon forget the courtesy and kindliness of the American officers there who made it possible for me to get 900 recruits for the Polish army that day, boys who did not know until I told them that Poland was free.

Moreover, there was the never-ending round of social duties. I think that all who were in Paris during the conference will agree that entertaining held a very subordinate place in the order of the day, but there was enough of it and to spare, an endless succession of *déjeuners*,[3] dinners, teas, and receptions, with now and then a gala at the opera or a fête. The giving of dinners, especially of official dinners, had its own trials. Precedence was all-important, and precedence was regulated by protocol, and the laws of the Medes and the Persians[4] were more elastic than the protocol. I remember that when we wanted to give a formal dinner for Marshal Foch,[5] we discovered that he and his wife followed in the wake of every ambassador and every minister, and the only way in which we could get around the difficulty was by having as our other

1. Violette Berger (b. 1888), physician from New York who joined the French army because, as a woman, she was refused commission by the US Army; she received both French and Polish decorations for her service.

2. These were ethnic Poles drafted into the German army and taken prisoner by the Allies. Most of them were soon released to join General Haller's Polish army.

3. The word *déjeuner* is French for breakfast, brunch, or lunch.

4. The once-popular expression "laws of the Medes and the Persians" was borrowed from the biblical book of Esther, where the ancient Babylonian laws are described as unalterable.

5. Ferdinand Foch (1851–1929), French general and military theorist; made supreme commander of the Allied Armies (1918).

guests none but French generals and staff officers so that the marshal and his wife were really the guests of honor. Had we had the minister from the tiniest and least important state at the conference, he would have had precedence over the marshal of France.

We gave several important dinners in addition to this one, three of which I particularly recall, the first to the Romanian delegation—it was the first of our official dinners—the second on the night of the signing of the treaty to the American delegation, and the third to the Duke and Duchess of Doudeauville[6] and others of our French friends who had shown us much kindness. The American dinner came on the evening that President Wilson was leaving Paris, and in the midst of it, Secretary Lansing, Mr. White,[7] General Bliss,[8] Mr. Grew,[9] and Mr. Gibson had to go to the station. As a great delicacy Mr. Paderewski had ordered ortolans[10] for the dinner, which some of the men had never tasted, and they begged us to keep them until they returned, so there was a recess in the dinner of nearly an hour.

I had seen Mr. Wilson that afternoon when he and Mrs. Wilson were making hurried farewell calls. As he stepped into his motorcar, a small boy on the walk near me shouted: "Look! He is smiling again!" I had not noticed particularly that he was very worn, perhaps because all the men at the conference by the end of June were so fearfully worn that to see a fresh, bright face among them would have created a sensation; but evidently that clever Parisian public had noticed that toward the end of the conference the famous presidential smile was seldom seen.

I could not then help remembering the last time I had had an interview with him, in Washington, a little more than a year before. I had gone to the White House to ask him if he would make it possible to have another Polish Day throughout the country in view of the fact that the one that he had authorized for New Year's Day, 1917, had amounted to little or nothing because

6. Armand de La Rochefoucauld, Duc de Doudeauville (1870–1963) and his wife, Princess Louise Radziwiłł (1877–1942).

7. Henry White (1850–1927), prominent American diplomat and one of the signers of the Treaty of Versailles.

8. Tasker H. Bliss (1853–1930), chief of staff of the US Army during 1917–1918.

9. Joseph C. Grew (1880–1965), American career diplomat with successive postings to Vienna, Copenhagen, Bern, Ankara, and Tokyo.

10. Ortolan bunting (*Euberiza hortulana*), small migratory bird, a French culinary delicacy. The birds were captured, force-fed in darkened boxes, roasted whole, and eaten, bones and all, while the diner draped his head and face with a napkin to absorb maximum flavor and aroma.

of the short notice. He was very kind and said that he would think it over. Two or three weeks passed without an answer, although every now and then during that time, Mr. Tumulty[11] would send me word saying that the president had not forgotten me and would write me as soon as possible. Finally the letter came, one that I shall always treasure, in which he told me that he could not grant my petition, but he said it so kindly, went so into his reasons for refusing me, that I was almost as pleased and flattered as if he had done what I asked.

My husband and I had a few words with him and his wife at the reception that preceded the great farewell dinner given for them by President Poincaré at the Elysée on the evening of June 26. Invitations for dinner were issued on a few hours' notice, and scores of engagements had to be cancelled by those who were invited. The dinner itself was a liberal education in how to handle affairs of that kind.

Everything seemed to be absolute perfection: the cooking, the wines, the china, the crystal, the plates, the napery, and, above all, the service. France was most fortunate in having at the Elysée during those months two such attractive and charming people as Mr. and Madame Poincaré, for they represented quite the best the country has to offer in culture, tact, and refinement, and that is saying very much. At this dinner two speeches were made, that in which President Poincaré bade Godspeed to President Wilson and the latter's response. Both of them were most effective, both of them models of their kind, the grace and beauty of Poincaré's French making a pleasing contrast with the rugged forcefulness of Wilson's English.

Over three hundred were present, and it would indeed have been difficult to gather into one room so many interesting and unusual personalities. And in the end, I think, the memory that will stay longest with those of us who were in Paris during the conference will be that of the men and women we met. Personally, I saw more or less all the leaders, for Mr. Paderewski was in constant demand not only because of his official position as premier of Poland but because there were always friends of his artistic days who wanted him. Of the many men I met there for the first time, two, at least, made an indelible impression on my mind, Foch and Venizelos.[12]

11. Joseph Patrick Tumulty (1879–1954), New Jersey lawyer and politician; private secretary to Wilson during 1911–1921.

12. Eleftherios Venizelos (1864–1936), prominent Greek statesman; known to his people as "the maker of modern Greece."

In Marshal Foch, there is a simplicity, a gentleness, and a kindly courtesy in all that he says and does that one hardly expects to find in the successful commander of great armies. But one is never with him, never even in the same room with him, without feeling the strength and power of his personality, nor can one talk with him without realizing the wonderfully keen and active mind that lies behind his broad brow and smiling blue eyes. He is a man who seems to impress one at once with his greatness and nobility of character, and yet he is the last man in the world, I truly believe, who would consciously work to make an impression on anyone, for his modesty of carriage and demeanor is as beautiful as it is rare.

My husband and I count it one of our greatest privileges that we may regard him and his charming wife as our very good friends. Certainly Marshal Foch had always been very good to me and to my country. Many times during the spring and summer, I had to go to him to ask favors, to get things done that I seemed to be unable to put through by any other means, for I never went to him except in cases of real stress. Never had he refused me his help, and sometimes my requests were not easy to fill. He made it possible for me to send directly to Poland a train of thirty-seven cars laden with supplies for the White Cross, a huge amount of everything necessary for our work in the Polish army, that I had bought from the American Liquidation Commission or had been given to me by the French, American, Canadian, and Australian Red Cross. In September he gave me another train, this time to take from Lyons to Warsaw close to a thousand refugees who had managed to escape from Odessa when the Reds had captured the city in the spring.

This train, incidentally, was in charge of two American women, Miss Mary Lane[13] of Flushing, New York, and Mrs. James Law[14] of San Francisco. They had been in the American Red Cross in France, serving with the First Division of Haller's Army after its arrival there, and when it was sent to the East Galician front in the spring of 1919, they went with it. While I was in Warsaw in August, they came to me and said that if I could make use of them, they would be glad to stay in Poland and work for me. Naturally I grasped the chance to have with me in my work two experienced and energetic American women, and ever since I have blessed the day they came to me. I took them back to Paris when I went in September, where they were demobilized from the Red Cross, and they returned to Poland with the refugees.

13. Unable to verify.
14. Unable to verify.

Their experiences with that train that was a fortnight going from Lyons to Warsaw would of themselves have made a fair-sized book. Only two such thoroughly resourceful women who had, besides, the rare gift of winning the loyalty and devotion of those whom they were serving could have got that train through without mishap. They even persuaded the former chief pastry cook of the tsar of all the Russians to make the cabbage soup that was the principal item on the daily menu of breakfast, dinner, and supper, and not only did he do it willingly but he took such pride in his desire to please his two commanders that often they doubted really that it was cabbage soup they were eating, so artistically had he disguised it.

Afterwards in Poland these two women were of invaluable help to me, Miss Lane really becoming my right hand, so to speak. To her I trusted the work of caring for the demobilized Polish Americans of Haller's Army. She established a canteen at Skierniewice, the demobilization base, organized a hospital there when some of the men brought typhus from the front, saw that they were all properly cared for when they left for America, and went home herself on the transport that carried the last detachment. A most remarkable woman, Miss Lane, sane, an energetic and indefatigable worker, with an unusual gift for organization, she had besides a most beautiful and inexhaustible sense of humor and an entrancing modesty that endeared her to all who knew her.

I think that the impression made on me by Venizelos was common to all who had anything to do with him or even met him. One of the most striking figures among the many who were in Paris at that time, it seems to be the general belief, which Mr. Paderewski warmly shares, that in him Greece furnished one of the truly great personalities of the conference. He is a man of most attractive manners, the possessor of a very shrewd wit and keen sense of humor, and I always counted it a treat when by chance I sat next to him at a dinner or a luncheon, for his conversation was always stimulating, rarely dropping into the hackneyed commonplaces of the table.

Another man for whom Mr. Paderewski had an immediate liking that soon developed into a strong friendship was Hugh Gibson, the first American minister to Poland. He was in Paris when we arrived for the first time in April, in reality waiting to see my husband before leaving for Warsaw. We met him first through Colonel House at a dinner given for Mr. Paderewski, and a little later he dined with us, the Schellings being the only other guests.

Whatever may have happened to her in other respects, Poland certainly has been happy with the Americans who have interested themselves in her or have been sent to Poland to represent the United States officially or semiofficially: Wilson, House, Hoover, Gibson, Kernan, Barber,[15] Gilchrist,[16] Fuller,[17] and the many others who have shown such fine, disinterested friendship. As to Gibson, my husband is wont to say that had President Wilson searched the United States from one end to the other he could not have found a man better fitted for the difficult and delicate task of establishing relations between America and the new republic. Not only did he show himself a man of exceptional experience, of unusual talent, of an enthusiasm rarely found in a diplomat and of a sane and sound judgment, but Warsaw quickly discovered in him a charm and attractiveness of personality that immediately made him most popular with all who had anything to do with him, the foreigners as well as the Poles. As for the Americans, they swore by him, and during the winter of '19–'20, the Blue Palace, which was his home, was the center of the social activities of the very pleasant American colony that was then in Warsaw. Mr. Paderewski has always felt that it was Colonel House who was ultimately responsible for the sending of Mr. Gibson to Warsaw, and, that being so, it is not the least item in the debt that my country owes to "Poland's providential man."

In Paris also we saw much of Mr. Hoover. I have so far carefully avoided mentioning his name lest I should forget the real subject of this narrative and devote undue space to this miracle worker from California, for as such do all of us people of Central Europe regard our great benefactor—Poles, Czechs, Austrians, Hungarians, Yugoslavs, Letts, Lithuanians, and all the others of those different peoples whose children he saved from hunger and the ills that go with it. Only those whose lot it was to be in Central Europe through the summer and fall of 1919 and the following winter can have any idea of the good this man has wrought, of the hundreds of thousands of young lives he has saved from sickness and death, of how his name is blessed in the largest cities and tiniest hamlets of the famine-scourged regions. He and the devoted young men who worked for him have done more in one year to make the name of America loved and understood than diplomats and wars could do in a century. During the past winter of 1919–1920 the American Relief Administration and its successors daily fed in Poland more than a million children, and for months this one meal meant the difference between comfort and actual starvation. Just

15. Colonel Alvin B. Barber (1883–1961), railway engineer with US Army Engineers; later with the American Relief Administration and technical adviser to Poland (1919–1922).

16. Colonel Harry L. Gilchrist (1870–1943), later general; specialist on medical management of chemical casualties; led American program to combat typhus in Poland (1919–1921).

17. William Parmer Fuller (1888–1969), administered American Relief Administration's European Children's Fund efforts in Poland during 1919–1921.

before Christmas Mr. Hoover sent to Poland 480,000 pairs of children's shoes, as many pairs of warm stockings, and as many overcoats for boys and girls.

It was as long ago as 1915 that Mr. Paderewski received a letter from Mr. Hoover, who was then in London, in which he expressed his deep interest in Poland and offered the use of his organization for the forwarding of food to the Polish sufferers. The offer was quite voluntary on his part, and that it came unsolicited from a man he did not know[18] made an unusually deep impression on Mr. Paderewski. Nothing came of it because Great Britain would not consent to the sending of foodstuffs to Poland by way of Germany, as they had to go, but this letter had much to do with the first interview my husband had with Colonel House.

During our stay in America, especially after the United States entered the war, they saw much of each other in Washington, and a strong friendship developed. Of Hoover, my husband does not hesitate to say that he regards him as one of the truly great men of our times, perhaps the greatest man made known to the world by the war. While we were in Warsaw, following the signing of the Treaty of Versailles, he came to Poland, and in both Warsaw and Kraków he received tributes that could have left no doubt in his mind as to the feelings of the Poles toward him. In Warsaw he was taken to the racetrack at Mokotow, and there assembled to greet him were the children of the city who had been fed by his bounty, a large part of whom unquestionably owed their lives to him, over sixty thousand of them. They ranged from four years to fourteen, only a few with shoes and stockings, although all were dressed in their best, most of them, it seemed, in clothes that for patches would have rivaled Joseph's coat; among them were Jews and Gentiles, Protestants and Catholics. It was tremendously inspiring but terribly sad.

In his honor, the same evening, the royal apartments in the Zamek were opened for the first time and a great dinner given. Notice was short and the task of preparing formidable, for what the Russians had not taken from the Zamek the Germans had, even to the brass handles on the doors, and prac-

---

18. In fact, Paderewski first met Herbert Hoover in February 1896, during the pianist's California concert tour. Hoover, then a senior at Stanford University, offered to organize a Paderewski concert in San Jose, which would in part benefit the students of Stanford. Poorly timed, the concert was not well attended, leaving Hoover and his associates unable to pay Paderewski's honorarium. Paderewski forgave the debt and promptly forgot the encounter. Hoover never did. When the two met again in 1919, Hoover thanked Paderewski for the magnanimous gesture. The incident certainly helped to forge a bond between the two men and played a role in Hoover's lifelong sympathy for Paderewski's homeland and its people.

tically nothing was left except the decorations on the walls, which could not be taken away, and the beautiful old parquet floors. But I had already discovered that things could be rushed through if there was great need, and at nine o'clock, more than two hundred sat down at the tables that had been laid in the magnificent salon: the principal members of the government and diet, men prominent in business and society, and members of the American colony.

Only two speeches were made, the greeting extended to Mr. Hoover by my husband and his reply. The latter made a very deep impression, especially on the Americans who were there, many of whom had never met him before. As one of them said later, it was so different from what they had expected, for in it Hoover had shown a strain of poetry, of real fancy, a gift of real eloquence, which was most unusual. A few days later we came with him to Kraków, where there was another demonstration followed by a gala at the opera, and there the enthusiasm was as high as it had been in Warsaw. In both cities the demonstrations were notable for their sincerity and spontaneity, for we had had only the shortest notice of his coming, and in Warsaw all preparations had to be made within twelve hours.

Of all the men who were in Paris for the conference, none was better known to the public at large than my husband, and during the spring and early summer, while the savor of novelty was still felt, wherever he went he was the object of demonstrations. During his artistic career, he had always been a figure who appealed to the imagination of the Parisians. They had regarded him almost as one of themselves and had shown their fondness for him innumerable times. Years before, he had been made an officer of the Legion of Honor without having to take the preliminary grade of chevalier, quite an unusual distinction for one who was not in public life; it was almost, I believe, without precedent. This had been done at the request of the leading French musicians headed by Saint-Saëns[19] and the professors of the conservatoire, a most wonderful tribute to Paderewski, the artist.

The Paris public adores the unexpected, and few things seem to have taken so strong a hold on its fancy as the idea of a world-famous pianist to whom it had listened off and on for nearly thirty years becoming the prime minister of a great country and joining the ranks of the statesmen who were deciding the fate of a large part of the world. Wherever he went during those months, there were always cordial greetings from the people with many a "Vive Paderewski,"

---

19. Camille Saint-Saëns (1835–1921), French composer, organist, conductor, and pianist. His opinion of Paderewski was that he "is a genius who happens to play the piano."

whether it was going to or returning from Quai d'Orsay, in a restaurant, at a theater, or at the opera. There were many amusing and flattering incidents. Shortly after his arrival there in the spring, the artists of the opera gave a gala performance for him followed by a reception that was particularly gratifying not only because of the personal compliment it implied, but with the decorations of the evening in the colors of Poland and with the playing of the Polish national anthem, it was another step toward this recognition of his country for which he had been working so long.

An amusing incident that illustrated his popularity with the Parisians and their interest in the fate of Poland that he had done so much to arouse occurred at the Armenonville in Bois de Boulogne on the evening following the news of the acceptance of the treaty by the Germans. We were dining there with Mr. Smulski and Mr. James C. White[20] of Washington, both of whom had just arrived from America, and as we entered, everybody rose and greeted him with cheers, with "Vive Paderewski," "Vive la Pologne." He was surrounded by a crowd of pretty women who demanded kisses as a reward for their enthusiastic demonstration, and even then his courage did not falter.

The time is not yet here when the story of his work at the conference can be told. He says that he gave to it the best that he had, and it was patent to all, however remotely connected with the negotiations and deliberations, that he was held in very high esteem by the leaders who had made policies, diplomacy, and statesmanship their life's work. Numberless incidents showed this, and never once was he compelled to feel that he was at more or less disadvantage because he was, compared with all the others there, new at the task. In June he was invited, together with Marshal Foch and Mr. Venizelos, to go to Oxford to receive the honorary degree of doctor of civil law. It was one of the greatest compliments that he said had ever been paid him, but fate decreed that he could not accept because on the day that he was to be in Oxford, he was to have a conference of vital importance with President Wilson and Lloyd George, and as these degrees are not granted in absentia he had to decline the honor. Happily, this has turned out to be only a postponement, for this year the invitation has been renewed by Lord Curzon,[21] the chancellor of the university, and Mr. Paderewski will be able to go to England to receive the degree.

20. James C. White, editor of the *Boston Herald*, hired by the Polish National Department to head its Washington, DC, press office.

21. George Curzon, 1st Marquess Curzon of Kedleston (1859–1925), secretary of state for foreign affairs during 1919–1924; chancellor of Oxford.

I was one of the few fortunate women who was in the great Salle des Glaces in Versailles on the afternoon of the twenty-eighth of June when the treaty was signed. It may be, as was said at the time, that the ceremony of the signing of the treaty lacked a certain impressiveness that one would have expected, but I think that only those who had nothing at stake would have found it so. For me personally, it was one of the great hours of my life, and so it must have been for the vast majority of people who were there. I cannot imagine what those who professed to find there a lack of solemnity and dignity could have expected. Truly, once within the hall, there was little of the spectacular. I can imagine nothing more gorgeous than what must have been the spectacle that was furnished, for example, by the signing of the Treaty of Vienna, placed as it was in a setting of gorgeous uniforms and ceremonial costumes of the imperial and royal courts of a century ago. There is little that is spectacular or beautiful about the civilian dress of the men of today, and such soldiers as were there were clad in the very practical but most unromantic garb of modern service. Save for the glistening helmets and breastplates of the cuirassiers who filled the great court leading to the entrance of the palace, there was little of the glitter, the pomp, and circumstance that one had always associated with functions of this kind.

All this made it for me the more impressive, and what was not the least thing to move me was that my husband was to be one of the signers that day of the document that was to make his country free. It surpassed the wildest flight of imagination that he who had given his whole life to the art of music should have been transported in five short years, in reality in six short months, into a position where he was one of those who decided the fate of nations. The significance of the day and the occasion overwhelmed me, and really the recollection of all that took place that afternoon is more or less of a blur, and so it must have been for any Pole. Other nations were created by that treaty, other peoples were set free, but none had waited so long for freedom, none had suffered so much for freedom, none had grown so heartsick for it as Poland and the Poles, and this day brought it to them. The one really distinct, sharp impression I carried away from Versailles was the appearance of the German delegates, how completely out of key they were with all the others there.

At the signing of the Treaty of St. Germain[22] in the autumn, there was a completely different atmosphere. There was none of the strain, the tension

---

22. Treaty of Saint-Germain-en-Laye dissolving the Austro-Hungarian Empire was signed between the victorious Allies and the Republic of German-Austria on September 10, 1919.

that seemed to fill Versailles, as if all must be in harmony with the sullen, ungracious attitude of the German delegates. At St. Germain everything was bright and cheerful, even the Austrian delegates coming to the palace with smiling faces. When they arrived, they were greeted cheerfully and cordially by the waiting crowd that was massed about the entrance, and when the ceremony was over, Dr. Renner,[23] who was at the head of the Austrian delegation, was fairly besieged by men and women asking for his autograph, and he was heartily cheered when he left. There was nothing like this at Versailles, for even had the people wanted to show any kindness toward the representatives of a beaten enemy, the attitude of the German delegates toward them and their conduct during their stay in the town had been more than sufficient to nip in the bud any feeling of kindliness.

There is little more to tell of our stay in Paris. We returned to Warsaw, as I have said, in the middle of July because it was necessary for Mr. Paderewski to appear before the diet, present the treaty, and secure its immediate ratification. We were, however, fortunate to be there on the fourth and fourteenth of July[24], to see on the former day the review of the American troops in the Place de la Concorde and on the latter day to see the memorable *défilé*[25] down the Avenue des Champs Elysées. I was a guest of Madame Poincaré[26] on the fourteenth and saw the procession from beginning to end. Three things I shall always remember of it: the heartbreaking spectacle of the *Mutilés*,[27] the gallant battalion of Polish troops, and the wonderful American soldiers. I do not pretend to be a connoisseur in things military, but it was a rare thrill I received from the sight of those thousands of brown-clad Americans who marched with the perfection of a great machine, and truly they were the sensation of the day.

23. Karl Renner (1870–1950), Austrian Social Democrat, first chancellor of Austria, 1918–1920.
24. July 14 is La Fête Nationale, otherwise known as Bastille Day, the French national holiday.
25. *Défilé* is French for "parade."
26. Henriette Benucci Poincaré (1858–1943), wife of President Raymond Poincaré of France
27. *Mutilés* is French for "disabled."

CHAPTER FOURTEEN

July 1919 – February 1920

By the time we returned to Warsaw in July, the apartments in the old Royal Palace that had been set aside for the use of the president of the council were ready to receive us. We traveled then by special train and with us went not only a carload of supplies for the White Cross and the personal luggage of our large party but all the silver, china, linen, glass, and the like for use in our new home, the selection and purchase of which had been one of the several tasks that enabled me to fill my spare time in Paris. As I have already said, the Zamek, when the Germans left, had nothing but its bare walls, and everything had to be bought for the residence of the prime minister, down to the humblest kitchen utensil.

Viewed from a distance, the idea of living in a palace that had been the home of the kings of Poland and, after them, of many Russian viceroys, has a certain enticing attractiveness, but it did not take me long to discover that such a residence entailed inconveniences and discomforts that more than offset its sentimental charms. Our forefathers, when they set about the task of building a palace for a king, seem to have rested content if they provided an imposing exterior and an interior containing a sufficient number of large salons for court functions. They seemed always to predicate an unlimited supply of servants. The Zamek is a huge quadrangular structure built around a great court, and if its exterior presents few features of real beauty, the building in its mass has a very certain dignity worthy of the purposes for which it was built and to which it has been put. Some of it goes back to the fourteenth century, but the greater part of it, the livable part, so to say, was built three hundred years later, and today it stands much as it did when Augustus III was king. It suffered a little during the fighting in '15 between the Russians and the Germans, and its eastern walls, facing the Vistula, will forever bear the marks of the bullets from the Russian guns that were posted in the suburb of Praga on the right side of the river.

Our apartments comprised a series of rooms on the first floor overlooking the square in which stands the statue of King Sigismund III, which is on the borderline between the new Warsaw and the ancient part of the city clustered about the Old Town (Stare Miasto), where some of the most beautiful specimens of sixteenth- and seventeenth-century houses anywhere in the world are to be found. We actually lived here less than three months, but that time was quite enough to make me forever a devout advocate of "modern improvements." Until I lived there, I had never realized how many steps one might take to get nowhere at all, and, frankly, not my least reason for thankfulness when Mr. Paderewski resigned from the government came from our return to our old quarters at the Bristol, confined and circumscribed as they were.

Of course, we were living in the Zamek when we celebrated my husband's fête on July 31. It was a day full of memories for him and one of great rejoicing. Although we had observed the day the three summers we were in Paso Robles and had even found time in New York the year before to have a few of our friends with us, this was really the first opportunity we had had for a real celebration since the fête at Morges on the eve of the outbreak of the war. We gave the whole day to it, beginning in the morning with a special mass celebrated in the cathedral. There was a great luncheon for the diplomatic corps, the members of the government, the leaders of the diet, and various functionaries from the Foreign Ministry. There was a review of the palace guard, a reception for the general staff, and finally in the evening, another reception for the general public, with dancing. On that day the diet had ratified the Treaty of Versailles, and in one sense the work that my husband had begun just five years before was finished.

I shall not attempt to tell in detail the happenings in Warsaw that followed our return from Paris in October, the political battles that were waged, the crisis that lasted for weeks, and finally Mr. Paderewski's resignation and retirement from the government, which came in early December. As I have already related, the cabinet that he had formed in January represented neither his wishes nor his judgment of what such a cabinet should be, and it was his intention to make many changes in it, but the months he was compelled to spend in Paris prevented him from doing many things in Poland that he would have liked to do. He never had the loyal support of some of the members of his cabinet, which he had the right to expect, and finally during his stay in Paris during the autumn, matters came to such a pass that it was a question in his mind whether he would not resign immediately on his return to Warsaw.

Very serious problems pressed for solution, and he felt that he could not carry on the work he had begun unless he had with him a united and loyal cabinet, backed by a substantial majority in the diet. Shortly after his return, he went before the diet, and in a speech in which he outlined his policy, he announced the conditions under which he would continue to serve as premier, the chief one being that a majority be formed that should give him its active support. For a time it looked as if this would be done, but after weeks of futile negotiations, he decided to retire and sent in his resignation to the chief of state. The latter, after having sought in vain for several days to find a successor, appealed to him once more to attempt to form a government, and he accepted, but three or four more days of conferences convinced him that it was useless for him to try to do more at this time, and he notified Piłsudski to this effect, his definite retirement coming in the first week of December.

It was with no small relief that I greeted his decision to retire, for a time at least, from public life. The unwonted strain he had been under continuously for five and a half years, especially the wear and tear, the anxieties and worries of this last year in Europe, had begun to make serious inroads on his health, how much neither of us realized until the reaction began to set in after the responsibilities had been taken from him. Leaving the Zamek immediately after his resignation, we returned to the Bristol, we thought for not more than a week or ten days, but one thing after another occurred that prevented us from leaving Warsaw until the early part of February, when we finally started for Riond-Bosson, where we were sure to find quiet and rest.

And here he has been all through this miraculous spring of 1920, the most beautiful spring I have memory of, resting quietly, preparing his body and mind for whatever new work the future may bring. What that may be only the future can tell, for only one thing seems to be certain. The chapter in his life story that had to do with music is closed forever. He will never play in public again; I doubt that he will ever compose. That he has settled definitely in his mind. His music was simply a stage in his development for him, in his preparation for the great work he was destined to perform, and it is irretrievably of the past.

And while we have been living quietly here in Switzerland, not a day passes that we do not speak of America and of the good and true friends we have left there. It is really our second home, and often when I look across the lake at the rugged line of the Savoyan Alps, those mountains seem to fade away and in their place rise the Sierras as we see them from our beloved Paso Robles in beautiful California.[1] My husband is a Pole, the duties of the future will probably make Poland his home, but the thought of the United States and the memory of his friends there always will tug at his heart strings, and he waits impatiently for the time that he can again cross the Atlantic, if only to tell to Americans his gratitude for their goodness to him and to his countrymen.

The story that I set out to tell really ended with the signing of the Treaty of Versailles on the twenty-eighth of June 1919, when the freedom of Poland was assured, I trust, for all time. I have undertaken merely to give a sketch of the work my husband did for his country during the years of the Great War, to tell the motives and impulses that animated him, to explain to his friends throughout the world how it came that he abandoned his art and his career to plunge into politics and to indicate how little he regards the sacrifice he has made. It had been my purpose also to show that in all he has done and has attempted to do he has never been influenced by personal ambition, by the desire to be in high places for the gratification of his own pride. I am not at all sure that it might not have been better for the cause for which he worked had he been more ambitious personally, better for his country and for his people, but I am content to leave all such questions to the decision of others when enough time has passed to allow the events of the last year to be viewed in a proper perspective. I simply know that he has given to Poland the best that was in him, and more than that can be asked of no man.

Riond-Bosson,
Morges, Switzerland,
May 29, 1920

1. This is dramatic license, as the Sierra Nevada range is more than two hundred miles to the east of Paso Robles.

Helena Paderewska, c. 1920.
[Hoover Institution Library & Archives]

Children waiting for a meal being sponsored by the American Relief Administration, 1919.
[Hoover Institution Library & Archives]

Helena and Ignacy Paderewski welcoming Herbert Hoover to Warsaw. Hoover was then the director of the American Relief Administration, August 1919.

[Ośrodek Dokumentacji Muzyki Polskiej. Jagiellonian University, Cracow]

Mass on the Saski Square. Sitting from the left: Józef Piłsudski, papal nuncio Achille Ratti, and Herbert Hoover. Ignacy Paderewski stands behind the nuncio, August 1919.

[Hoover Institution Library & Archives]

Reception in the Belvedere palace in honor of Herbert Hoover. In the middle: Paderewski, Hoover, Piłsudski, and Hugh Gibson, USA representative, August 1919 [inset: detail]. [Hoover Institution Library & Archives]

*Hugh Gibson speaks to the American Poles, soldiers of the Blue Army,
in Warsaw, 1919.* [Hoover Institution Library & Archives]

*Handwritten invitation
to dinner from Helena
Paderewska to Hugh Gibson,
Warsaw, 1919.* [Hoover
Institution Library & Archives]

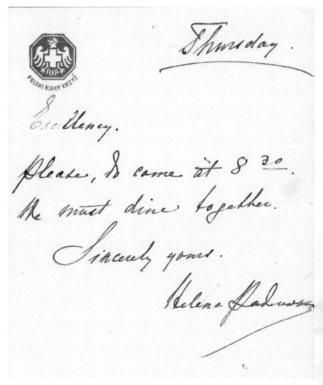

Blue Army soldiers playing baseball, Warsaw, 1919.
[Hoover Institution Library & Archives]

Ignacy and Helena Paderewski in Poznań, December 1919.
[Muzeum Powstania Wielkopolskiego 1918–1919, Poznań]

4th of July celebration in Warsaw.
Statue of Liberty is on the balcony of
the Grand Theatre, 1921.
[Hoover Institution Library & Archives]

Unveiling of the Monument of Gratitude of the United States on the Hoover Square. The sculptor of the monument, Xawery Dunikowski is in the first row (with a scarf). October 1922. [Hoover Institution Library & Archives]

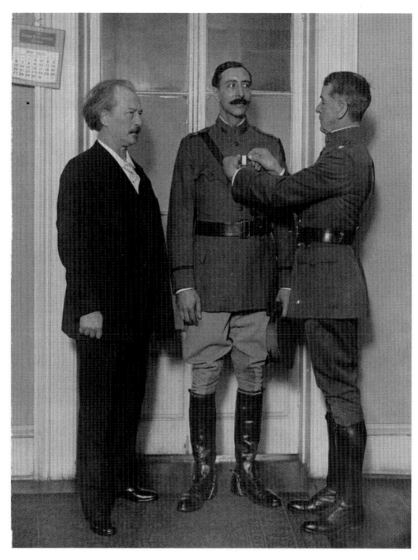

Major Ernest Schelling receives the Distinguished Service Medal for his intelligence work, in the presence of his teacher Ignacy Paderewski, May 1923. [Hoover Institution Library & Archives]

The Paderewskis at Riond-Bosson, Morges, Switzerland, 1929.
[Source: Maciej Siekierski]

Poster of General Jozef Haller, commander of the Polish "Blue Army," 1919.
[Hoover Institution Library & Archives]

"Follow the Impulse," poster for the Home for Polish Girls Fund, 1917; artist: W. T. Benda. [Hoover Institution Library & Archives]

"Come to the Polish Booth" poster/sign, New York, 1917.
[Hoover Institution Library & Archives]

"Armia Polska we Francyi. Polish Army in France," Polish recruitment poster, *1917; artist: W. T. Benda.* [Hoover Institution Library & Archives]

"Polacy! Idźcie na bój na prawy. Under the Polish flag on to the fight." Polish poster, 1917; artist: Witold D. Gordon. [Hoover Institution Library & Archives]

Editor's Epilogue

The relaxed country living of Riond-Bosson, after years filled with travels and politics, did not last very long for the Paderewskis. Helena had barely finished writing her reminiscences when Poland found itself in another mortal crisis. In the summer of 1920, the Bolsheviks repelled the Polish offensive from Ukraine and were rapidly advancing on Warsaw and western Europe. Much as he was against Piłsudski's "eastern adventure," Paderewski, because of his sense of responsibility, felt compelled to approach the Polish government and volunteer his services. He was appointed Poland's representative to the League of Nations as well as to the Conference of Ambassadors in Spa, Belgium, which was to enforce the execution of peace treaties and mediate territorial disputes. Paderewski was quickly disappointed by the inertia of the organizations and his inability to assure more support for Poland in the hour of its greatest need, even after its decisive victory over the Russian armies at the gates of Warsaw. He resigned both positions by mid-1921. In 1924 the Paderewskis visited Poznań, which was to be their last visit to Poland. That same year, Paderewski sold his Warsaw daily, *Rzeczpospolita* (Republic), marking a near-complete withdrawal from Polish politics. He would later, after Marshal Piłsudski's death in 1935, meet with some of the opposition leaders to discuss a unified front against Piłsudski's more authoritarian, less charismatic, and less competent successors, but the proposed alliance of centrist political parties, named "Front Morges" after the town where Paderewski lived and where the alliance was founded, never gained significant support in Poland.

Withdrawal from politics was accompanied by serious financial difficulties. The Paderewskis were living on credit since 1917. Investments were ruined by the war, and there was no income from concerts. For several years during and after the war, the Paderewskis were traveling and working at their own expense. The maintenance of Riond-Bosson and of the ranchos in California was very costly. After politics, it was time to return to the world of music and to the United States. They did so, already in 1921, arriving in New York City in February. The Paderewskis' principal social engagement was a reception in their honor given by their friends Lucie and Ernest Schelling at New York's exclusive Colony Club. They spent much of the remainder of that year in Paso Robles in the magnificent El Paso de Robles Hotel. Here Paderewski began practicing in earnest and preparing his new repertoire for the 1922 concert tour. That tour and the succeeding ones were very successful and brought millions of dollars in income and hundreds of thousands for various charities. Helena accompanied Ignacy on all of his tours until 1928. She also continued her charity and social programs in Poland, albeit with increasing difficulty because of deteriorating health. She died January 16, 1934, at the age of seventy-seven, in Riond-Bosson. Ignacy took her body to Paris to be buried next to his son, Alfred, in the Montmercy cemetery. The death of his lifetime partner and closest collaborator was a great blow to Ignacy. He continued to perform, but less frequently and with more difficulty. And then came the war, more horrible and devastating for the Paderewskis' homeland than the previous one. Ignacy made his final trip to the United States in 1940, pleading for help for his countrymen. He died of pneumonia in New York City's Buckingham Hotel on June 29, 1941. He was eighty years old. President Roosevelt directed a state burial at Arlington National Cemetery until such time as the remains could be returned to Poland. Ignacy Paderewski returned to a free Poland in 1992 and was buried in a crypt of St. John's Cathedral in Warsaw.

The Paderewskis' Timeline, 1910–1920

Note: This timeline is based in part on Małgorzata Perkowska, *Diariusz koncertowy Ignacego Jana Paderewskiego* [Concert datebook of Ignacy Jan Paderewski] (Kraków: Polskie Wydawnictwo Muzyczne, 1990).

1910

January	12, Vienna
	14, Budapest
February	14, Lausanne
	17, Paris
March	9, Lausanne
July	15–17, Kraków, unveiling of the Grunwald Monument
October	23, Lwów, First Congress of Polish Musicians
November	Warsaw

1911

March	29, Berlin
May	26, Fribourg
June	14, London
August	1–13, Rio de Janeiro
	17–21, São Paolo
September	10–31, Buenos Aires
October	1–6, Buenos Aires
	18, Paris

1912

February	13–14, Paris
March	5–30, South Africa: Capetown, Kimberley, Bloemfontein, Johannesburg, Pretoria, Maritzburg, Durban
June	17–28, Great Britain: London, Harrogate, Brighton
October	23–26, Great Britain: Bristol
November	12–18, Great Britain: London, Sheffield, Torquay
December	9, Lausanne

1913

February	6, Monte Carlo
March	6, Leipzig
	9, Kraków
	14, Lwów
	19, Kraków
	25, Łódź
	28–30, Warsaw
May	18–21, Vevey, Switzerland
June	London
October	16, US tour begins in Trenton, NJ
November	New York City; Buffalo; Worcester, MA; Boston; Baltimore; Washington, DC; Scranton, PA; Philadelphia; Brooklyn, NY; Springfield, OH
December	Columbus, OH; St. Louis; Milwaukee; Boston; Minneapolis; Fargo, ND; St. Paul; Madison, WI; Cleveland; Pittsburgh

1914

January	Colorado Springs, CO; Salt Lake City; Boise; Vancouver, BC; Seattle; San Francisco; Paso Robles
February	Paso Robles, Paderewski signs affidavit denying that he ever provided support for an anti-Jewish newspaper in Warsaw; purchases Rancho Ignacio; Fort Worth, TX; Wichita, KS; St. Joseph, MO;

	Springfield, MO; Cedar Rapids, IA; Lincoln, NE; Birmingham, AL; Louisville; Cincinnati; Chicago
March	Ann Arbor, MI; Detroit; New York City; Toronto; Boston; Philadelphia; Washington, DC; Baltimore; Brooklyn, NY; Newark, NJ; Providence, RI; Troy, NY; Harrisburg, PA
April	Philadelphia; Hartford, CT; Boston; Rochester, NY; Erie, PA; Chicago; Kansas City; Knoxville, TN
May	2, New York, dinner honoring Paderewski given by the Bohemians (New York Musician's Club) at the Ritz-Carlton Hotel
June	Great Britain: London, Harrogate
July–December	Riond-Bosson in Morges, Switzerland

1915

January	Paris
March	London
April	15, New York
	30, Chicago, "Decoration Day" speech to Polish Americans near the Kosciuszko monument in Humboldt Park; famous photo
July–August	Paso Robles
Late August	San Francisco, including concert at the Panama Pacific International Exhibition, garden party in the Crockers' Burlingame home
September	New York City; Bar Harbor, ME, summer home of Ernest and Lucie Schelling
October–November	Schenectady, NY; Boston; New York City; Wilkes-Barre, PA; Binghamton, NY; Newark, NJ; Pittsfield, MA; Philadelphia
December	Hartford, CT; Boston; Milwaukee; New York City

1916

January	Chicago; Milwaukee; Minneapolis; Des Moines, IA; Columbia, MO; Moline, IL; Omaha; Detroit; Toledo, OH; St. Louis; Kansas City; Joplin, MO

February	Oklahoma City; Tulsa; Chicago; Pittsburgh; Wheeling, WV; New York City 22, Washington, DC, Paderewski plays for President Wilson at the White House
March	New York City; Albany, NY; Boston; Chicago; Springfield, MA; Brooklyn, NY; New Haven, CT; Providence, RI; Reading, PA; New York City; Waterbury, CT
April	Youngstown, OH; Bridgeport, CT; Wilmington, DE; Syracuse, NY; New York City
May	7, New York City, Paderewski, along with Fritz Kreisler and Pablo Casals, plays at a benefit concert for the children of Enrique Granados
June–September	Paso Robles
September	San Francisco
October	San Francisco; Los Angeles; San Diego; Salt Lake City; Denver; Buffalo; Philadelphia
November	6, Princeton, NJ, Paderewski's private visit with President Wilson on the eve of his election for the second term New York City; Cleveland; Boston; Elmira, NY; Rochester, NY; Chicago; Indianapolis; Dayton, OH; Chicago; Cincinnati; Charleston, WV
December	Washington, DC; New York City; Brooklyn, NY; Boston; Providence, RI

1917

January	9–11, New York City, Paderewski writes his memorandum on Poland for President Wilson, as requested by Colonel House Boston; Baltimore; Spartanburg, SC 22, President Wilson's "Peace without Victory" speech to the Senate with reference to a "united, independent, and autonomous Poland" Raleigh, NC; Columbia, SC; Jacksonville, FL; Miami
February	6–12, Havana, Cuba

March	New York City
April	4, Pittsburgh, speech at the Congress of Polish Falcons of America
	6, US declaration of war against Germany
	Boston; Canton, OH; Detroit; Chicago; St. Louis
May	10, New York, Paderewski plays for the "last" time at the Metropolitan Opera House gala in honor of Marshal Joffre
June	Chicago
	New Haven, CT, Paderewski receives honorary doctorate from Yale University
June–September	Paso Robles
October	14, Chicago, Paderewskis at the meeting honoring the Polish Military Commission and the presentation of the flag to the first contingent of Polish soldiers
November	17, Niagara-on-the-Lake, Ontario, Paderewskis visit the Polish army camp in Canada

1918

January	8, President Wilson's "Fourteen Points" speech to Congress
March	3, New York City, Paderewski addresses the National Security League
June–July	Washington, DC, launching of the Polish White Cross
July	4, Columbus, OH
	14, New York City, French national holiday celebration
August	26, Detroit, meeting of the Polish Diet
October	Paso Robles; Chicago
November	11, New York, Armistice Day
	23, sailing on the *Megantic* for England
December	London; Paris; London
	19, Harwich, departure on the *Concord* for Gdańsk
	25, Gdańsk
	26–30, Poznań

1919

January	1, arrival in Warsaw
	6–7, Kraków
	16, Warsaw, Paderewski's government formed with Paderewski taking both the premiership and the foreign ministry
April	Paris
	Riond-Bosson (Easter)
May	Warsaw
June	28, Versailles, signing of the treaty with Germany
July	Warsaw
August	Warsaw
September	10, Saint-Germain-en-Laye, signing of the treaty with Austria
December	9, resignation of the Paderewski government accepted by Piłsudski

1920

February	Paderewskis depart for Riond-Bosson, Morges

Guide to Names

Adamowski, Timothee (Tymoteusz) (1857–1943), Polish-born American conductor, composer, and violinist; first conductor of the Boston Pops Orchestra.

Adlington, William, piano teacher, one of Paderewski's representatives in London; nicknamed "Governor," he accompanied the Paderewskis on several tours in America and Australia.

Alexander, Sir George (1858–1918), English actor and theater producer.

Alma-Tadema, Laurence (1865–1940), Belgian-born English novelist and poet; friend of Paderewski and supporter of Polish causes.

Askenazy, Szymon (1866–1935), Polish historian; professor at the University of Lwów.

Asquith, Herbert (1852–1928), Liberal prime minister of the United Kingdom, 1908–1916.

Asquith, Mrs., born Margot Tennant, Herbert Asquith's second wife.

Balfour, Arthur (1848–1930), Conservative prime minister of the United Kingdom, 1902–1905; foreign secretary, 1916–1919.

Barber, Colonel Alvin B. (1883–1961), railway engineer with US Army Engineers; later with the American Relief Administration and technical advisor to Poland, 1919–1922.

Barrientos, Maria (1883–1946), Spanish opera singer, one of the most eminent sopranos of her time.

Barthou, Louis (1862–1934), French politician; prime minister in 1913.

Beck, James M. (1861–1936), American lawyer and politician from Philadelphia.

Bedford, Duchess of, was Mary Russell (1865–1934), English aviatrix, ornithologist, and founder of hospitals.

Benckendorff, Count Alexander Konstantinovich (1849–1917), Russian ambassador to the United Kingdom during 1903–1917.

Bendix, Max (1866–1945), American composer, conductor, and violinist.

Beresford, Lady Charles (d. 1922), wife of Lord Beresford; born Mina Gardner.

Beresford, Lord Charles (1846–1919), British admiral and member of Parliament.

Berger, Violette (b. 1888), physician from New York who joined the French army because, as a woman, she was refused commission by the US Army; she received both French and Polish decorations for her service.

Bergson, Michał (1831–1919), president of the Warsaw Jewish community during 1896–1918; banker, philanthropist, and civic leader.

Bertie, Francis, 1st Viscount Bertie of Thame (1844–1919), British ambassador to France, 1905–1918.

Beseler, Hans Hartwig von (1850–1921), German general; governor of German-occupied Russian Poland from 1915 until October 1918.

Bismarck, Otto von (1815–1898), chancellor and foreign minister of Germany; his anti-Catholic *Kulturkampf* ("culture struggle") and anti-Polish measures alienated the Polish population of the country.

Blaine, Anita (1866–1954), born McCormick, the wife of Emmons Blaine (1857–1892), son of the US secretary of state and presidential candidate, president of Baltimore and Ohio Railroad.

Bliss, Mildred Barnes (1879–1969), art collector and philanthropist, wife of Robert Woods Bliss (1875–1962), secretary of the US embassy in Paris, 1912–1916, and counselor of the embassy, 1916–1919.

Bliss, Tasker H. (1853–1930), general, chief of staff of the US Army during 1917–1918.

Blodgett, Eleanor (1855–1930), New York philanthropist; godmother of Franklin Delano Roosevelt.

Bok, Edward William (1863–1930), Dutch-born American editor and Pulitzer Prize–winning author; editor of the *Ladies' Home Journal.*

Borden, Ellen, born Waller, married to John Borden, a Chicago socialite and financier.

Bourn, Agnes, born Moody, married William Bowers Bourn II (b. 1857), San Francisco entrepreneur; they built the Filoli country estate in San Mateo County, California, where both died and are buried (1936).

Bourne, Francis (1861–1935), archbishop of Westminster, 1903–1935; made cardinal in 1911.

de Brancovan, Princess Rachel (1847–1923), pianist and socialite; born Mussuros, she was the widow of Prince Gregoire Bibesco-Bessaraba de Brancovan (1827–1886) and mother of Princess Anne de Noailles (1876–1933), writer.

Branner, John Casper (1850–1922), geologist; president of Stanford University during 1913–1916.

Brennan, W. C., of Boston, one of Paderewski's US managers.

Briand, Aristide (1862–1932), prime minister of France eleven times.

Cambon, Paul (1843–1924), French ambassador in London, 1898–1920.

Car, Stanisław (1882–1938), Warsaw lawyer and politician, very close to Piłsudski; during 1918–1920 he was the chief of the civilian chancery of the head of state.

Caraman-Chimay, Princess de (1873–1916), born Clara Ward, American socialite married to a Belgian prince.

Carton de Wiart, Adrian (1880–1962), British officer and war hero; member of the British military mission to Poland.

Casals, Pablo (1876–1973), Catalan cellist and conductor; considered one of the greatest cellists of all time.

Chamberlain, Austen (1863–1937), British statesman, half-brother of Neville; chancellor of the exchequer, 1903–1905 and 1919–1921.

Chełkowska, Mrs., a member of a prominent landowning family in the area south of Gdańsk.

Chimene, Mr., Paderewski's French manager and agent.

Chopin, Frédéric (Fryderyk) (1810–1849), Poland's greatest composer.

Churchill, Lady Randolph (1854–1921), born Jeanette Jerome; the American wife of Lord Randolph and mother of Winston.

Churchill, Winston (1874–1965), home secretary, 1910; first lord of the admiralty, 1911–1915; minister of munitions, 1917–1919; secretary of state for war, 1919–1921.

Ciechanowski, Jan (1887–1973), Polish diplomat; last posting was as ambassador to the United States during 1941–1945.

Cincinnatus, Lucius Quinctius (519–430 BC), the "savior of Rome"; in 458 BC, according to tradition, was plowing his land when he was asked to lead the forces of the republic against invading enemies; became Rome's symbol of virtue and simplicity.

Cochin, Denys (1851–1922), French writer and Catholic politician; during 1893–1919 he represented Paris in the French National Assembly.

Comstock, Elinor, former student of Theodor Leschetizky; founder of the Elinor Comstock School of Music in New York.

Copper, James, Paderewski's chef during their travels in Pullman Company cars.

Coppet, Edward J. de (1855–1916), American banker and music enthusiast; owned a villa on Lake Geneva called Flonzaley.

Cox, James M. (1870–1957), US congressman, 1909–1913; governor of Ohio, 1913–1915 and 1917–1921; Democrat candidate for president, 1920.

Crewe-Milnes, Robert, 1st Marquess of Crewe (1858–1945), British Liberal politician and writer.

Crocker, Ethel (1861–1934), born Sperry, wife of William Crocker.

Crocker, William Henry (1861–1937), president of Crocker National Bank.

Culp, Julia (1880–1970), known as the "Dutch Nightingale," an internationally celebrated mezzo-soprano.

Curtis, Cyrus Hermann Kotzschmar (1850–1933), publisher of magazines and newspapers, including the *Ladies' Home Journal* and the *Saturday Evening Post*; major philanthropist.

Curzon, George, 1st Marquess Curzon of Kedleston (1859–1925), secretary of state for foreign affairs during 1919–1924; chancellor of Oxford University.

Damrosch, Walter (1862–1950), German-born American conductor and composer.

Daniels, Josephus (1862–1948), North Carolina politician and publisher; secretary of the navy during 1913–1921.

De Forest, Robert (1845–1929), Connecticut politician; US congressman.

Dmowski, Roman (1864–1939), Polish politician and statesman with an anti-German nationalist orientation; one of the founders of the National Democratic Party; one of the leaders of the Polish National Committee in Paris and, along with Paderewski, a signatory of the treaties of Versailles and Saint-Germain-en-Laye.

Doheny, Edward L. (1856–1935), American oil tycoon based in Southern California.

Duke, Mrs. James Buchanan, formerly Nataline Holt Inman, the second wife of the tobacco and electric power industrialist and philanthropist; they married in 1907, and he died in 1925.

Dunne, Edward Fitzsimmons (1853–1937), former mayor of Chicago; governor of Illinois during 1913–1917.

Edison, Thomas A. (1847–1931), American inventor and businessman.

Ehlers, Nellie S., Polish White Cross executive, formerly with the American Red Cross.

Elgar, Sir Edward William, 1st Baronet (1857–1934), British composer.

Eliot, Charles William (1834–1926), president of Harvard University during 1869–1906.

Ellis, Charles, Paderewski's manager since 1902; also administered the Boston Symphony Orchestra during 1882–1918.

Fabbri, Alessandro, American filmmaker; younger brother of Ernesto Fabbri.

Fabbri, Ernesto G., associate of J. Pierpont Morgan; married to Edith Shepard, great-granddaughter of Commodore Cornelius Vanderbilt.

Farley, John Murphy (1842–1918), Catholic archbishop of New York during 1902–1918; made cardinal in 1911.

Fiedler, Max (1859–1939), German conductor.

Fischer, Emil C., Paderewski's "piano doctor" who traveled with him during several seasons; responsible for the movement and tuning of his pianos.

Flagler, Harry Harkness (1871–1952), philanthropist and music promoter; president of the Symphony Society of New York.

Fleishhaker, Herbert (1872–1957), San Francisco banker and philanthropist.

Fleishhaker, Mortimer (1866–1953), San Francisco banker and philanthropist.

Foch, Ferdinand (1851–1929), French general and military theorist; made supreme commander of the Allied armies in 1918.

Forgan, David R. (1862–1931), Scottish-born Chicago banker; president of Union National Bank and its successors; championship golfer.

Forgan, James B. (1852–1924), older brother of David R. Forgan; president of the First National Bank of Chicago and later a director of the Chicago Reserve Bank.

Foster, Lieutenant R. C., 1911 Harvard graduate; reported to Professor A. C. Coolidge's committee in Vienna (the committee, a unit of the US Peace Commission, studied political, social, and economic situation in East Central Europe); interviewed Piłsudski, Paderewski, and others.

Frampton, Sir George (1860–1928), British sculptor.

Franklin-Bouillon, Henry (1870–1937), French politician.

Fronczak, Franciszek E. (1874–1955), Polish American doctor from Buffalo; member of the Polish National Committee in Paris.

Frye, John C., Steinway executive.

Fudakowski, Leonida (1881–1941), born Krajewski, a piano student of Theodor Leschetizky; short marriage to Jerzy Fudakowski was the result of Paderewski's matchmaking.

Fuller, William Parmer (1888–1969), administered American Relief Administration's European Children's Fund efforts in Poland during 1919–1921.

Ganz, Rudolph (1877–1972), Swiss American pianist, conductor, and teacher.

Gąsiorowski, Wacław (1869–1939), Polish novelist and journalist.

George, Dame Margaret Lloyd (1866–1941), born Margaret Owen.

George, David Lloyd (1863–1945), 1st Earl of Dwyfor, British Liberal politician; prime minister during 1916–1922.

Gericke, Wilhelm (1845–1925), Austrian-born conductor and composer.

Gibbons, James (1834–1921), Catholic archbishop of Baltimore during 1877–1921; made cardinal in 1886.

Gibson, Hugh Simons (1883–1954), American diplomat; US minister plenipotentiary to Poland, 1919–1924; close associate and friend of Herbert Hoover.

Gilchrist, Colonel Harry L. (1870–1943), later general, specialist on medical management of chemical casualties; led American program to combat typhus in Poland (1919–1921).

Gluck, Alma (1884–1938), born Reba Feinsohn in Bucharest, Romania; world-famous American soprano.

Goerlitz, Hugo (b. 1854), German-born international music agent; Paderewski's secretary for several years in the 1890s.

Gompers, Samuel (1850–1924), English-born American labor leader; founder and president of American Federation of Labor (AFL).

Górski, Wacław Otton (1877–1936), journalist, Helena Paderewska's son from her first marriage to violinist Władysław Górski.

Gosse, Sir Edmund (1849–1928), English poet, author, and critic.

Granados, Enrique (1867–1916), Spanish pianist and composer.

Greer, David Hummell (1844–1919), Episcopal bishop of New York during 1903–1919.

Grew, Joseph C. (1880–1965), American career diplomat with successive postings to Vienna, Copenhagen, Bern, Ankara, and Tokyo.

Grey, Edward, 1st Viscount Grey of Fallodon (1862–1933), British Liberal statesman; foreign secretary, 1905–1916; ambassador to the United States, 1919–1920.

Grove, William H., US Army colonel; headed US government relief efforts in Poland during 1919–1921.

Haller, Józef (1873–1960), former Austrian officer, later one of the commanders of Polish units fighting on the side of Austria against Russia; renounced allegiance to the Central Powers after signing the Brest-Litovsk treaty and made his way to France, where he arrived in July 1918 to command the Polish "Blue Army."

Hanna, Edward Joseph (1860–1944), Catholic archbishop of San Francisco during 1915–1935.

Hanotaux, Gabriel (1853–1944), French statesman and historian.

Hardy, Thomas (1840–1928), English novelist and poet.

Hawk, Samuel, co-owner of the Windsor and Manhattan hotels in New York City.

Heliński, Teodor (1857–1921), banker, Polish American activist; during World War I chaired the Military Commission of the National Department, responsible for organizing a Polish army in America.

Heyman, "Sir" Henry (1855–1924), Jewish American violinist and director; knighted by the king of Hawaii.

Higginson, Henry Lee (1834–1919), businessman, philanthropist, and founder of the Boston Symphony Orchestra.

Hill, David Jayne (1850–1932), American diplomat and historian; ambassador to Switzerland, the Netherlands, and, during 1908–1911, Germany.

Hill, James J. (1838–1916), Canadian American railroad executive, Great Northern Railway.

Hofmann, Josef (Józef Kazimierz) (1876–1956), Polish American virtuoso pianist, composer, teacher, and inventor.

Horodyski, Jan (1881–1948), Polish count and former Austrian subject; active in émigré affairs while serving as a British secret service agent.

House, Edward Mandell (1858–1938), American diplomat and politician; foreign policy advisor to President Woodrow Wilson.

Howard, Esme, 1st Baron Howard of Penrith (1863–1939), British diplomat; final posting was as ambassador to the United States during 1924–1930.

Hughes, Charles Evans (1862–1942), New York politician and lawyer; governor of New York, 1907–1910; associate justice of the US Supreme Court, 1910–1916; secretary of state, 1921–1925; judge on the Court of International Justice, 1928–1930; chief justice of the US Supreme Court, 1930–1941.

Iwanowska, Helena (1882-1941), American singer, wife of Major Iwanowski.

Iwanowski, Zygmunt (or Sigismund de Ivanowski) (1876–1944), Polish American painter and illustrator; military aide to Paderewski with the rank of major.

Izvolsky, Alexander (1856–1919), Russian foreign minister during 1906–1910; ambassador to France during 1910–1917.

Jaurès, Jean (1859–1914), French Socialist leader.

Joffre, Joseph (1852–1931), French general most famous for stopping the Germans at the first battle of the Marne in 1914.

Johnston, Sir Charles, 1st Baronet (1848–1933), Lord Mayor of London, 1914–1915.

Joubert, Eldon, Paderewski's (Weber and later Steinway) piano tuner and travel companion for more than three decades starting in 1906.

Judson, Harry Pratt (1847–1927), historian; president of the University of Chicago during 1907–1923.

Jusserand, Jean Jules (1855–1932), author and diplomat; French ambassador to the United States, 1902–1925.

Kamieński, B. S., Polish American journalist; before joining Haller's Army was the editor of Buffalo's *Dziennik dla Wszystkich* (Everybody's Daily); in Haller's Army, edited *Biuletyn Wojskowy* (Military Bulletin) and served as a liaison officer with the Polish White Cross.

Kauser, Alice (1872–1945), theatrical agent.

Kellogg, Charlotte, author and biographer of Paderewski; widow of Vernon Kellogg (1867–1937); Stanford biologist; member of the American Commission for Relief in Belgium and, in the first months of 1919, the American Relief Administration's representative in Warsaw.

Kellogg Fairbank, Mr., probably a relative of Nathaniel Kellogg Fairbank (1829–1903), industrialist and philanthropist.

Kelman, John (1864–1929), English-born Presbyterian minister; pastor in New York City.

Kerensky, Alexander (1881–1970), Russian lawyer and politician; prime minister of the provisional government from July to November 1917; deposed by the Bolsheviks.

Kern, John Worth (1849–1917), senator from Indiana; Democrat majority leader during 1913–1917.

Kernan, Francis J. (1859–1949), general; technical military advisor to the US Commission to Negotiate Peace during 1918–1919.

Klein, Charles (1867–1915), British American playwright and actor.

Kościuszko, Tadeusz (1746–1817), Polish general; veteran of the American Revolutionary War; leader of the abortive 1794 national uprising against Russia.

Krajewski, Rose Schnell (1859–1943), American-born widow of Tomasz Florian Krajewski (1851–1913), Polish-born inventor, industrialist, and music enthusiast.

Kreisler, Friedrich "Fritz" (1875–1962), Austrian-born violinist and composer.

Kucharzewski, Jan (1876–1952), Polish historian; prime minister of German-occupied Kingdom of Poland during 1917–1918.

de Lalaing, Count Charles (1856–1919), Belgian minister in London.

Lambert, Alexander (1862–1929), pianist and composer; friend of Paderewski since student days in Berlin; later director of New York College of Music.

Langford, Mr., British Foreign Office employee.

Lankester, Sir Ray (1847–1929), British zoologist.

Lansing, Robert (1864–1928), American lawyer and politician; secretary of state during 1915–1920.

Łapowski, Bolesław, dermatologist in the New York Good Samaritan Dispensary.

de La Rochefoucauld, Armand (1870–1963), Duc de Doudeauville; his wife was Princess Louise Radziwiłł (1877–1942).

Lathrop, Bryan (1844–1916), Chicago real estate investor, art collector, and patron; married to Helen Lynde Aidis Lathrop (1849–1935).

Latinik, Franciszek (1864–1949), colonel of Austrian-Hungarian infantry during World War I; later Polish general commanding the military district of Cieszyn; military governor of the Polish capital during the Battle of Warsaw in August 1920.

Law, Andrew Bonar (1858–1923), British politician; leader of Conservative opposition, 1911–1915; chancellor of the exchequer, 1916–1919; Lord Privy Seal, 1919–1921.

Lawrence, William (1850–1941), Episcopal bishop of Boston during 1893–1927; known as the "banker bishop" because of his successful fund-raising drives.

Łazarska, Stefania (Krautler) (1887–1977), Paris doll maker and painter.

LePan, Colonel Arthur D'Orr (1885–1976), Canadian commander of Niagara-on-the-Lake Polish army camp.

Longhena, Giovanni Romei, Italian general with Allied mission in Russia in 1917, later in Poland.

Loubet, Emile (1838–1929), president of the French Republic during 1899–1906.

Lübke, Helena (1893–1987), Paderewska's secretary from 1919 until 1934.

Lutosławski, Wincenty (1863–1954), Polish philosopher and author; member of the Polish National League.

Lvov, Prince Georgy (1861–1925), Russian statesman; prime minister in 1917.

Lynam, Edward B., 1895 graduate of Yale University; journalist and author of "The Jan and Halka Happy-Here Helpers," a booklet about the cloth dolls for the Polish Victims' Relief Fund (1916).

Mackenzie, Thomas (1854–1930), prime minister of New Zealand in 1912; later New Zealand high commissioner in London.

Manteuffel, Reverend Juliusz, pastor of St. Joseph parish in Passaic, New Jersey.

Marshall, Helen "Peggy" (1918–2007), married Ernest Schelling several months before his death in December 1939; during the war and immediately after, was active in the Paderewski Testimonial Fund, which financed the Polish hospital in Edinburgh, Scotland.

Martin, Colonel James, chief of the French military mission to Washington, DC.

Martin, William, chief of protocol of the French Ministry of Foreign Affairs during the Peace Conference.

Masaryk, Thomas Garrigue (1850–1937), Czech sociologist and philosopher; founder and first president of Czechoslovakia.

Mayer, Daniel, Paderewski's musical agent until about 1901.

McBride, Sir Peter (1867–1923), Australian politician and industrialist; Victorian agent-general in London.

McCormack, John (1884–1945), world-famous Irish tenor.

McKenna, Reginald (1863–1943), British banker and Liberal politician; home secretary, 1911–1915; chancellor of the exchequer, 1915–1916.

Melba, Dame Nellie (1861–1931), born Helen "Nellie" Porter Mitchell, Australian operatic soprano.

Mickiewicz, Adam (1798–1855), Poland's national poet.

Mickiewicz, Marie (1868–1952), granddaughter of Adam; Polish émigré activist in Paris.

Mickiewicz, Władysław (1836–1926), son of Adam, Polish émigré activist and publisher in France.

Mitchel, John Purroy (1879–1918), mayor of New York, 1913–1917; killed in a training accident as an army air officer.

Modjeska-Modrzejewska, Helena (1840–1909), renowned Polish and American actress specializing in Shakespearean roles.

Montgana, Giulio-Cesare (1874–1953), Italian diplomat.

Moore, Charles Caldwell (1868–1932), prominent San Francisco businessman.

Morax, Jean (1869–1939), Swiss painter and theater and costume designer.

Morax, Rene (1873–1963), Swiss poet and playwright.

Morgan, Anne Tracy (1873–1952), American philanthropist; daughter of John Pierpont Morgan.

Morgan, Herbert Edward, business executive; author of the 1914 book *The Dignity of Business*; later assistant to Lloyd George in Ministry of Munitions.

Morgan, Louise Pierpont (1866–1946), older sister of Anne Tracy Morgan; Herbert Satterlee's spouse.

Morrow, William W. (1843–1929), US representative from California for three terms; also served as a US judge.

Moschziesker, Robert von (1870–1939), chief justice of the Pennsylvania Supreme Court.

Muck, Karl (1859–1940), German-born conductor.

Napieralska, Emilia (1882–1947), Polish American activist; president of the Chicago-based Polish Women's Alliance of America for the years 1918–1935.

Neumann, Anna (1860–1947), president of the Polish Women's Alliance of America for the years 1902–1906 and 1909–1918.

Nicholas Nikolaevich, Grand Duke of Russia (1856–1929), cousin of Tsar Nicholas II, commander in chief of Russian forces during 1914–1915.

Nichols, William Ford (1849–1924), Episcopal bishop of California.

Niessel, Henri Albert (1866–1955), leader of French military mission to Russia in 1917; oversaw withdrawal of German *Freikorps* (volunteer military units) from the Baltic area.

Nikisch, Arthur (1855–1922), Hungarian conductor.

Nilan, John Joseph (1855–1934), Catholic bishop of Hartford during 1910–1934.

Norfolk, 15th Duke of, was Henry Fitzalan-Howard (1847–1917), married to Gwendolen Constable-Maxwell.

Northcliffe, Lord 1st Viscount, was Alfred Harmsworth (1865–1922), British newspaper and publishing magnate.

Noulens, Joseph (1864–1944), French diplomat and politician; ambassador to Russia during 1917–1918; in 1919, president of the Inter-Allied Commission for Poland; later, president of an international association of creditors of Russia.

O'Connell, William Henry (1859–1944), Catholic archbishop of Boston during 1907–1944; made cardinal in 1911.

O'Donnell, James E. (b. 1874), manager of American Oilfields Company of Edward Doheny and other Southern California oil companies.

Opieński, Henryk (1870–1942), Polish composer, violinist, teacher, and musicologist.

Orłowski, Mieczysław (b. 1865), from Jarmolince in Podolia, married to an American, Mabel Ledyard Stevens (b. 1872).

Painleve, Paul (1863–1933), French mathematician and politician; prime minster in the fall of 1917.

Parrott, John, Jr. (1859–1918), San Mateo, California, businessman.

Paton, William Douglas, British naval officer; first captain of HMS *Concord*, 1916–1919.

Patten, James A. (1852–1928), American financier and grain merchant.

Patterson, Mrs. Robert Wilson (1853–1933), born Nellie Medill, widow of Patterson (d. 1910), Chicago newspaper publisher and editor; daughter Eleanor "Cissy" married Polish count Józef Giżycki.

Paur, Emil (1855–1932), Austrian-born conductor.

Pavlova, Anna (1881–1931), Russian ballerina; performed with her Russian Ballet Company in the United States during 1914–1917.

Perley, Sir George Halsey (1857–1938), American-born Canadian politician and diplomat; Canadian high commissioner to the United Kingdom during 1914–1922.

Phillips, Anna Mary Laise, principal and owner of the Laise-Phillips girls' boarding school in Washington, DC; Paderewska's close collaborator in the Polish Victims' Relief Fund and the Polish White Cross; American hooked-rug designer and collector; owner of Hearthstone Studios of New York.

Piłsudski, Józef (1867–1935), Polish statesman; chief of state during 1918–1922; leader of the Second Polish Republic during 1926–1935; imprisoned in Germany from July 1917 to November 1918.

Piltz, Erazm (1851–1929), Polish journalist and politician; member of the Russian Duma in 1914.

Piotrowski, Nikodem L. (b. 1863), Chicago city attorney, 1911–1915; in 1918 elected president of the Polish Roman-Catholic Union of America.

Poincaré, Henriette Benucci (1858–1943), wife of president Raymond Poincaré of France.

Poincaré, Raymond (1860–1934), four-time French conservative prime minister; president, 1913–1920.

de Polignac, Princess Edmond (1865–1943), American-born Winnaretta Singer, heiress to the Singer sewing machine fortune; musical patron.

Poniatowski, Princess Elizabeth (d. 1911), born Elizabeth Sperry, sister of Mrs. William Crocker.

Poniatowski, Stanislas (1895–1970), son of Prince Andre and Elizabeth Sperry Poniatowski.

Potocki, Count Michael, later in the war organized the League for the Care of Polish Soldiers.

Poynter, Sir Edward (1836–1919), English painter; president of the Royal Academy of Arts.

Radziwiłł, Prince Ferdynand (1834–1926), Polish aristocrat and one of the leaders of the Polish minority in the German Empire.

Rawlings, (Henry) Bernard (Hughes) (1889–1962), Royal navy officer; later admiral.

Reading, Lord, 1st Marquess of Reading, was Rufus Isaacks (1860–1935), English lawyer and politician; lord chief justice of England, 1913–1921; later secretary of foreign affairs.

Rejer, Stefan (1874–1940), union organizer of Polish coal miners in Westphalia and northern France.

Renner, Karl (1870–1950), Austrian Social Democrat; first chancellor of Austria, 1918–1920.

de Reszke, Jean (Jan Reszke) (1855–1925), internationally renowned Polish operatic tenor.

de Reszke, Maria, born de Goulaine, wife of Jean; earlier married to Count Mailly-Nesle.

Rhode, Paul Peter (1871–1945), Catholic bishop of Green Bay, 1915–1945; first Polish-born American bishop.

Ripon, 2nd Marquess, was Frederick Robinson (1852–1923), married to Gwladys Herbert, Marchioness of Ripon (1859–1917), patron of the arts.

Roca, Julio Argentino (1843–1914), president of Argentina, 1880–1886 and 1898–1904.

Rolph, James (1869–1934), mayor of San Francisco during 1912–1931.

Rosebery, 5th Earl of, was Archibald Primrose (1847–1929), Liberal statesman and prime minister in 1886; married to Hannah de Rothschild.

de Rothschild, Edmond (1845–1934), of the French banking family; philanthropist and supporter of Zionism.

de Rothschild, Mrs. Leopold, born Marie Perugia (1862–1937), daughter of a Trieste merchant.

Rutherford, Ernest, 1st Baron Rutherford of Nelson (1871–1937), New Zealand–born British physicist and chemist; dubbed the "father of nuclear physics."

Ryerson, Martin, Jr. (1857–1932), Chicago philanthropist and art collector.

Saint-Saëns, Camille (1835–1921), French composer, organist, conductor, and pianist.

Samaroff, Olga (1880–1948), American pianist, music critic, and teacher; married to Leopold Stokowski, 1911–1923.

Sargent, John Singer (1856–1925), American portrait painter.

Satterlee, Herbert (1863–1947), American lawyer, writer, and businessman; son-in-law of John Pierpont Morgan; during 1908–1909 was assistant secretary of the navy.

Schaad, Herman, secretary of the Aeolian Company; Paderewski endorsed the company's organs and pianos.

Schäfer, Dietrich (1845–1929), German historian and political scientist, nationalist.

Schelling, Ernest (1876–1939), American conductor and composer; student and friend of Paderewski; during the war, served as a major in the Military Intelligence Service in the American legation in Bern.

Schelling, Lucie How (1872–1938), French-born wife of Ernest Schelling.

Selfridge, Harry Gordon (1856–1947), American-born British retail magnate.

Sembrich, Marcella (1858–1935), stage name of Prakseda Marcelina Kochańska, coloraturo soprano, with an international singing career chiefly with the New York Metropolitan and the Royal Opera House in London.

Seyda, Marian (1879–1967), Polish politician and journalist; member of the National Democratic Party.

Sharpe, L. G., Paderewski's London manager after the retirement of William Adlington; went with him on several tours of the United States, South America, and South Africa.

Sienkiewicz, Henryk (1846–1916), journalist and Nobel laureate novelist.

Skulski, Leopold (1878–1940), mayor of Łódź during 1917–1919; succeeded Paderewski for a few months as prime minister, 1919–1920; interior minister during 1920–1921.

Smulska, Jadwiga (Harriet), operatic singer in her youth; wife of John F. Smulski.

Smulski, John F. (1867–1928), Chicago banker and Polish American leader.

Somerset, 15th Duke of, was Algernon St. Maur (later Seymour) (1846–1923), married to Susan Margaret Richards Mackinnon (d. 1936); philanthropist.

Starzyński, Teofil Antoni (1878–1952), first Polish American doctor in Pittsburgh; principal organizer and national leader of the Falcon (Sokół) organization.

Steed, Henry Wickham (1871–1956), historian and journalist; editor of the *Times* of London, 1919–1922.

Stengel, Wilhelm, Sembrich-Kochańska's teacher at the Lwów Conservatory and later husband.

Stojowski, Zygmunt (1870–1946), student of Paderewski; Polish American pianist and composer.

Strakacz, Sylwin (1892–1973), Polish diplomat; Paderewski's personal secretary and political aide during 1919–1941.

Strzelecki, Monsignor Jan H. (1863–1918), pastor of St. Stanislaus parish in New York City.

Święcicki, Julian Adolf (1850–1932), Polish writer and translator of Romance languages.

Świrski, Czesław (1885–1973), aide and associate of Piłsudski going back to pre–World War I anti-tsarist underground; aide to Paderewski during the Paris Peace Conference.

Szaniawski, Waldemar or Włodzimierz, second lieutenant; member of the Polish military mission to the United States.

Szebeko, Lieutenant Witold (b. 1889), aide to General Dowbór-Muśnicki of the Poznań-area forces.

Szeptycki, Count Stanisław Maria (1867–1950), Polish general; chief of staff, 1918–1919; later an opponent of Piłsudski.

Szumowska-Adamowska, Antonina (1868–1938), Polish American pianist and student of Paderewski; taught at the New England Conservatory of Music in Boston; along with her husband, Joseph (cellist), and brother-in-law, Tim (violinist), made up the Adamowski Trio.

Szymanowski, Wacław (1859–1930), Polish sculptor and painter; his Chopin monument, designed in 1909, was unveiled in 1929.

Taft, Henry W. (1859–1945), antitrust lawyer; brother of President William Howard Taft.

Tardieu, Andre (1876–1945), French politician, later prime minister.

Thompson, William Hale (1869–1944), the last Republican mayor of Chicago, 1915–1923 and 1927–1931.

Tobin, Richard M. (1866–1952), San Francisco banker, philanthropist, and diplomat.

Trąmpczyński, Wojciech (1860–1953), Polish lawyer and National Democratic politician from the Poznań area.

Tretbar, Charles F. (1832–1909), German-born concert organizer and executive at Steinway and Sons.

Tumulty, Joseph Patrick (1879–1954), New Jersey lawyer and politician; private secretary to Woodrow Wilson during 1911–1921.

Urchs, Ernest (d. 1928), manager of Steinway and Sons and concert promoter.

d'Uzes, Duchess, Marie Therese d'Albert de Luynes (1876–1941), French aristocrat and socialite.

Vanderlip, Frank A. (1864–1937), president of the National City Bank of New York, 1909–1919.

Vandervelde, Lalla, organizer of Belgian relief; the first wife of Emile Vandervelde, Belgian socialist minister.

Van Sinderen, Howard, New York lawyer.

Venizelos, Eleftherios (1864–1936), prominent Greek statesman; known as "the maker of modern Greece."

Volpe, Arnold (1869–1940), Lithuanian-born American conductor and composer.

Wade, Harry A. L. H. (1873–1959), British lieutenant colonel in 1918; later with the League of Nations and the World Court.

Wanamaker, John (1838–1922), American businessman, religious leader, and political figure; pioneer in modern advertising and marketing.

Weingartner, Felix (1862–1943), Austrian composer, conductor, and pianist.

Wetherbee, Gardner, co-owner of the Windsor and Manhattan hotels in New York City.

Wheeler, Benjamin Ide (1854–1927), philology professor; president of University of California during 1899–1919.

White, Henry (1850–1927), prominent American diplomat and one of the signers of the Treaty of Versailles.

White, James C., American journalist, head of the Polish National Department's press bureau in Washington, DC; former editor of the *Boston Herald*.

Wierusz-Kowalski, Józef (1866–1927), Polish physicist and diplomat; Polish envoy to the Holy See, 1919–1921.

Wilkońska, Antonina (1858–1941), Ignacy Paderewski's sister.

Wiwulski, Antoni (1877–1919), architect and sculptor.

Wojciechowski, Stanisław (1869–1953), Polish politician and scientist; interior minister, 1919–1920; president of Poland during 1922–1926.

Wroński, Tadeusz (1887–1965), Polish basso opera singer; came to the United States in 1913 and performed in Boston and later Detroit; dubbed "Father of Detroit Opera."

Young, Canadian major; the camp adjutant at Niagara-on-the-Lake Polish army camp.

Zamoyski, Count Maurycy Klemens (1871–1939), conservative politician and diplomat; member of the Polish National Committee in Paris; Poland's ambassador to France during 1919–1924.

Zapała, Father Władysław (Ladislaus) (1874–1948), pastor of the St. Stanislaus Kostka parish in Chicago; later superior general of the Congregation of the Resurrection.

Zimbalist, Efrem (1889–1985), Russian-born American concert violinist, composer, and conductor.

Znamiecki, Alexander, in charge of Russia Division of the Foreign Trade Department of the National City Bank of New York in 1916; later worked as secretary of the American Relief Administration mission in Poland.

Żychliński, Kazimierz (1854–1927), Polish American activist; leader of the Polish National Alliance of Chicago during the years 1913–1927.

About the Author

Helena Paderewska was born Helena Rosen in 1856 in Warsaw, the daughter of a Polish father and a Greek mother, who died shortly after giving birth to Helena. Brought up mostly by her grandmother and aunt, Helena had little formal education but excelled in foreign languages, especially French. In 1899, after an unhappy marriage that ended in an annulment, Helena married her old friend and lover, Ignacy Paderewski. The couple moved to a palatial villa, Riond-Bosson, in Morges, Switzerland, overlooking Lake Geneva. Although they spent most of their remaining years on concert tours and political missions, including summer months in the hot springs and wine country of California's Paso Robles, they called Riond-Bosson home, a place where they rested and entertained neighbors and international visitors. It was there that Helena died in 1934. Helena Paderewska's memoirs, recently discovered in the Hoover Archives, chronicle the years 1910 to 1920, a crucial decade that, in large measure thanks to the efforts of Ignacy and Helena, brought the cause of Polish independence to the international arena and saw its successful achievement. Ignacy and Helena worked as a team: he wrote memoranda, delivered eloquent speeches, and met with the high and mighty: President Wilson, Colonel House, Herbert Hoover, and the American and European political and economic elites; she worked at the grassroots level, meeting parish priests, leaders of women's organizations, and anyone else willing to help. Paderewska's flagship endeavor, which she founded and directed, was the Polish White Cross, which enlisted almost twenty thousand members in bringing assistance to victims of war, a humanitarian and patriotic effort on a scale previously unknown.

About the Editor

Maciej Siekierski is curator of European Collections at the Hoover Institution Library and Archives at Stanford University. A specialist on Poland and eastern Europe, he has been a member of the staff since 1984, with the principal responsibility for acquiring European archival materials. From 1991 to 1993, Siekierski directed the Hoover Institution's Warsaw office, overseeing the collection and shipment to Stanford of a massive number of publications and documents released by the revolutions and transitions to democracy taking place in eastern Europe. Siekierski's publications include works in modern and early modern history as well as archival guides and commentaries. He edited Wiktor Sukiennicki's two-volume *East Central Europe during World War I: From Foreign Domination to National Independence*, published by East European Monographs in 1984. His doctoral dissertation, "Landed Wealth in the Grand Duchy of Lithuania: The Economic Affairs of Prince Nicholas Christopher Radziwill (1549–1616)," was published by the Polish Academy of Science in *Acta Baltico-Slavica*, volumes 20–21, in 1992 and 1993. Siekierski is the compiler of *Polish Independent Publications: Guide to the Collection in the Hoover Institution Archives* (Hoover Institution Press, 1999). His most recent book is *I Saw the Angel of Death: Experiences of Polish Jews Deported to the USSR during World War II*, published in Polish by the Jewish Historical Institute in Warsaw in 2006. In June 2001, Polish prime minister Jerzy Buzek honored Siekierski with the Laurel Award for his work on the preservation of Polish historical records. In May 2013, he was recognized by the Lithuanian Ministry of Culture for his contributions to the restoration of Lithuanian cultural and archival heritage. Siekierski holds a PhD in history from the University of California, Berkeley.

Index